The Forex Chartist Companion

The Forex Chartist Companion

A Visual Approach to Technical Analysis

MICHAEL D. ARCHER
JAMES L. BICKFORD

John Wiley & Sons, Inc.

332.632042
A67f

Copyright © 2007 by Michael D. Archer and James L. Bickford. All rights reserved.

Published by John Wiley & Sons, Inc., Hoboken, New Jersey.
Published simultaneously in Canada.

No part of this publication may be reproduced, stored in a retrieval system, or transmitted in any form or by any means, electronic, mechanical, photocopying, recording, scanning, or otherwise, except as permitted under Section 107 or 108 of the 1976 United States Copyright Act, without either the prior written permission of the Publisher, or authorization through payment of the appropriate per-copy fee to the Copyright Clearance Center, Inc., 222 Rosewood Drive, Danvers, MA 01923, (978) 750-8400, fax (978) 646-8600, or on the web at www.copyright.com. Requests to the Publisher for permission should be addressed to the Permissions Department, John Wiley & Sons, Inc., 111 River Street, Hoboken, NJ 07030, (201) 748-6011, fax (201) 748-6008, or online at http://www.wiley.com/go/permissions.

Limit of Liability/Disclaimer of Warranty: While the publisher and author have used their best efforts in preparing this book, they make no representations or warranties with respect to the accuracy or completeness of the contents of this book and specifically disclaim any implied warranties of merchantability or fitness for a particular purpose. No warranty may be created or extended by sales representatives or written sales materials. The advice and strategies contained herein may not be suitable for your situation. You should consult with a professional where appropriate. Neither the publisher nor author shall be liable for any loss of profit or any other commercial damages, including but not limited to special, incidental, consequential, or other damages.

For general information on our other products and services or for technical support, please contact our Customer Care Department within the United States at (800) 762-2974, outside the United States at (317) 572-3993 or fax (317) 572-4002.

Wiley also publishes its books in a variety of electronic formats. Some content that appears in print may not be available in electronic books. For more information about Wiley products, visit our web site at www.wiley.com.

Library of Congress Cataloging-in-Publication Data:

Archer, Michael D. (Michael Duane)
    The forex chartist companion : a visual approach to technical analysis / Michael
  D. Archer and James L. Bickford.
      p.   cm.—(Wiley trading series)
    Includes index.
    ISBN-13: 978-0-470-07393-3 (pbk.)
    ISBN-10: 0-470-07393-4 (pbk.)
    1. Stocks—Charts, diagrams, etc.   2. Investment analysis.   3. Foreign
  exchange market.   I. Bickford, James L.   II. Title.
    HG4638.A73   2007
    332.63'2042—dc22   2006032777

Printed in the United States of America.

10 9 8 7 6 5 4 3 2 1

Contents

University Libraries
Carnegie Mellon University
Pittsburgh, PA 15213-3890

Acknowledgments

We would like to thank our personal friends Susan L. Cress and Paul J. Szeligowski for their meticulous assistance in design layout, organization, and editing. It is not surprising to find out that both have become avid small-cap forex traders since editing this book.

Introduction

Trading in the foreign exchange (forex) currency markets has recently exceeded $2 trillion a day and this figure is expected to double within the next five years. The reason for this astonishing surge in trading popularity is quite simple: no commissions, low transaction costs, easy access to online currency markets, no middlemen, no fixed lot order sizes, high liquidity, low margin with high leverage, and limited regulations. These factors have already attracted the attention of both neophyte traders and veteran speculators in other financial markets.

ABOUT THIS BOOK

Immediately following the publication of *Getting Started in Currency Trading* (also by Mike Archer and Jim Bickford, John Wiley & Sons, 2005), the authors received an overwhelming number of inquiries and requests for more detailed information on the mechanics of currency day trading, market entry timing, and which positions to initiate in forex markets.

The authors hope to fill that void with the publication of the current volume. We have concentrated our primary focus on the most lethal weapons in the technical analysis arsenal: the traders' charts, pristine in their concept and dynamic in their visual presentation of both raw and processed data. Numerous groundbreaking and innovative additions to charting theory have been included here. Also several well-known classical charting types have been updated and modified to scrutinize the unique characteristics of forex data.

HOW THIS BOOK IS ORGANIZED

There are six major divisions in this book:

Part I: Forex-Specific Charting Techniques

Much of the material in this section originally appeared in a collection of technical currency studies called *Forex Charting Companion: Innovative Charting Techniques for*

Currency Traders (Syzygy Publishing, 2005) by the same co-authors. Many of the charts along with the corresponding data have been revised to reflect the current personality of the spot currency market.

Part II: Point and Figure Charting

Point and figure (P&F) charting was invented in the 1890s and has since evolved into a highly respectable technical analysis tool for detecting market entry signals. Although P&F was originally designed for use on the stock exchange, all the examples in Part II focus directly on the spot currency markets (with some startling results). This section is actually a revised update of *The Point & Figure Chartist's:Companion: The Computer-Side Reference for Currency Traders and Analysts*, also by the co-authors (Syzygy. Publishing, 2005).

Part III: Forex Swing Charting

Like their sibling P&F charts, swing charts are also members of that genre of charts normally referred to as reversal charts. Their shared *advantage* is their ability to filter out minor price fluctuations and highlight the critical inflection points in a price chart. This section is also an update of an earlier work entitled *The Swing Trader's Companion: The Computer-Side Reference for Swing Traders and Analysts* (Archer and Bickford, Syzygy Publishing, 2005).

Part IV: Other Reversal Charts

Both Western and Japanese reversal charts are examined in detail in this section. Knowledge of unusual and exotic charting techniques can only benefit the currency day trader since this knowledge assists in scrutinizing the same data through a different perspective.

Part V: Goodman Swing Count System

In this section, the authors examine the actual trading system of veteran trading guru Charles B. Goodman. His unique theories and hypermodern principles are accompanied by numerous practical studies and examples.

Appendixes

We have gone to extreme measures to ensure that readers will have more than ample study materials to assist them in their daily trading sessions. To this extent we have supplied a very exhaustive appendix, which essentially mirrors the contents of the book. This section is intended to be a computer-side reference guide to be used while traders are working online in their currency platforms. We have also included some Microsoft

Visual Basic 6.0 source code in the appendixes for those traders who home-brew their own forecasting programs.

DISCLAIMER

We wish to emphasize that spot currency trading may not be suited to everyone's disposition. All investors must be keenly aware of the risks involved and of the consequences of poor trading habits and/or mismanaged resources. Neither the publisher nor the authors are liable for any losses incurred while trading currencies.

PART I

Forex-Specific Charting Techniques

CHAPTER 1

Streaming Data

OVERVIEW

The smallest time unit between changes in the price of any currency pair is called a single *tick*, and a sequence of consecutive ticks is referred to as streaming data. During periods of heavy trading, there may be as many as three hundred ticks in a single minute. Conversely, during periods of low trading (such as in certain minor currency pairs over the weekend), several hours can elapse between individual ticks.

Tick data does not have an open, high, low, or close quote—it simply tells the prevailing price. The OHLC quotes occur only after tick data has been collected and coerced into interval data, such as one minute, one hour, one day, or any other selected duration.

TICK CHART

By definition, interval data is represented along the x-axis as equally spaced time segments. By contrast, tick data almost always distorts the representation of time along the x-axis, although it does remain continuous. Between January 1, 2000 and December 31, 2005, the number of ticks in a single minute in the EURUSD currency pair ranged from zero to three hundred. These variations produce an accordion effect on the x-axis. (See Appendix A for a list of world currency codes.)

In the tick chart of the euro/U.S. dollar currency pair shown in Figure 1.1, a continuous line represents the price, while the time scale at the bottom of the chart fluctuates by the number of ticks per time interval. This is the sole criterion that distinguishes tick charts from other line charts. The chart clearly shows a variation in the number of ticks per minute as time progresses.

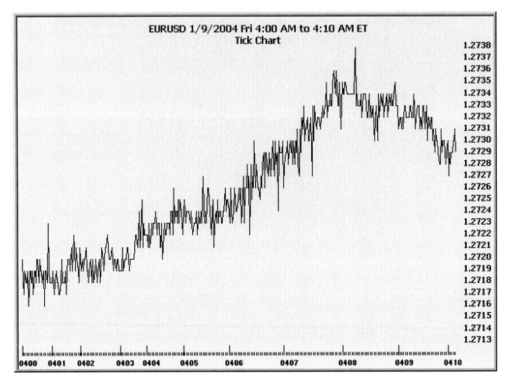

FIGURE 1.1 EURUSD Tick Chart

SPREAD CHART

Nearly all financial vehicles can be plotted as some form of a spread chart based on some unique properties of the underlying instrument. In futures markets, a spread chart usually implies the comparison of a forward expiry month with a distant expiry month in the same commodity. Within spot currency markets, a spread chart is defined specifically as the difference between the bid price and the ask price, which currency dealers use as the transaction cost for a round-turn trade in that currency pair.

The ask price is the price that the trader pays when entering the market in a long position; the bid price is used when the trader enters the market short.

The currency spread chart is plotted as a channel chart in which the upper boundary is the bid price and the lower boundary is the ask price. (See Figure 1.2.)

The importance of the spread chart is that it is the most common method used to display streaming data in online trading platforms. The trader can readily see the buying price (the lower boundary) and the selling price (the upper boundary).

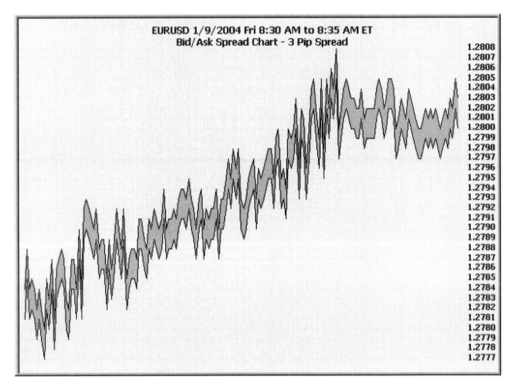

FIGURE 1.2 EURUSD Spread Chart

CONCLUSION

Understanding the nature of spot currency data in its most primitive form (raw streaming tick data) is requisite knowledge for all traders.

CHAPTER 2

Activity

OVERVIEW

When analyzing spot currency interval data, it should be noted that all six quote fields (open, high, low, close, upticks, and downticks) can be derived directly from the streaming tick data. An uptick occurs every time the current price exceeds the magnitude of the previous price within the prescribed interval. Similarly, a downtick occurs whenever the current price is lower than the previous price.

ACTIVITY BAR CHART

Given the two fields upticks and downticks, we define activity as shown in Figure 2.1, where x is the array index in the time series.

Activity is displayed as vertical bars in the lower portion of the five-minute chart in Figure 2.2. The empty rectangles are upticks, while the shaded rectangles are downticks.

In the long-term chart (Figure 2.3), note that activity in the EURUSD currency pair nearly tripled during the 2000–2004 period.

$$\text{Activity}_x = \text{Upticks}_x + \text{Downticks}_x$$

FIGURE 2.1 Activity Formula

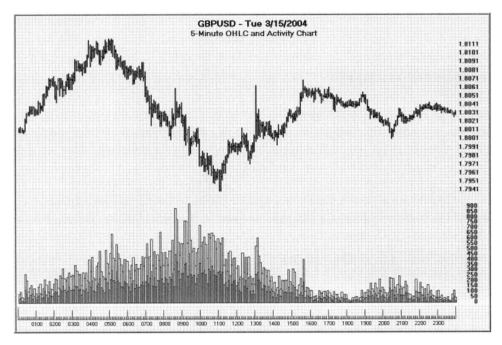

FIGURE 2.2   Activity Expressed as Vertical Bars

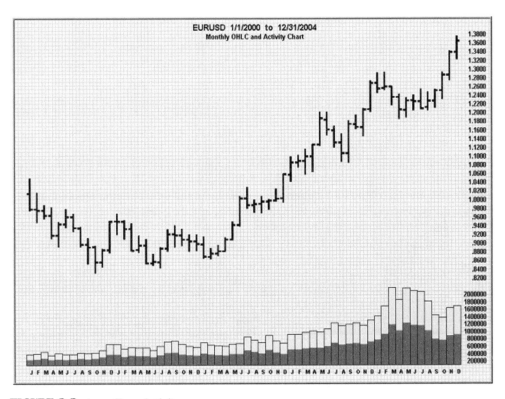

FIGURE 2.3   Long-Term Activity

COMPOSITE ACTIVITY

The foreign exchange is a 24/7 global market (with reduced liquidity on Saturdays and Sundays, of course). The importance of activity is extremely useful for traders in determining when to trade. For this purpose, we developed two composite charting techniques to show traders when trading activity is at its highest and lowest for each currency pair: the time of day chart and the day of week chart. Composite charts are simply the average activity for each time interval sampled over a long time frame.

TIME OF DAY ACTIVITY CHART

In Figure 2.4, multiple time intervals have been plotted where each average value has been centered. That is, the three-minute average for 10:00 A.M. is the mean of the activity for 9:59 A.M., 10:00 A.M., and 10:01 A.M. rather than front-based averaging (9:58 A.M., 9:59 A.M. and 10:00 A.M.).

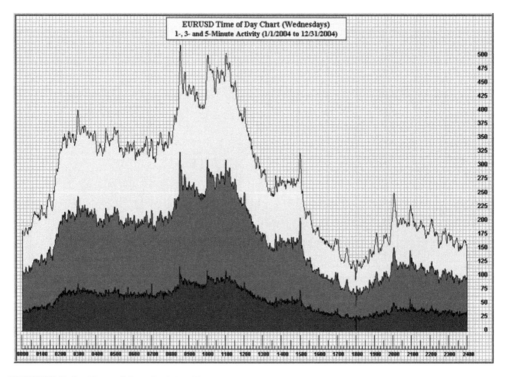

FIGURE 2.4 Time of Day Activity Chart

DAY OF WEEK ACTIVITY CHART

The time of day chart is excellent for examining the activity over a single 24-hour period. For the purpose of scrutinizing the activity over an entire week, we created the day of week chart, which is simply the concatenation of six time of day charts. (See Figure 2.5.) Because of the increased time frame, we also increased the time interval. Because New York City is conventionally considered to be the global center for currency trading, the bottom time scale of all time of day and day of week charts is expressed in terms of U.S. eastern time (ET) or Greenwich mean time (GMT) minus five hours.

Several time of day and day of week charts for the most frequently traded currency pairs appear in Appendixes E, F, and G. These charts have been updated to mirror the prevailing market's characteristics and are intended as a computer-side reference guide while traders are working in their online currency platforms.

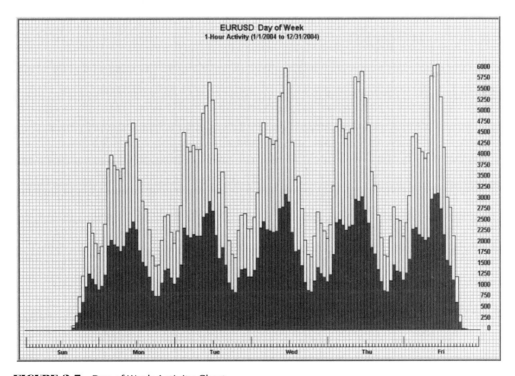

FIGURE 2.5 Day of Week Activity Chart

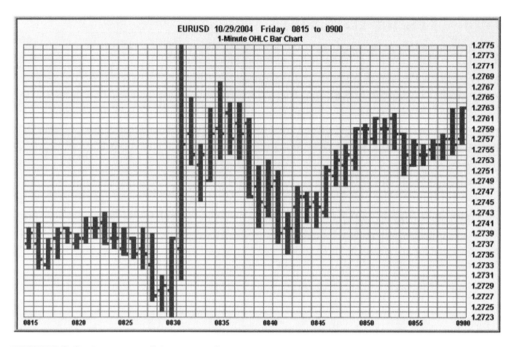

FIGURE 2.6   Conventional OHLC Bar Chart

EQUI-ACTIVITY CHART

The equi-activity chart is the brainchild of co-author Jim Bickford, who wanted to incorporate the activity property directly into the OHLC bar chart rather than displaying activity at the bottom of the chart as an afterthought. The concept is similar to that of analyst and author Richard W. Arms Jr., who in the early 1970s introduced the equivolume chart in his book *Volume Cycles in the Stock Market.*

The basic principle is that, since the height and range of each vertical bar define the high and low prices for that interval, the width of the vertical bar can be used to represent the activity for the same interval. The chart in Figure 2.6 displays the raw data as a conventional OHLC vertical bar chart with equal spacing along the x-axis, whereas the chart in Figure 2.7 displays the accordion-like property of the equi-activity chart: Column widths increase proportionately with an increase in activity during that interval.

ACTIVITY MERCURY CHART

The mercury chart is another creation that Jim Bickford also conceived while trying to utilize the vertical bars for more than just open, high, low, and close information. This charting technique first appeared in *Chart Plotting Algorithms for Technical Analysts* (Syzygy Publishing, 2002). (See Figure 2.8.)

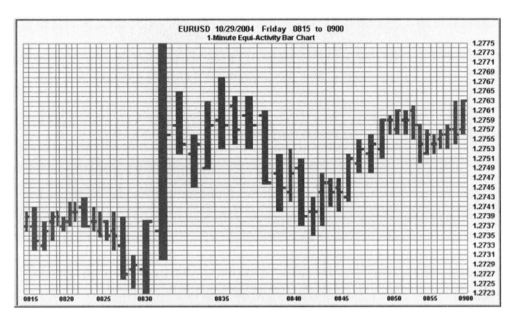

FIGURE 2.7 Corresponding Equi-Activity Chart

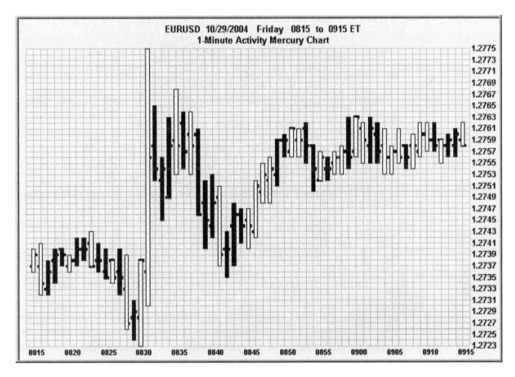

FIGURE 2.8 Activity Mercury Chart

The crux of the mercury chart is the shading inside the vertical bars. If the activity for the current interval is greater than the activity of the previous interval, then the inside of the vertical bar is left empty. If the activity for the current interval is less than the activity of the previous interval, then the inside of the vertical bar is shaded.

UPTICK-DOWNTICK MERCURY CHART

An important variation to the activity mercury chart is its sibling counterpart, the uptick-downtick mercury chart. (See Figure 2.9.) In the uptick-downtick mercury chart each vertical bar is divided into two equal parts and shaded according to the following rules:

A—If the current uptick is greater than the previous uptick, then the upper half of the bar is left empty.

B—If the current uptick is less than the previous uptick, then the upper half of the bar is shaded.

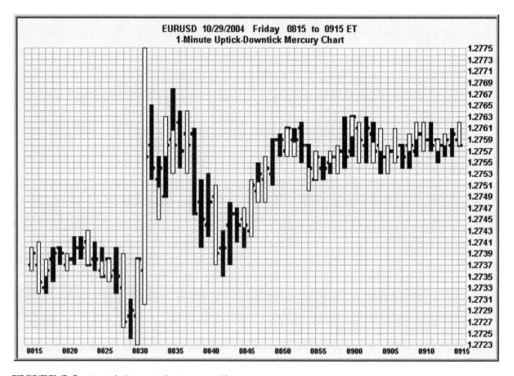

FIGURE 2.9 Uptick-Downtick Mercury Chart

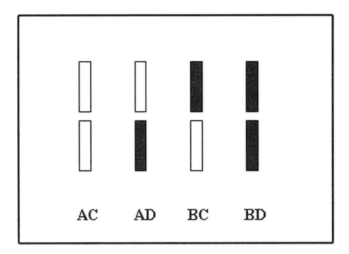

FIGURE 2.10 Uptick-Downtick Mercury Bar Types

C—If the current downtick is greater than the previous downtick, then the lower half of the bar is left empty.

D—If the current downtick is less than the previous downtick, then the lower half of the bar is shaded.

Not surprisingly, types AC and BD are much more frequent than types AD and BC. Incidentally, the mercury chart derives its name from the thermometer-like appearance of the four bar types in Figure 2.10.

CONCLUSION

The examination of the activity of targeted currency pairs can be very insightful in assisting traders in determining when to schedule their trading sessions. The addition of the equi-activity chart and the mercury chart to the trader's arsenal may also provide a technical edge in the selection of currency pair candidates.

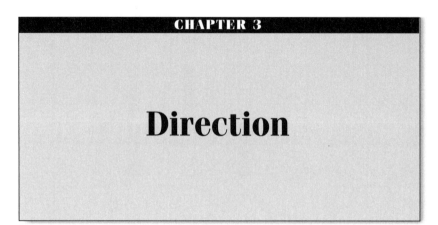

CHAPTER 3

Direction

OVERVIEW

For the purpose of this book, we define direction as the difference between the number of upticks and the number of downticks over a specified period of time for a single currency pair. (See Figure 3.1, where x equals the array index inside the time series array.)

We wish to clarify that there is no intended correlation between our arbitrary definition of direction and that of J. Welles Wilder, the noted trader and author of the 1970s who developed the Average Directional Index (ADX), which uses a positive directional indicator and a negative directional indicator to evaluate the strength of a trend. Further information on Wilder's method can be found in his highly acclaimed book entitled *New Concepts in Technical Trading Systems* (Trend Research, 1978).

DIRECTION CHART

Like its sibling counterpart the activity oscillator, the direction oscillator is unique to currency markets or more accurately, unique to those financial markets where the number of upticks and downticks for each time interval is recorded and readily accessible.

The moving direction oscillator is calculated as shown in Figure 3.2.

$$\text{Direction}_x = \text{Upticks}_x - \text{Downticks}_x$$

FIGURE 3.1 Direction Formula

14

$$\text{Direction Oscillator} = 100 \times \frac{\text{Upticks} - \text{Downticks}}{\text{Upticks} + \text{Downticks}}$$

FIGURE 3.2 Direction Oscillator Formula

Due to its ratio nature (dividing the difference by the sum), this indicator can oscillate between +100 and –100, as expressed in the lower right vertical scale of Figure 3.3.

It is not, per se, a volatility indicator, although sharp incursions into the extremes (say above +50 or below –50) imply an increase in volatility. Instead, it serves as a trend confirmation indicator.

We note that Figure 3.3 employs a one-minute time interval while Figure 3.4 uses a one-hour time interval. From this we determine the following rule: As the time interval increases, the absolute magnitude of the direction oscillator decreases. Although the direction oscillator has potential in unraveling a currency pair's hidden behavior, it should not be used as the sole criterion in justifying a market entry signal. We intend to delve a lot deeper into its analysis. One important aspect to note

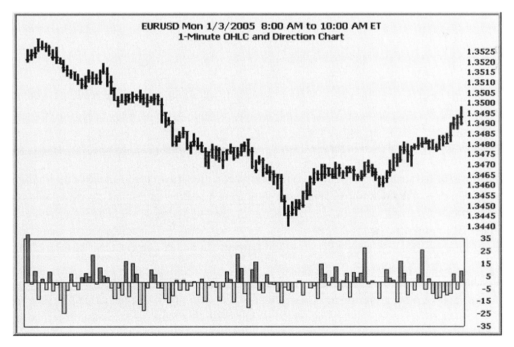

FIGURE 3.3 One-Minute OHLC and Direction Chart

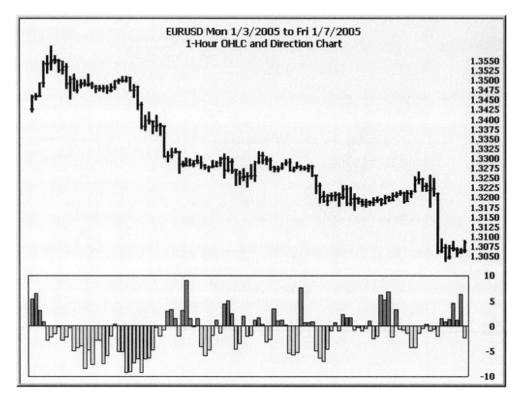

FIGURE 3.4 One-Hour OHLC and Direction Chart

about the direction oscillator is that the magnitude of its deviation from the mean line of zero is not necessarily most significant. Rather it is the length of time that it stays above or below the zero mean.

DIRECTION MERCURY CHART

Figure 3.5 compares the direction of the current bar with the direction of the previous bar. If the direction has increased, then the current bar is left empty. If the direction has decreased, then the current bar is shaded.

One interesting phenomenon is the instance where the high and low of the current day are both greater than the high and the low respectively of the previous bar yet the direction of the current bar is negative. The study of direction for one-minute intervals has potential.

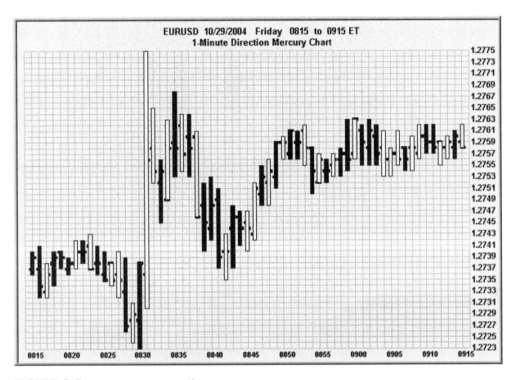

FIGURE 3.5 Direction Mercury Chart

ACTIVITY-DIRECTION MERCURY CHART

In order to take full advantage of the mercury chart concept, we combined the OHLC quote data, the change in activity, and the change in direction into a single chart.

Each vertical bar is divided into two equal parts and shaded according to the following rules (see Figure 3.6):

A—If the current activity is greater than the previous activity, then the upper half of the bar is left empty.

B—If the current activity is lower than the previous activity, then the upper half of the bar is shaded.

C—If the current direction is greater than the previous direction, then the lower half of the bar is left empty.

D—If the current direction is less than the previous direction, then the lower half of the bar is shaded.

These rules generate the resulting chart shown in Figure 3.7.

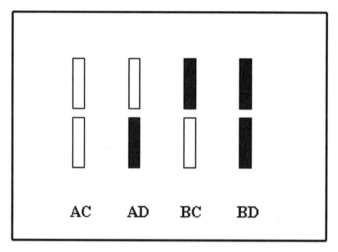

FIGURE 3.6 Activity-Direction Mercury Bar Types

FIGURE 3.7 Activity-Direction Mercury Chart

CONCLUSION

We feel that the chart in Figure 3.7 is the most important variation of all the mercury charts presented in this book because of the amount of information that has been compressed into a single vertical bar chart.

CHAPTER 4

Forex versus Futures

OVERVIEW

In our original *Currency Trader's Companion: A Visual Approach to Technical Analysis of Forex Markets* (2004) in the chapter entitled "Spot Currency Prices versus Currency Futures," we presented two tables that rank currency futures in order of their futures trading volume. A complete list of all commodity futures is published monthly by *Active Trader* magazine, which we again gratefully acknowledge. That chapter was included simply to give the reader an idea of the magnitude of volume and open interest in the commodities market since these figures are not currently available in forex spot markets.

PIP DIFFERENTIAL CHART

In this current book, we prefer to go one step farther and compare spot prices with futures prices graphically over the same time frame. For this purpose, we have created the pip differential chart, which compares a spot currency pair with the analogous futures currency pair.

Figures 4.1 and 4.2 are the charts for the EURUSD and the GBPUSD currency pairs. In both cases, the spot currency prices are displayed in the upper third of the chart. In the center is displayed the corresponding futures currency. In the lower section of the chart is displayed the pip differential oscillator, derived as shown in Figure 4.3.

First, the explanation of the Chicago Mercantile Exchange (CME) ticker symbols is:

ECM4 = Eurocurrency June 2004
BPM4 = British Pound June 2004

where June 2004 is the expiration (or delivery) month.

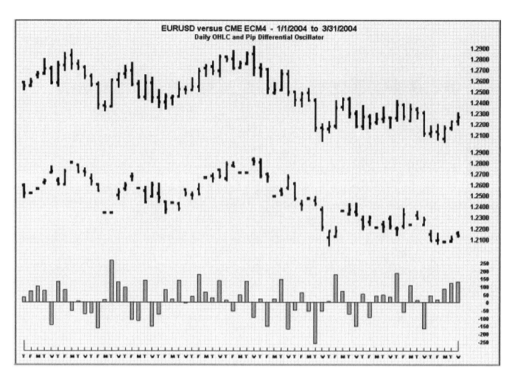

FIGURE 4.1 EURUSD Pip Differential Chart

FIGURE 4.2 GBPUSD Pip Differential Chart

20

$$\text{Pip Differential Oscillator} = (10,000 \times \text{Spot Close}) - (10,000 \times \text{Futures Close})$$

FIGURE 4.3 Pip Differential Oscillator Formula

Our first observation is that the spot data has a greater daily range than the futures data, which we attribute to its greater trading activity. Also, futures contracts are usually thin markets during their infancy and grow more liquid as they mature, the result of increased volume and open interest.

Interesting to note is that in Figure 4.1 the price differential oscillates on both sides of a zero mean, while in the Figure 4.2 the spot price is almost always higher than the futures price. This anomaly can probably be explained, though with some tedious research, by the changes in short-term interest rates between the three currencies involved (USD, EUR, and GBP). Veteran commodity traders will probably recognize this phenomenon as a variation of so-called backwardization.

Also, the fact that the pip differential chart for EURUSD/ECM4 does in fact undulate around a zero mean brings up an important point. There may be a very profitable leader/lagger relationship between the two financial vehicles if a discernible pattern can be uncovered.

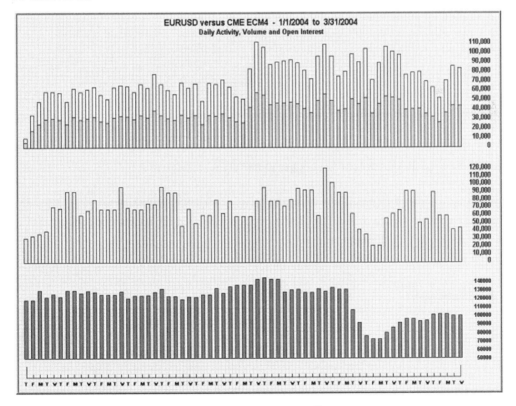

FIGURE 4.4 EURUSD Activity-Volume and Open Interest Chart

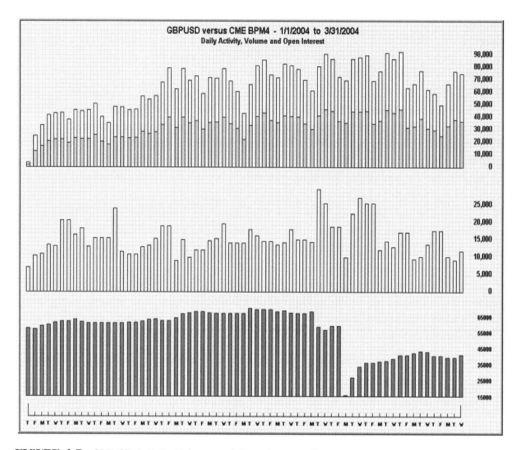

FIGURE 4.5 GBPUSD Activity-Volume and Open Interest Chart

ACTIVITY VERSUS VOLUME AND OPEN INTEREST

In Figures 4.4 and 4.5, the upper section displays the daily activity of the forex currency pair. The volume and open interest of the currency futures contract are displayed in the middle and bottom sections respectively.

CONCLUSION

This chapter offers only a preliminary visual comparison between forex activity and futures volume/open interest. An exhaustive study between spot and futures currencies that includes multiple delivery months and cross correlations, both historical and recent, is obviously an important weapon in the active currency trader's arsenal.

CHAPTER 5

Arbitrage

OVERVIEW

The somewhat esoteric trading strategy known as arbitrage is sometimes employed by currency day traders with a home computer. However, this arena of trading is normally left to the experts and financial managers with highly specialized software and private streaming data sources. Nonetheless, this discussion is included because arbitrage trading almost always guarantees a profit if the market entry and exiting trades are executed with utmost precision, and knowledge of the arbitrage mechanisms can benefit the small-cap day trader.

In general, arbitrage is the purchase or sale of any financial instrument and simultaneous taking of an equal and opposite position in a related market, in order to take advantage of small price differentials between markets. Essentially, arbitrage opportunities arise when currency prices go out of sync with each other. There are numerous forms of arbitrage involving multiple markets, future deliveries, options, and other complex derivatives. A less sophisticated example of a two-currency, two-location arbitrage transaction follows.

Bank ABC offers 170 Japanese yen for one U.S. dollar, and Bank XYZ offers only 150 yen for one dollar. Go to Bank ABC and purchase 170 yen. Next go to Bank XYZ and sell the 170 yen for $1.13. In a little more than the time it took to cross the street that separates the two banks, you earned a 13 percent return on your original investment. If the anomaly between the two banks' exchange rates persists, repeat the transactions. After exchanging currencies at both banks six times, you will have more than doubled your investment.

TRANSITIVITY

Within the forex market, *triangular arbitrage* is a specific trading strategy that involves three currencies, their correlation, and any discrepancy in their parity rates.

Thus, there are no arbitrage opportunities when dealing with just two currencies in a single market. Their fluctuations are simply the trading range of their mutual exchange rate. This fluctuating property of any three corresponding currency pairs is referred to as *transitivity* and is the necessary ingredient in all profitable arbitrage trades.

The actual trading mechanism requires executing three market entry trades simultaneously the exact moment that the exchange rate anomaly appears, then liquidating all three trades simultaneously as soon as the previous exchange rate parity has been reestablished.

TRIANGULAR ARBITRAGE CHART

In Figure 5.1, we examine the EURUSD, the GBPUSD, and their corresponding cross rate the EURGBP for Tuesday, January 14, 2003, 12:00 A.M. to 11:59 P.M. using one-minute closing quote data.

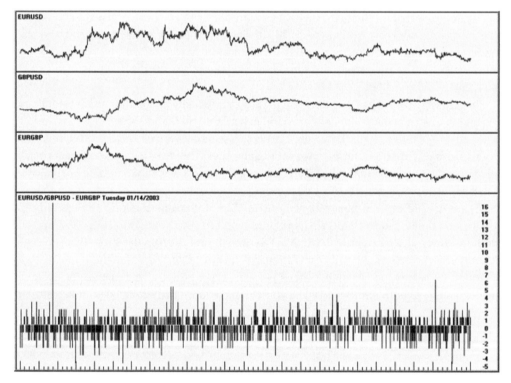

FIGURE 5.1 EUR-GBP-USD Triangular Arbitrage Chart

EQUILIBRIUM

The upper three charts in Figure 5.1 are simply line charts of the three underlying currency pairs, while the bottom chart illustrates any arbitrage opportunities present. The formula to calculate the data in the bottom chart is based on the theoretical identity known as the equilibrium formula, shown in Figure 5.2, which means the value of a cross rate should equal the ratio of the two corresponding USD pairs. In turn, that can be used to plot the corresponding arbitrage oscillator. (See Figure 5.3.)

To determine if an arbitrage opportunity does exist and is in fact profitable, we must first consider the transaction cost. We will assume that most reputable currency dealers will charge three pips for the transaction cost of the major currency pairs and four pips for the transaction cost of a major cross rate. Therefore, the cost to execute one round-turn arbitrage trade in the EUR-GBP-USD triangle is 10 pips.

If we had executed such a trade at 1:45 A.M. when the arbitrage oscillator hit 18 pips and liquidated as soon as the arbitrage oscillator returned to zero or less, we would have earned an 8-pip profit with minimal risk.

The chart in Figure 5.1 illustrates an instance of where only one major anomaly occurred within a 24-hour time frame. Figure 5.4, whose time range is one week later (Tuesday, January 21, 2003, 12:00 A.M. to 11:59 P.M.), illustrates numerous arbitrage opportunities.

There are more than a dozen instances within a 24-hour time frame where the arbitrage oscillator exceeds the transaction cost requirement. Notice that the cross rate chart (EURGBP, third from top) begins relatively smoothly but after 2:30 P.M., it becomes very spiky (i.e., less smooth). It is during these periods that numerous arbitrage opportunities may present themselves in a single triangle. Also interesting to note is the fact that all of the anomalies after 2:30 P.M. occurred on the same side of the zero mean line.

Figure 5.5 is an example of the CHF-JPY-USD triangle for Thursday January 9, 2003, 12:00 A.M. to 11:59 P.M., where there are at least six arbitrage opportunities with the 24-hour time frame using one-minute closing quotes.

$$EURGBP = \frac{EURUSD}{GBPUSD}$$

FIGURE 5.2 EURGBP Equilibrium Formula

$$Arbitrage\ Oscillator = \frac{EURUSD}{GBPUSD - EURGBP}$$

FIGURE 5.3 Arbitrage Oscillator Formula

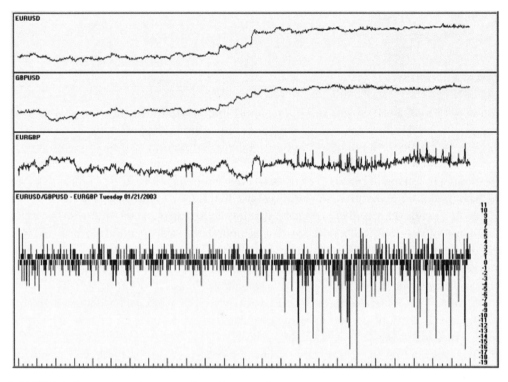

FIGURE 5.4 EUR-GBP-USD Triangular Arbitrage Chart

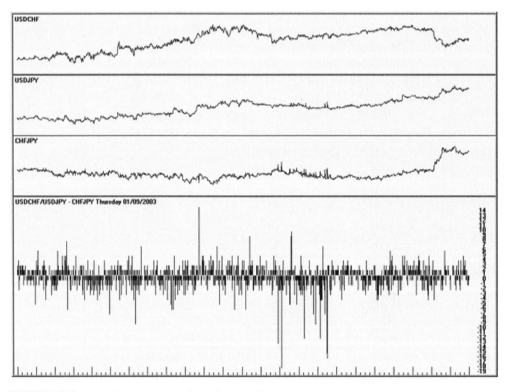

FIGURE 5.5 USD-CHF-JPY Triangular Arbitrage Chart

We selected this specific triangle because the equilibrium formula differs slightly from the previous triangle: EURGBP = EURUSD/GBPUSD. This formula is applicable only when the USD is the quote currency in both the USD currency pairs. However, in the CHF-JPY-USD triangle, the USD is the base currency in the two USD currency pairs. This difference determines which pair is in the numerator and which is in the denominator. The equilibrium formula for the CHF-JPY-USD triangle is shown in Figure 5.6.

In the preceding examples, we noticed that when anomalies do occur, the arbitrage oscillator normally returns to or near the zero mean shortly thereafter. In the next chart (Figure 5.7), we see a not-too-common phenomenon where a 14-pip anomaly occurs only to be immediately followed by a 19-pip anomaly in the opposite direction. Technically, both anomalies could have been trapped with a single arbitrage trade, which would have netted the trader a 33-pip profit before transaction costs.

$$\text{CHFJPY} = \frac{\text{USDJPY}}{\text{USDCHF}}$$

FIGURE 5.6   CHFJPY Equilibrium Formula

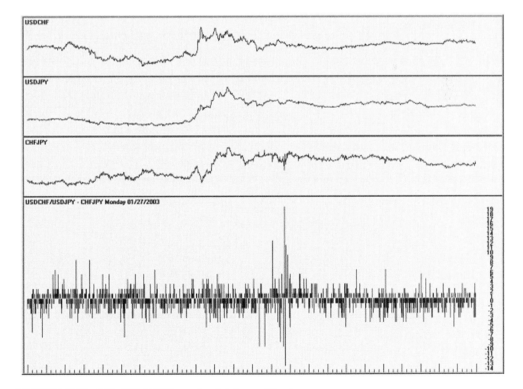

FIGURE 5.7   USD-CHF-JPY Triangular Arbitrage Chart

TABLE 5.1 Equilibrium Formulas for Major Currencies

Currency	Formula
EURGBP	EURUSD/GBPUSD
EURCHF	EURUSD × USDCHF
EURJPY	EURUSD × USDJPY
GBPCHF	GBPUSD × USDJPY
GBPJPY	GBPUSD × USDJPY
CHFJPY	USDJPY / USDCHF

MAJOR CURRENCIES

In any currency pair, the currency listed on the left is called the base currency and the currency on the right is the quote currency. Central banks and currency dealers have more or less arbitrarily established a relationship condition that determines the base/quote positions for each pair. It is this relationship that dictates what the mathematical formula will be on the right side of the equation. (See Table 5.1.) Note the importance of the arithmetic operators / and x.

OBSERVATION

As mentioned earlier, we included this chapter in the belief that, in currency trading, any information on the inner working of the market can be illuminating or at least helpful. However, the small-cap day trader should be aware that even though arbitrage opportunities are always present, they are unfortunately very short-lived and correct themselves in less than a minute or so. Automated trading software is the only realistic method of trapping risk-free arbitrage profits.

CHAPTER 6

The Mundo

OVERVIEW

In *Currency Trader's Companion: A Visual Approach to Technical Analysis of Forex Markets* (2004), we introduced the synthetic global currency, the Mundo, to which we gave an International Organization for Standardization (ISO) symbol of ICU for international currency unit. We arbitrarily defined the prevailing price of the Mundo as the arithmetic average price of the 10 most frequently traded major and minor USD currency pairs: EURUSD, GBPUSD, USDJPY, USDCHF, USDCAD, AUDUSD, NZDUSD, USDSEK, USDNOK, and USDDKK.

All pairs are treated with equal weight, which means six of the pairs must be adjusted so that the USD is the quote currency. The reciprocals (divide the exchange rate into 1) of the USDJPY, USDCHF, USDCAD, USDSEK, USDNOK, and USDDKK must be calculated to create the JPYUSD, CHFUSD, CADUSD, SEKUSD, NOKUSD, and DKKUSD pairs. This ensures that any price change in any of the 10 pairs is measured in pips of the same currency unit, the USD.

Summing the most recent values of these 10 pairs and dividing by 10 yields the current price of the Mundo.

FOREX BETA

We can now use an analogous coefficient to compare the volatility of a single currency pair to the volatility of the overall forex market as described in terms of the volatility of the Mundo.

Rather than using the ratio of the slope of a single currency pair and the slope of the ICUUSD pair, we will use the standard deviation of each. We can justify this change because of a major difference in the trading philosophies of stocks and spot currencies. Nearly all stock traders use a buy-and-hold strategy in which they hope that their investment will more than better the current inflation rate over a long period of time. Thus stock traders hold a long position in their trades and, in nonleveraged positions, they own the shares of stock outright.

Spot currency traders, by contrast, are not buying shares in a corporation or a mutual fund. They feel equally comfortable on either side of a currency trade, long or short. A forex trade is, in fact, the simultaneous buying of one currency while selling another currency. Spot currency traders (particularly scalpers) may initiate a long trade, follow a five-minute rally, liquidate the long position at its peak, and then initiate a short position in the same currency pair and follow that security's decline to the next trough.

Therefore, spot currency traders are not particularly interested in the long-term slope of any currency pair. Instead they are more interested in the number of significant peaks and troughs that occur during their trading sessions. The standard deviation is therefore employed in our model for forex beta (though many may agree that this is a misnomer).

To calculate the forex beta of, say, the EURUSD pair see Figure 6.1.

A running calculation of this statistic using streaming data informs the forex day trader which currency pairs are showing the highest volatility relative to the whole spot market. This identifies the pairs with the highest risk/reward factor. The order of these pairs may change throughout the day as central banks around the world open and close.

Table 6.1 illustrates the standard deviation and beta coefficient for each of the 10

$$\text{Beta(EURUSD)} = \frac{\text{StdDev(EURUSD)}}{\text{StdDev(ICUUSD)}}$$

FIGURE 6.1   Forex Beta Formula

TABLE 6.1   Forex Beta for Mundo Pairs

Currency Pair	Standard Deviation	Beta
EURUSD	802.61	2.28
GBPUSD	745.48	2.11
CHFUSD	570.65	1.62
JPYUSD	570.19	1.62
NZDUSD	506.27	1.44
AUDUSD	437.44	1.24
ICUUSD	352.70	1.00
CADUSD	253.73	0.72
NOKUSD	124.65	0.35
DKKUSD	109.26	0.31
SEKUSD	94.43	0.27

pairs for the time range 1/1/2000 through 6/30/2003. During this period, the Mundo exhibited a standard deviation of 352.70 pips (or 3.53 U.S. cents).

Thus, when compared to the aggregate currency pair ICUUSD, the EURUSD showed the highest beta coefficient and therefore carries the greatest risk/reward factor. In other words, for the time period examined, the EURUSD was 2.28 times more volatile than the average of all 10 currencies.

MUNDO LINE CHART

Figure 6.2 is the line chart for the Mundo during the same time frame.

The first aspect to note is that the Mundo has a lower parity rate than the USD, roughly 53 to 67 U..S cents. Second, slight changes in the same price direction in the 10 underlying currency pairs may cause an exaggerated price change in the Mundo. This phenomenon is also partially due to the use of reciprocals in six of the currency pairs.

This study is in no way definitive or authoritative. It is simply a novel approach to currency pair selection using aggregate standard deviations.

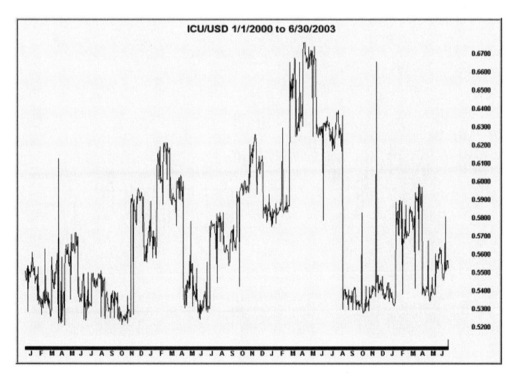

FIGURE 6.2 Unweighted Mundo Chart

TABLE 6.2 Mundo Currency Weights

Currency Pair	Upticks	Downticks	Activity	Weight
USDCHF	2,419,490	2,570,069	4,989,559	18.69%
EURUSD	2,394,304	2,511,721	4,906,025	18.38%
GBPUSD	2,120,519	2,153,168	4,273,687	16.01%
USDJPY	1,563,400	1,607,036	3,170,436	11.88%
AUDUSD	932,126	968,878	1,901,004	7.12%
USDCAD	839,353	829,357	1,668,710	6.25%
USDSEK	803,501	800,648	1,604,149	6.01%
USDNOK	808,156	793,129	1,601,285	6.00%
USDDKK	700,413	694,882	1,395,295	5.23%
NZDUSD	600,077	587,156	1,187,233	4.45%
Totals	13,181,339	13,516,044	426,697,383	100.00%

WEIGHTING

The preceding example illustrates the calculation of the Mundo as the simple arithmetic mean of the 10 most frequently traded USD currency pairs. A more realistic approach is to weigh each component USD currency pair using its corresponding activity as the weighting factor. For this purpose, we have used the daily activity data for 1/1/2004 through 3/31/2004. (See Table 6.2.)

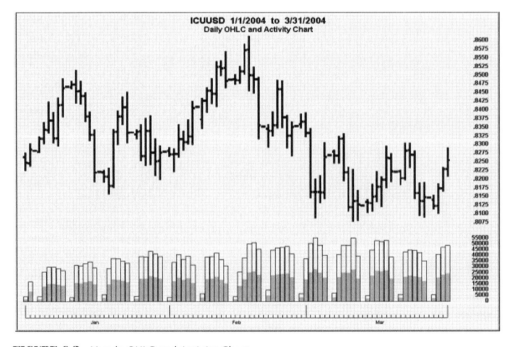

FIGURE 6.3 Mundo OHLC and Activity Chart

MUNDO BAR CHART

The price of the Mundo ranged from 0.80 USD to 0.86 USD during the first quarter of 2004 (See Figure 6.3.). Activity was calculated by summing the upticks and downticks of each component currency pair and dividing by 10. The standard deviation of the ICUUSD currency pair over this time period was 0.01147 USD. The beta coefficients for the ten component currency pairs using activity weighting are shown in Table 6.3.

Examples of usage for this table are: The GBPUSD is 2.5 times more volatile than the Mundo. The CADUSD pair is almost identical to the Mundo in volatility. The JPYUSD pair occupies the bottom position probably because of its low parity exchange rate (110 JPY = 1 USD).

OBSERVATION

The effect of weighting the currencies by their corresponding activity is illustrated in the fact that the order of the currency pairs has changed, somewhat dramatically, from the order in Table 6.1 in which simple arithmetic averaging was employed.

The classical tools of technical analysis are well revered and time-tested. Our approach here has been to capitalize on characteristics indigenous to a specific security group (spot currency prices) and to develop unique tools to assist the trader in the uncovering of security properties that may prove enlightening and profitable. We are continually tweaking these new methods and apologize for any infractions that may appear to violate any nuances of mathematical rigor.

TABLE 6.3 Mundo Standard Deviation

Currency Pair	Standard Deviation	Beta
GBPUSD	0.0287	2.5079
EURUSD	0.0207	1.8118
NZDUSD	0.0166	1.4508
AUDUSD	0.0152	1.3254
CHFUSD	0.0127	1.1112
ICUUSD	0.0115	1.0000
CADUSD	0.0114	0.9934
SEKUSD	0.0030	0.2598
DKKUSD	0.0028	0.2430
NOKUSD	0.0023	0.2042
JPYUSD	0.0001	0.0145

CHAPTER 7

Range Charts

OVERVIEW

Traditionally range has been defined as the difference between the highest high and the lowest low over a selected period of time (see Figure 7.1). In Figure 7.2, the vertical scale on the right is expressed in pips while the horizontal scale at the bottom is expressed in minutes, and x is the day number inside the price array.

The study of range has always provided technical analysts with vital information on the volatility and the trending properties of a time series.

RANGE BAR CHART

Graphically, there is nothing very exotic about a range bar chart. It is simply a vertical bar chart of the OHLC quotes at the top of the chart while range is represented as vertical columns at the bottom of the chart. (See Figure 7.2.)

The vertical scale in the lower right portion is expressed in terms of the quote currency of the underlying currency pair. Close examination of the vertical bars will

$$\text{Range}_x = \text{Highest High}_x - \text{Lowest Low}_x$$

FIGURE 7.1 Range Formula

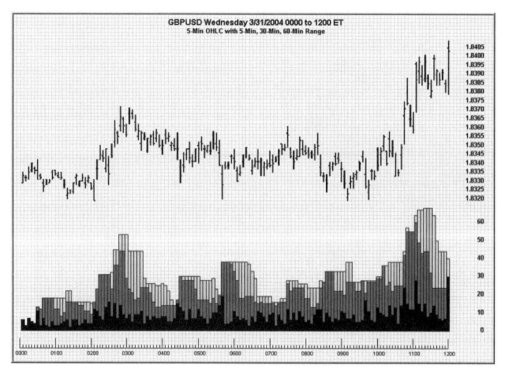

FIGURE 7.2 OHLC with Range Bar Chart

reveal the timing of trending cycles and lateral congestion in the corresponding OHLC chart.

COMPOSITE RANGE CHARTS

In an analogous manner to the one described in Chapter 2 on activity, range sampled over a long time frame can be used to create time of day and day of week charts. Simple arithmetic averaging is employed to create interval range values.

TIME OF DAY RANGE CHART

The time of day charts shown in Figures 7.3 and 7.4 were designed by averaging 2-, 7-, and 15-minute range statistics for the time frame 1/1/2004 through 12/31/2004 for

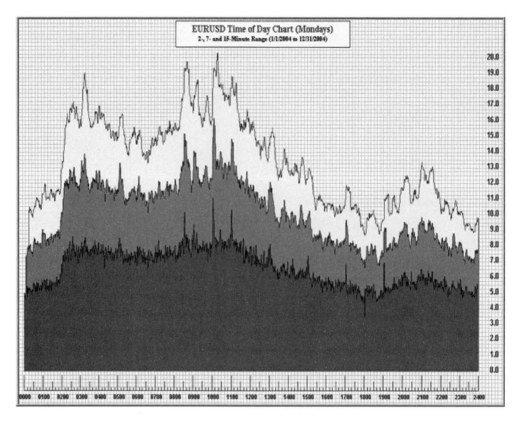

FIGURE 7.3 Time of Day Range Chart (Mondays)

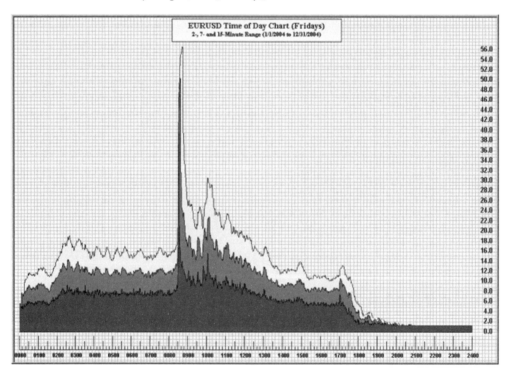

FIGURE 7.4 Time of Day Range Chart (Fridays)

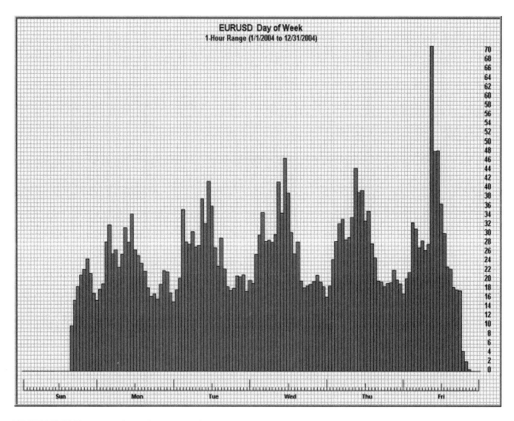

FIGURE 7.5 Day of Week Range Chart

each weekday except Saturday. The vertical scale on the right is expressed in terms of USD pips.

DAY OF WEEK RANGE CHART

In a similar fashion, the time of day range charts can be concatenated to create a day of week range chart. The distinguishing time interval must be increased accordingly. (See Figure 7.5.)

AVERAGE INTERVAL RANGE CHART

Figure 7.6 uses one-minute high/low data from 1/1/2000 to 12/31/2003 in the EURUSD currency pair. We calculated the average range (high minus low) for each integer time interval from 1 minute to 60 minutes.

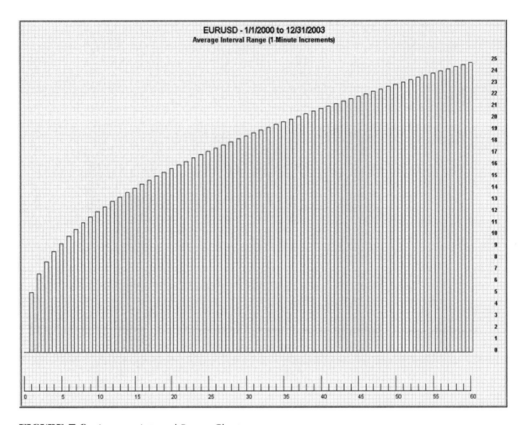

FIGURE 7.6 Average Interval Range Chart

OBSERVATIONS

The chart in Figure 7.6 provides the trader with some interesting theoretical information. Note on the far left, the height of the first vertical bar is 5.14 pips tall. This means that for every one-minute interval in the horizontal scaling of the dealer's trading platform there is a high statistical expectancy that the price movement will span 5.14 pips.

Within every half hour representation in the trading platform, the price movement should cover a range of 18.5 pips. Every hour in the trading window, prices should span 21.2 pips.

CHAPTER 8

Absolute Momentum

OVERVIEW

Within technical analysis, momentum has traditionally been defined as the difference between the current closing price and a closing close that occurred *lag* time units earlier. (See Figure 8.1.)

ABSOLUTE MOMENTUM

Running momentum generates a stream of data consisting of both positive and negative numbers whose mean approaches zero in large samples. To rectify this intrinsic mathematical property for the purpose of plotting composite charts, it is necessary to use the absolute values of the momentum data streams. That is, all negative numbers are converted to positive numbers. (See Figure 8.2.)

$$\text{Momentum}_x = \text{Close}_x - \text{Close}_{x-lag}$$

FIGURE 8.1 Momentum Formula

$$\text{Absolute Momentum}_x = \sum \frac{\text{Abs}(\text{Close}_x - \text{Close}_{x-lag})}{n}$$

FIGURE 8.2 Absolute Momentum Formula

Thus in composite time of day momentum charts, we are not concerned about the direction of the processed data since all absolute momentum values are positive. We are, however, very concerned about the magnitude of the processed data. Extreme values in the absolute momentum oscillator inform us at what time of day breakouts are most likely to occur, although we do not know which direction. This is, nonetheless, valuable information to traders, particularly those who subscribe to trend following techniques.

TIME OF DAY MOMENTUM CHART

The time frame 1/1/2004 to 12/31/2004 was examined in Figures 8.3 and 8.4. Running one-minute OHLC data was employed with a five-minute absolute momentum calculated every minute.

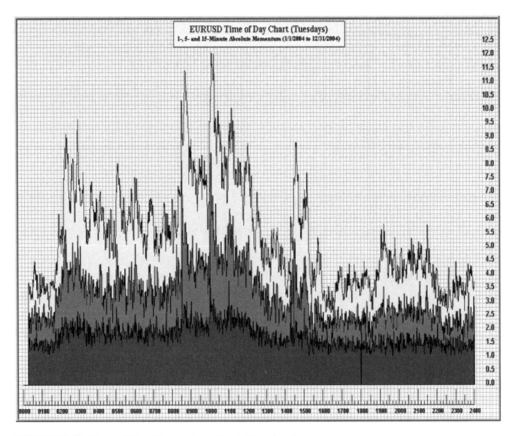

FIGURE 8.3 Time of Day Momentum Chart (Tuesdays)

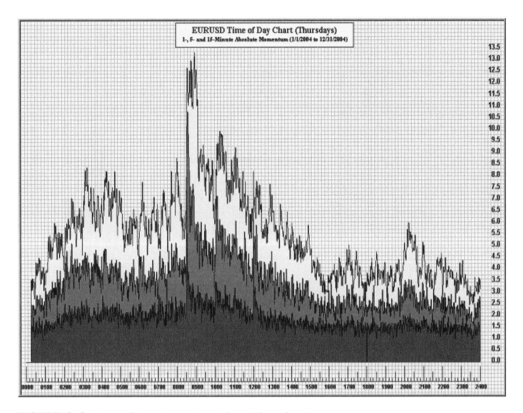

FIGURE 8.4 Time of Day Momentum Chart (Thursdays)

DAY OF WEEK MOMENTUM CHART

Individual time of day charts can be concatenated (this is, linked together sequentially) to create a single day of week chart. (See Figure 8.5.)

A simple visual examination of the absolute momentum charts reveals a distinct difference from the time of day range charts. Momentum charts exhibit a spiky quality while range charts show a more smoothed quality. Obviously, trading during these spiky periods offers the highest potential for profit (and loss) since bold breakouts and unexpected reversals tend to manifest themselves during these extremes. Forewarned is forearmed.

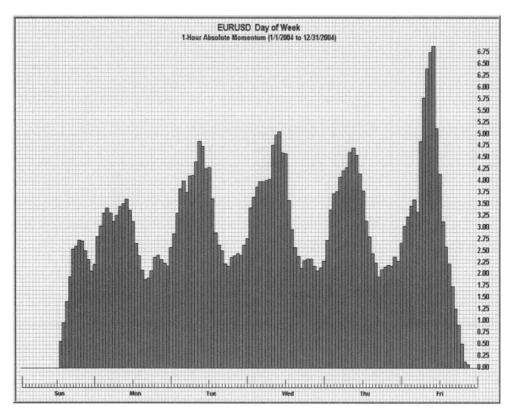

FIGURE 8.5 Day of Week Momentum Chart

CONCLUSION

The employment of time of day and day of week charts can greatly benefit forex currency traders. These activity, range, and absolute momentum charts assist traders in scheduling trading sessions based on desired volatility. For intrinsic mathematical reasons, the composite absolute momentum chart tends to exhibit slightly greater spikiness than the corresponding composite range chart covering the same time period.

CHAPTER 9

Two-Dimensional Momentum

OVERVIEW

The study of momentum is a valuable tool when scrutinizing serial price fluctuations. Historically, standard momentum charts displayed a running series of the differences between one closing price and another closing price that occurred x time units earlier, where x is referred to as the momentum or lag index. Selecting the optimum value for the number of time units in the momentum index is frequently a difficult and haphazard decision, particularly when visible cycles are present in the time series.

In Figure 9.1, a momentum index of 15 days was arbitrarily selected. The vertical scale in the lower right section of the chart is expressed in terms of quote currency pips (USD). To view the output of a 30-day momentum index, it would be necessary to print an additional momentum chart.

TWO-DIMENSIONAL MOMENTUM \CHART

As a plausible solution in the search for determining the optimum momentum index value, we have created an innovative variation to the classical momentum charting method, which we have named the two-dimensional momentum chart (Figure 9.2).

The most distinctive feature of the two-dimensional momentum chart is the trapezoidal shape at the bottom of the chart. Each cell in the quadrangle is shaded according to one of five unique gradations representing the magnitude of momentum. These gradations are described in the legend area directly beneath the chart header. A white cell means that the current close is significantly higher than a specific previous close while a

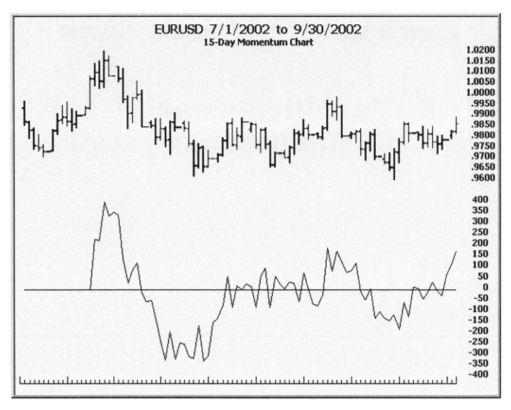

FIGURE 9.1   OHLC with 15-Day Momentum Chart

black cell means that the current close is significantly lower than a specific previous close. A medium gray cell indicates that the difference between the two closes, which are separated by a known lag index, is relatively near the zero mean. The light and dark gray shades are interpolated values explained in the legend.

The bottom row of the trapezoid is equivalent to a one-dimensional one-day momentum chart but the magnitude of momentum is expressed in terms of intensity of the cell shading rather than deviations from the x-axis. The row immediately above the bottom row represents a two-day running momentum of closes, and so on. The vertical scale to the right identifies the momentum index (the lag between the current closes and a previous close). The top row of the matrix represents a 15-day momentum chart. Thus, all momentum indexes between one and the maximum number of time units (15 days in this example) can be visualized in a single chart.

Additionally, the quadrangular nature of the two-dimensional momentum chart has another advantage beyond the horizontal display of multiple momentum indexes in a single chart. Specifically, this is the vertical interpretation of the matrix. Each column displays the differentiating relationship of a single close with all its predecessors in ascending magnitude of momentum indexes.

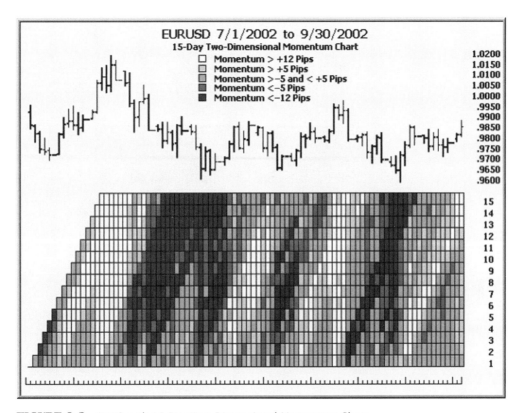

FIGURE 9.2 OHLC with 15-Day Two-Dimensional Momentum Chart

ISLANDS

In the two-dimensional momentum charts shown in Figures 9.3, 9.4, and 9.5, the maximum momentum index has been increased gradually to illustrate an interesting charting phenomenon.

Note that as we increase the size of the momentum index, the top left cell of the momentum matrix scoots to the right. As the momentum index approaches the number of intervals along the x-axis, the matrix becomes a right triangle.

We have, for want of a better term, called this phenomenon *streaking*, which denotes the presence of diagonal island patterns, which are prevalent in all momentum matrices. The length and width of each island can be directly correlated to a trending pattern in the underlying data, where black patterns indicate a downward trend and white patterns indicate upward trending. The number of vertical cells that separate two distinct like-colored islands (white versus white and black versus black) indicates the size of a wavelength prevalent in an underling cycle in the raw data. The vector direction of each island pattern is always a 45-degree angle (northeast) from the point of origin.

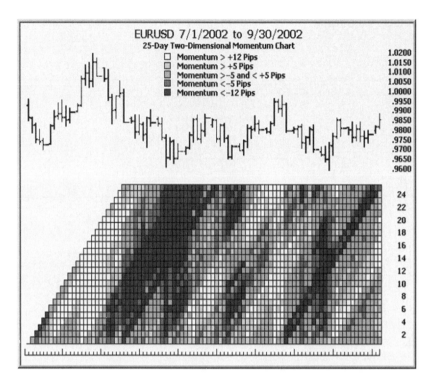

FIGURE 9.3 OHLC with 25-Day Two-Dimensional Momentum Chart

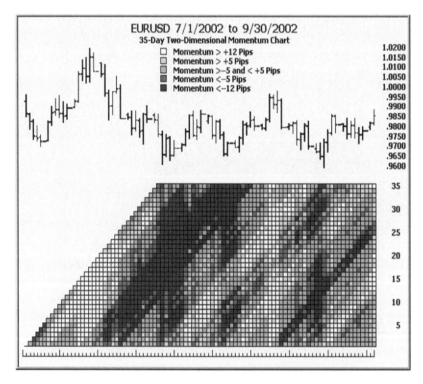

FIGURE 9.4 OHLC with 35-Day Two-Dimensional Momentum Chart

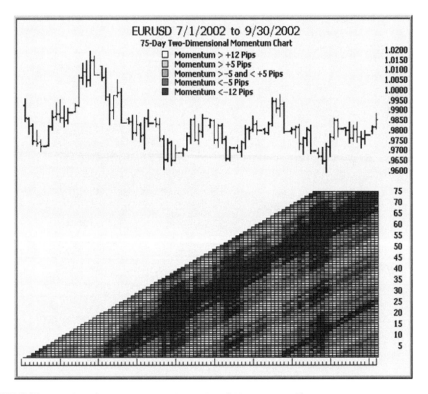

FIGURE 9.5 OHLC with 75-Day Two-Dimensional Momentum Chart

SMOOTHING

In an effort to enhance the clarity of the islands in the momentum matrix, a mild prewhitening of the raw data was employed in Figure 9.6, and the daily midrange (high plus low divided by 2) was substituted for the daily close.

The obvious result is that the visibility of the islands is only slightly improved using the midrange values. Therefore a more drastic technique is necessary. In Figure 9.7, a five-day arithmetic moving average of the raw daily closes was employed.

Smoothing the daily closes prior to plotting the two-dimensional momentum quadrangle has a pronounced effect on the visualization of the island patterns. The number of vertical cells between the center of each island and the center of a vertically adjacent island of the same shade (white or black) is equal to half the wavelength predominant in the raw time series. An example of this occurs on days 77 and 78 in Figure 9.7.

OBSERVATION

The interpretation of two-dimensional momentum charts is a topic for extended research, particularly with regard to the identification of dominant cycles in any financial time series.

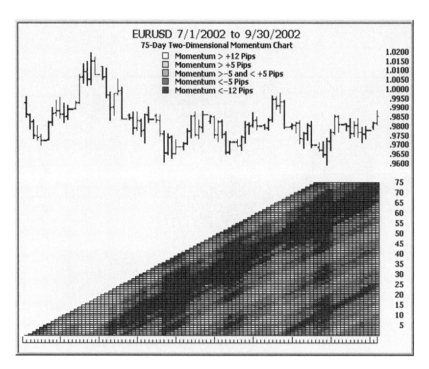

FIGURE 9.6 OHLC with 75-Day Two-Dimensional Momentum Chart Using Midrange

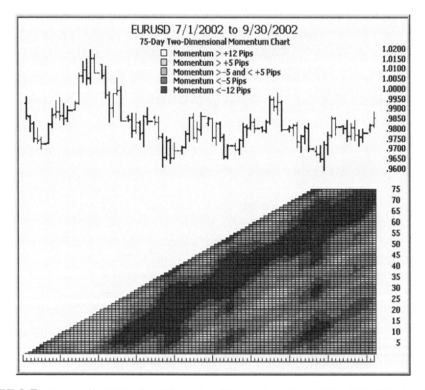

FIGURE 9.7 OHLC with 75-Day Two-Dimensional Momentum Chart Using 5-Day Moving Average

CHAPTER 10

Moving
Trend Analysis

OVERVIEW

Trend analysis is a somewhat nebulous term when applied to the science of forecasting price movements. Some traders will probably think of J. Welles Wilder's Relative Strength Index or George Lane's stochastic oscillators. In this chapter we define a trend in terms of its most basic mathematical properties.

LINEAR REGRESSION

A linear regression is a statistical tool that traders can use to determine how closely a data set (say, a stream of sequential closing prices) fits a straight-line model. From elementary geometry, we recall the diagram and formula shown in Figure 10.1.

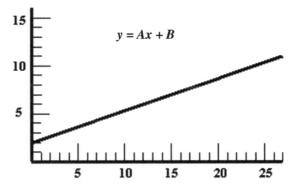

$$y = Ax + B$$

FIGURE 10.1 Straight-Line Model

The general formula for the straight-line model is:

$$y = Ax + B$$

where x = independent variable (time units)
         y = dependent variable (prices)
         A = slope
         B = intercept

The straight-line model has only two regression coefficients: intercept and slope.

The intercept is the point where the y-axis and the straight line intersect. In this example, the intercept equals +2.

The slope is the ratio of the y-axis value less the intercept to the x-axis value for every point along the straight line:

$$\text{Slope} = \frac{(y - \text{Intercept})}{x}$$

One observed point on the straight line is $x = 15$ and $y = 7$. Therefore:

$$\text{Slope} = \frac{(7 - 2)}{15}$$

$$= \frac{5}{15}$$

$$= \frac{1}{3} \text{ or } .333333$$

In other words, for every unit of price that the model advances along the y-axis, three time units are advanced along the x-axis.

An alternate (and more accurate) definition of slope is the quotient of the *change* in the y-axis divided by the *change* in the x-axis for any two points along the straight line:

$$\text{Slope} = \frac{y_2 - y_1}{x_2 - x_1}$$

Note that the slope can be positive, negative, or zero.

ORDINARY LEAST SQUARES METHOD

The slope and intercept for any set of continuous data can be calculated by using the ordinary least square (OLS) regression model for a straight line seen in Figures 10.2 and 10.3.

$$\text{Slope} = \frac{n\Sigma xy - \Sigma x\Sigma y}{n\Sigma x^2 - \Sigma x\Sigma x}$$

FIGURE 10.2 Slope Regression Formula

$$\text{Intercept} = \frac{\Sigma x^2\Sigma y - \Sigma x\Sigma xy}{n\Sigma x^2 - \Sigma x\Sigma x}$$

FIGURE 10.3 Intercept Regression Formula

$$r = \frac{n\Sigma xy - \Sigma x\Sigma y}{[(n\Sigma x^2 - \Sigma x\Sigma x)(n\Sigma y^2 - \Sigma y\Sigma y)]^{1/2}}$$

FIGURE 10.4 Coefficient of Correlation Formula

COEFFICENT OF CORRELATION

Calculating the regression coefficients for the estimated slope and intercept for a data set is only half the battle. We also need to know how well our estimated values match the raw data. For this purpose, we use another statistical tool called the coefficient of correlation or simply r. (See Figure 10.4.)

Any introductory text on descriptive statistics will supply traders with additional information on these and other regression techniques, their purpose and usage.

TREND OSCILLATORS

The whole purpose behind burdening traders with this refresher course in elementary statistics is to provide a method for scrutinizing trending properties in actual forex data. In Figure 10.5, we present two new oscillators: the moving slope oscillator and the moving correlation oscillator.

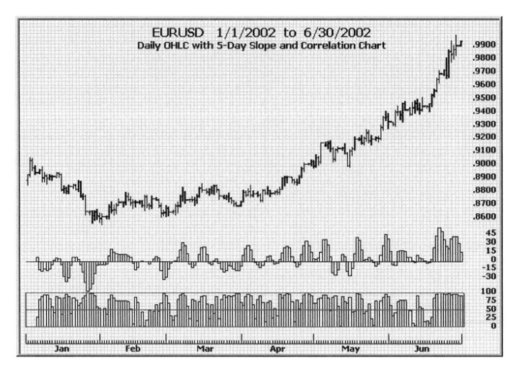

FIGURE 10.5   Five-Day Moving Slope and Correlation Oscillators

MOVING SLOPE OSCILLATOR

In a sufficiently large set of closing prices, the moving slope oscillator will fluctuate around a mean of zero. Positive values represent uptrends and negative values represent downtrends. The magnitude indicates how sharply the prices are trending. The vertical scale to the right of the oscillator is expressed in terms of pips in the quote currency per time units.

MOVING CORRELATION OSCILLATOR

The quality or reliability of a trend is represented by the oscillator at the bottom of the chart, the moving correlation oscillator, which has been adjusted to fluctuate between 0 and +100 as seen in the vertical scale to the right. When the correlation value drops below 85, a change in trend is normally indicated.

MOVING TREND INDEX

The moving trend index is analogous to a moving average index. It defines the number of elements to include in each sample moving across the x-axis. The same moving trend index must be used for both oscillators. In Figures 10.6 through 10.8, gradually increasing moving trend indexes are employed.

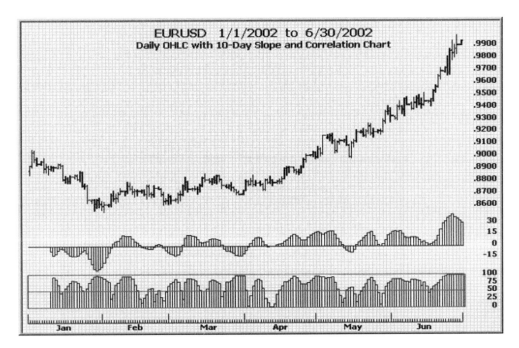

FIGURE 10.6 OHLC with 10-Day Moving Slope and Correlation Oscillators

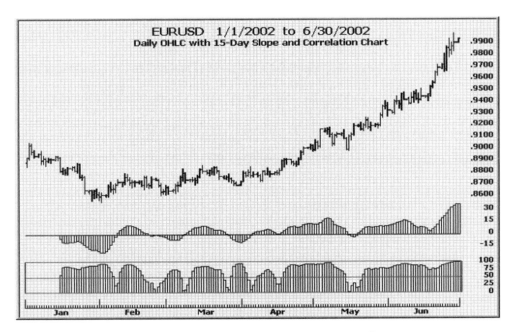

FIGURE 10.7 OHLC with 15-Day Moving Slope and Correlation Oscillators

FIGURE 10.8   OHLC with 25-Day Moving Slope and Correlation Oscillators

OBSERVATIONS

The obvious effect of increasing the size of the moving trend index is a corresponding decrease in the number of peaks and valleys in the moving slope oscillator and in the moving correlation oscillator. Another rather logical result is the fact that the values for the moving slope oscillator tend to decrease as the moving trend index increases. Coincidentally, moving trend analysis may also be employed to extract information on the wavelengths of dominant cycles indigenous to the time series.

PART II

Point and Figure Charting

CHAPTER 11

History of Point
and Figure Charting

OVERVIEW

In this section we concentrate a genre of charts referred to as reversal charts and, more specifically, a subset known as the point and figure (P&F) chart in which the raw financial data is converted into vertical columns of Xs and Os. A column of Xs represents advancing prices while a column of Os indicates declining prices. (See Figure 11.1.)

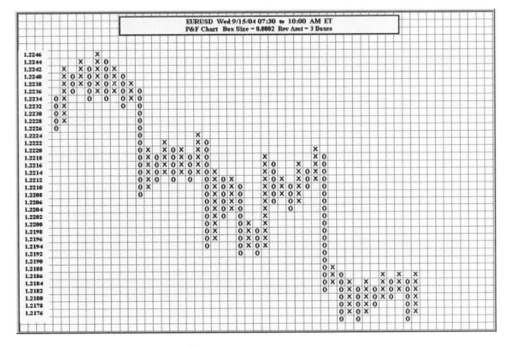

FIGURE 11.1   Point and Figure Chart

HISTORY

The point and figure chart (also called the three box reversal method) was created in the later nineteenth century. Roughly 15 years older than the bar chart, it is probably the oldest Western method of charting prices around. Its roots date way back into trading lore, as it has been intimated that this method was successfully used by the legendary trader James R. Keene during the merger of the Carnegie Steel Company into U.S. Steel in 1901. Keene was employed by Andrew Carnegie to distribute his holding, as Carnegie refused to take stock as payment for his equity interest in the company. Keene, using point and figure charting and tape readings, managed to promote the stock and get rid of Carnegie's sizable stake without causing the price to crash.

The point and figure method derives its name from the fact that price is recorded using figures (Xs and Os) to represent a point hence point and figure. Charles Dow, the founder of the *Wall Street Journal* and the inventor of stock indexes, was rumored to be a point and figure user, and the practice of point and figure charting is alive and well today on the floor of the Chicago Board of Trade. Its simplicity in identifying price trends, support, and resistance and its ease of upkeep have allowed this method to endure the test of time, even in the age of web sites, personal computers, and the information explosion.

CHAPTER 12

The Point and Figure Algorithm

OVERVIEW

Point and figure (P&F) charts are members of a genre of charts normally referred to as reversal charts. A reversal chart is any chart that filters the raw data in order to accentuate significant points of interest while ignoring points of less interest. All technical analysts find peaks and valleys of great interest while areas of lateral price movements are less interesting. Peaks and valleys are those points of inflection where price directions reverse and the slope of an existing trend changes its arithmetic sign (minus to plus and plus to minus).

P&F ANATOMY

Price advances are represented as vertical columns of Xs while price declines are represented as columns of Os. (See Figure 12.1.)

Two user-supplied variables are required to plot a point and figure chart, box size, and reversal amount.

BOX SIZE

Traditionally, the minimum price unit is the smallest fractional price increment by which the quote currency (or underlying security) can change. In the currency markets, this increment is a single pip. For example, if the EURUSD currency pair is currently trading at 1.2451, a single pip is 0.0001 USD.

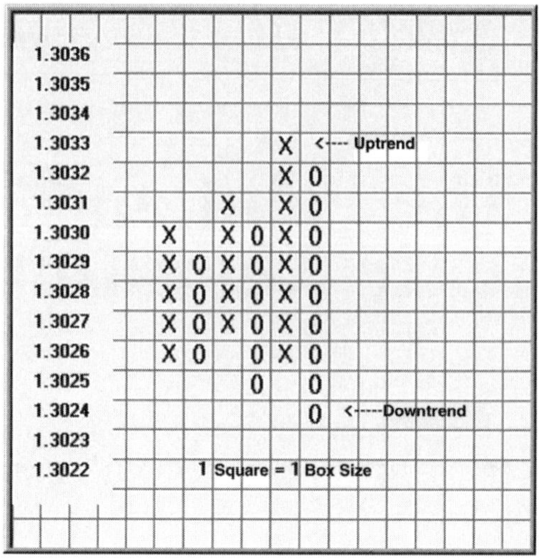

FIGURE 12.1 P&F Anatomy

There are cases where a box size greater than one pip might be used such as when the parity rate between two currencies is very wide and causes a very large bid/ask spread. For example, if the bid/ask spread (transaction cost) for the EURCZK currency pair is 350 koruny, then a one-pip box size will have very negligible filtering power.

A second reason for using a box size greater than one pip occurs when performing historical analysis and a longer time frame is being analyzed. In this case, the analyst will probably be scrutinizing major reversals and may have little interest in minor reversals. This pertains more to position traders than session or day traders.

REVERSAL AMOUNT

The reversal amount is the number of boxes necessary to plot a reversal in price direction. For instance, if the current trend is upward and the reversal amount is set at three boxes, then a decline of three box units must be reached before the downward movement is plotted. If instead, a new price continues in the direction of the existing trend, then single boxes are automatically added to the last extreme (either a peak or a valley).

It is the mutual interaction between the box size and the reversal amount that triggers the reversal mechanism in the reversal algorithm necessary to plot new columns of Xs and Os while ignoring lateral price movements.

There is one final case for increasing the box size. If an analyst, for whatever reason, has become very partial to one specific reversal amount, it is possible to increase the box size instead of the reversal amount when market conditions change.

For example, a three-box reversal amount is favored by many traders. If traders wish to filter out some of the minor reversals, they can increase either the reversal amount or the box size. However, keep in mind that although a two-pip box size with a three-box reversal amount algorithm will generate results very similar to a one-pip box size with a six-box reversal amount algorithm, they will not be identical. This requires some reflection. The reason is that, when plotting a continuation of an existing trend, smaller distances can be plotted when a smaller box size is used.

UNRAVELING BAR QUOTE DATA

Before we explain the intricacies of the P&F reversal algorithm, we need to massage the OHLC quote data into a stream of single values (closes only). The four bar quotes (open, high, low, and close) must be stretched out and ordered according to which occurred first. Actually, this applies only to the high and low quotes, and the Visual Basic 6.0 "unraveling" routine is given in Appendix N. This greatly simplifies the reversal algorithm in the next section.

P&F ALGORITHM

Upward trends are represented as a vertical column of Xs, while downward trends are displayed as an adjacent column of Os.

New figures (Xs or Os) cannot be added to the current column unless the increase (or decrease) in price satisfies the minimum box size requirement. A reversal cannot be plotted in the subsequent column until the price has changed by the reversal amount times the box size.

Programmatically, this first step to plotting a point and figure chart is to determine the number of Xs and Os in each alternating column and to store the values in a global array. A separate function was written to accomplish this goal.

Given the information and user-supplied variables, we will now define the swing reversal algorithm as follows (this algorithm assumes we are using daily OHLC quotes as the input data):

Step 1: Initialize BoxSize and ReversalAmount variables.
Step 2: Create a new variable called Direction.
Step 3: Create an array variable called Price(MAX_PRICES).
Step 4: Set Price(1) = Close(1).
Step 5: If Close(2) – Price(1) > BoxSize * ReversalAmount Then
        Set Price(2) = Close(2)
        Set Direction = UP
   ElseIf Price(1) – Close(2) > BoxSize * ReversalAmount Then
        Set Price(2) = Close(2)
        Set Direction = DOWN

```
        Else
                Increment day number and repeat Step 5
        End If
Step 6: Increment DayNo
        If DayNo = Number of Closes Then
                Go to Step 9
        If Direction = DOWN Then
                Go to Step 8
        End If
Step 7:  If Close(DayNo) – Price(Idx) > BoxSize Then
                Set Price(Idx) = Close(DayNo)
        ElseIf Price(Idx) – Close (DayNo) > BoxSize * ReversalAmount Then
                Increment Swing Idx
                Set Price(Idx) = Close (DayNo)
                Set Direction = DOWN
        End If
                Go to Step 6
Step 8:  If Close (DayNo) – Price(Idx) > BoxSize * ReversalAmount Then
                Increment Swing Idx
                Set Price(Idx) = Close (DayNo)
                Set Direction = UP
        ElseIf Price(Idx) – Close (DayNo) > BoxSize Then
                Set Price(Idx) = Close (DayNo)
        End If
                Go to Step 6
Step 9:  Set Number of Swings = Swing Idx
                Exit
```

At this point the array Price() has been populated with the necessary P&F data. The complete code for the preceding algorithm written in Microsoft Visual Basic 6.0 is provided in Appendix N.

TIME REPRESENTATION

Adherents of the point and figure charting method believe that the compression of time along the x-axis is an advantage since the trader can then focus solely on price movements. Proponents of swing charts, by contrast, are more comfortable viewing the points of inflection (peaks and valleys) as they occur in real time.

CHAPTER 13

Trend Lines

SUPPORT AND RESISTANCE

A support level indicates the price at which most traders feel that prices will move higher. There is sufficient demand for a security to cause a halt in a downward trend and turn the trend up. You can spot support levels on the point and figure (P&F) charts by looking for a sequence of daily lows that fluctuate only slightly along a horizontal line. When a support level is penetrated (the price drops below the support level) it often becomes a new resistance level; this is because traders want to limit their losses and will sell later, when prices approach the former level.

Like support levels, resistance levels are horizontal lines on the P&F chart. They mark the upper level for trading, or a price at which sellers typically outnumber buyers. When a resistance level is broken and the price moves above the resistance level, it often does so decisively.

The area between the support line and the resistance line is frequently referred to as the security's current trading range. (See Figure 13.1.)

TREND LINES

A trend can be up, down, or lateral and is represented by drawing a straight line above the highest Xs in a downward trend and a straight line below the lowest Os in an upward trend. (See Figure 13.2.)

A common trading technique involves the intersection of the trend line with the most recent prices. If the trend line for a downward trend crosses through the most recent prices, a buy signal is generated. Conversely, if the trend line for an upward trend passes through the most recent prices, then a sell signal is generated.

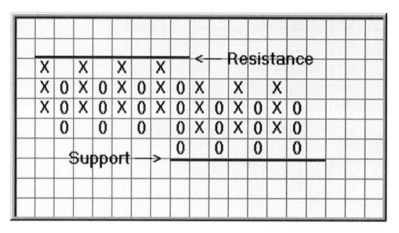

FIGURE 13.1 Support and Resistance

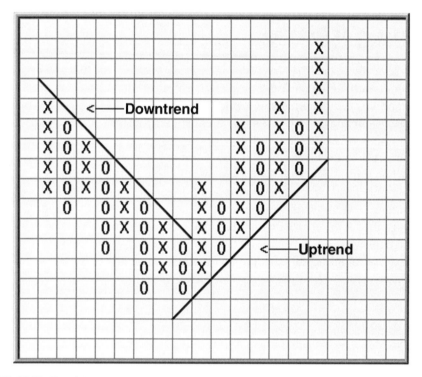

FIGURE 13.2 Trend Lines

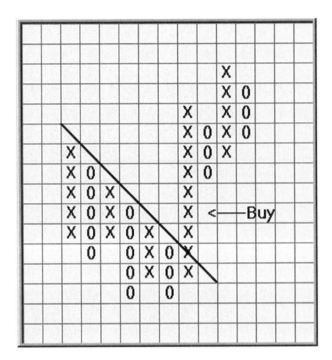

FIGURE 13.3 Buy Signal

BUY SIGNALS

Many traders feel that when a downward trend line crosses through a vertical column of Xs, a buy signal is generated. The market entry point is the first X that is above the highest X in the previous column of Xs. (See Figure 13.3.)

SELL SIGNALS

The converse is true regarding an upward trend line crossing through a column of Os; that is, a sell signal is generated. The market entry point is the first O that is below the lowest O in the previous column of Os. (See Figure 13.4.)

We recommend that traders confirm trend lines' buy and sell signals using other formation signals before entering the market. Paper trading is the safest way to hone one's skills at signal identification.

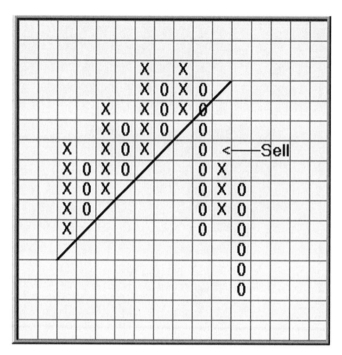

FIGURE 13.4 Sell Signal

CHAPTER 14

Double Tops and Bottoms

OVERVIEW

Pattern recognition is essential to profitable point and figure charting. In this chapter, we examine two of the most basic P&F formations.

DOUBLE TOP PATTERN

One of the easiest P&F chart formations to identify is the double top pattern which consists of two X columns and one O column. (See Figure 14.1.) The highest Xs in both

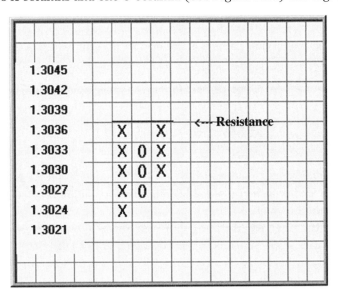

FIGURE 14.1 Double Top

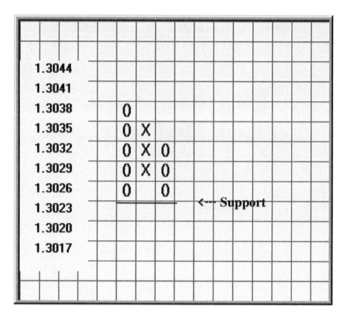

FIGURE 14.2 Double Bottom

the X columns must be in the same row, thus forming a local (and temporary) line of resistance.

DOUBLE BOTTOM PATTERN

The inverse to the double top pattern is the double bottom, which has two O columns and one X column. (See Figure 14.2.) The lowest Os in both columns must be in the same row, thus forming a local line of support.

DOUBLE TOP SIGNALS

In the double top pattern displayed in Figure 14.1, the stage is set for a potential buy or sell market entry signal. If the price can exceed the local line of resistance, then a buy signal is generated. (See Figure 14.3.)

Coversely, if the price can decline below the lowest O in the previous columns of Os, then a sell market entry signal is triggered. (See Figure 14.4.)

There is a third alternative in which the price does in fact decline but does not go lower than the lowest O in the previous O column. (See Figure 14.5.) The pattern

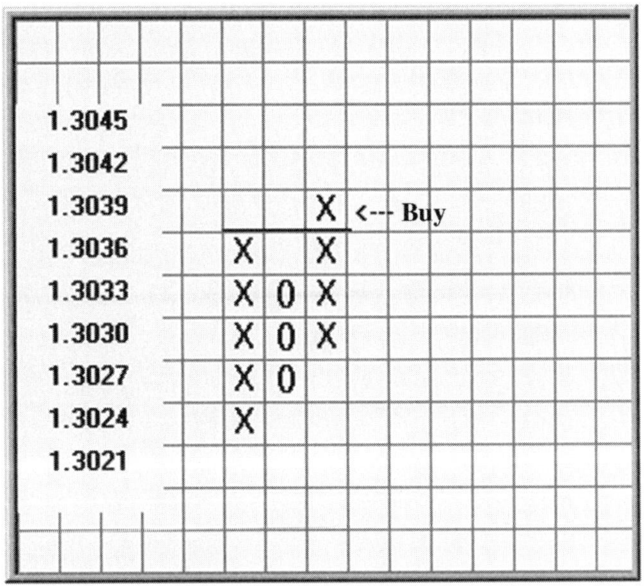

FIGURE 14.3 Double Top Buy Signal

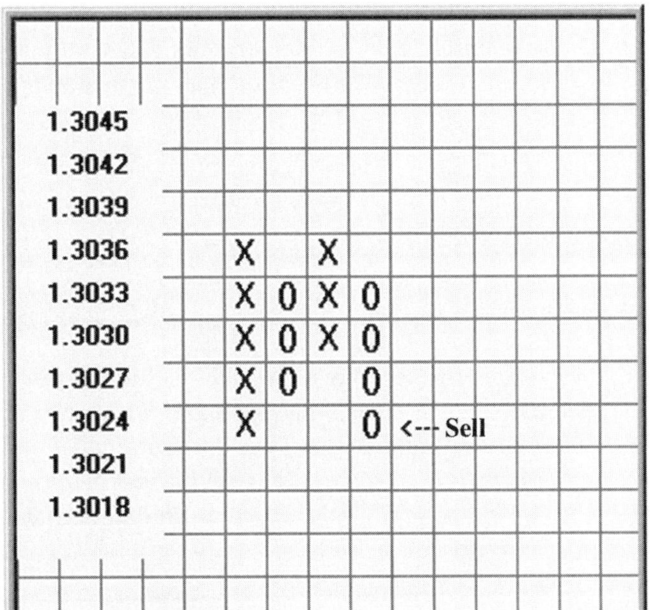

FIGURE 14.4 Double Top Sell Signal

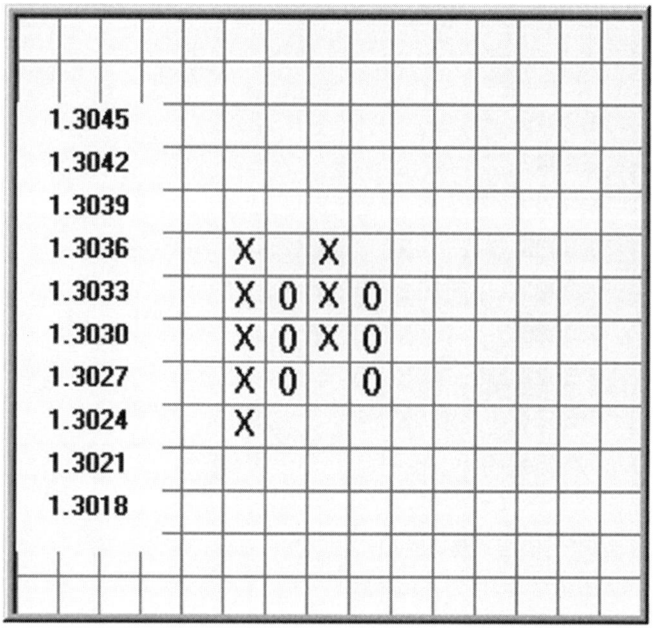

1.3045					
1.3042					
1.3039					
1.3036	X		X		
1.3033	X	O	X	O	
1.3030	X	O	X	O	
1.3027	X	O		O	
1.3024	X				
1.3021					
1.3018					

FIGURE 14.5   Double Top No Signal

does not generate an immediate signal. In fact, traders will note that with the latest price movement the original double top formation has now become a double bottom pattern.

DOUBLE BOTTOM SIGNALS

If the price can extend below the local line of support in a double bottom pattern, then a sell signal is generated. (See Figure 14.6.)

However, if the price can advance above the highest X in the previous columns of Xs, then a buy market entry signal is triggered. (See Figure 14.7.)

Analogous to the double top pattern, there is a third alternative in which the price does in fact advance but does not go higher than the highest X in the previous X column. (See Figure 14.8.) In the diagram, no immediate trading signals have been triggered. The latest price movement has transformed the double bottom into a double top formation.

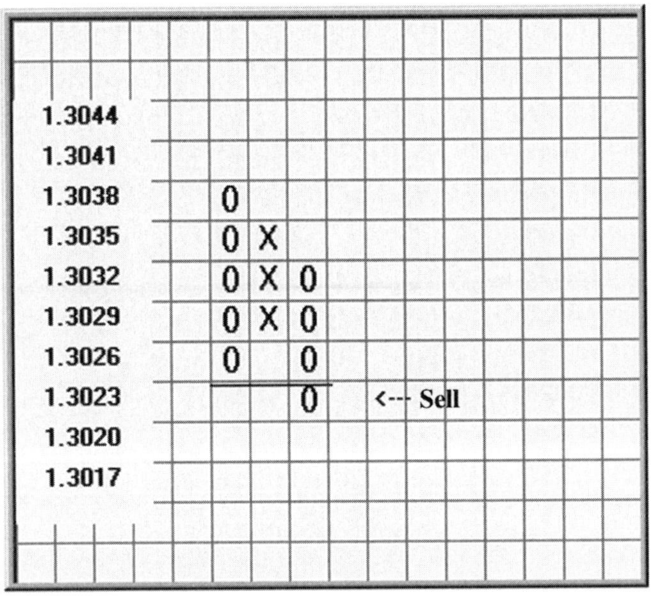

FIGURE 14.6 Double Bottom Sell Signal

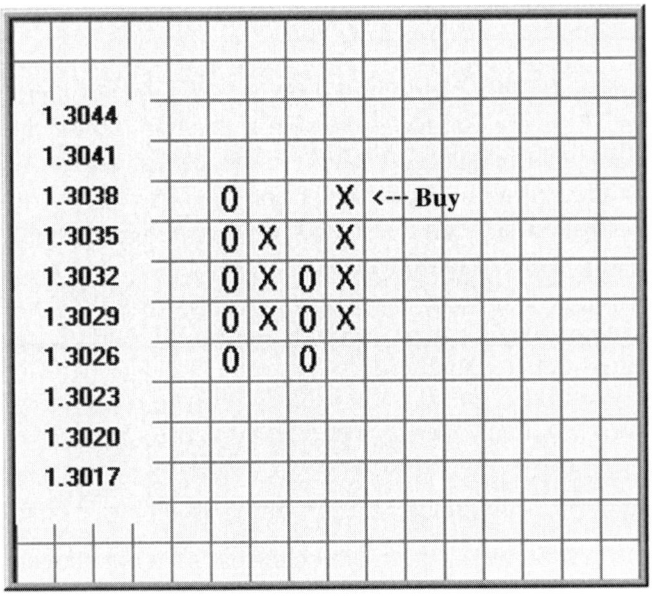

FIGURE 14.7 Double Bottom Buy Signal

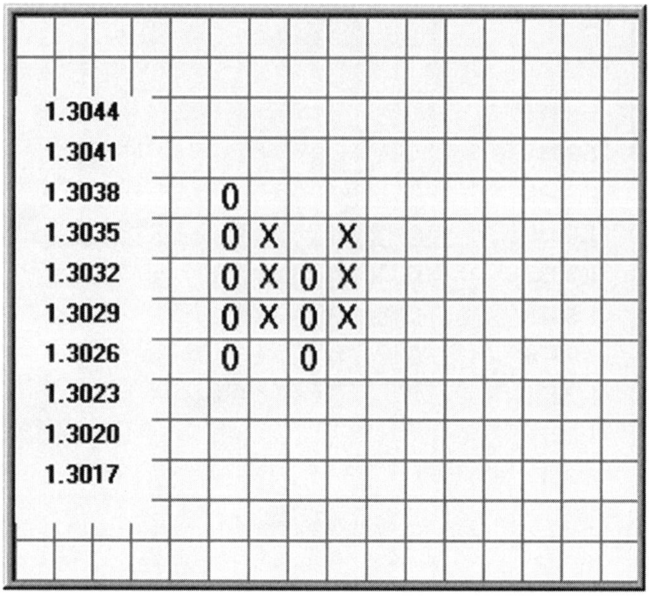

FIGURE 14.8 Double Bottom No Signal

FALSE SIGNALS

All traders are familiar with the concept of false signals, perhaps more intimately than they wish to admit. This undesirable phenomenon involves the following sequence of events: (1) a buy or sell signal is generated by some mechanical means, (2) the trader enters the market at the designated price level, and (3) a breakout in the opposite direction occurs. False signals have also been labeled failures. Regardless of the nomenclature, they can be very disheartening and costly.

Although the effect of false signals can never be completely eliminated, their detrimental impact can be significantly reduced by the use of confirming signals and the proper positioning of stop-loss limit orders.

SIGNAL PERCENTAGES

We will be using the diagrams in Figure 14.9 as the basis for our statistical calculations.

On the left is a double top pattern and on the right is a double bottom pattern. Both employ a three-box reversal amount that will remain constant throughout this analysis. We will vary the box size from one pip to five pips. The sample data is our 7,000,000+ quotes in our SQL (structured query language) database, which consists of the streaming tick closes for the calendar year of 2002 in the EURUSD currency pair.

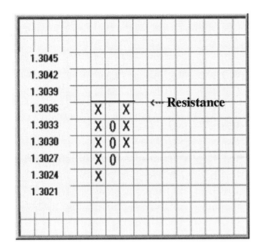 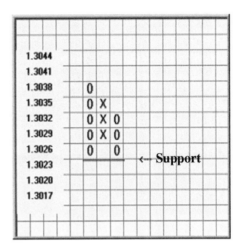

FIGURE 14.9 Resistance and Support

Likelihood of a Reversal

The likelihood of a reversal in price direction after the basic double top or double bottom pattern is as shown in Table 14.1.

The results in the table are not particularly impressive since it is a common belief that there is a 50:50 chance that the next price will go either up or down anyway. It is interesting, though, when we consider that a change in price direction must satisfy the minimum reversal amount of three boxes, while a single box is all that is necessary to continue the trend in the most recent column.

Continuation Percentages

In Table 14.2, the leftmost column lists the number of boxes required to continue the trend in the current column in either of the two patterns in Figure 14.9. The numbers in the top row indicate the box size for the reversal algorithm.

For example, assume a double bottom pattern with a four-box reversal amount. The likelihood that the price movement will decline exactly two boxes is 24.40 percent (the

Box Size	Percentage
1	48.67
2	50.52
3	50.66
4	50.60
5	50.56

TABLE 14.1 Reversal Percentages

Boxes	1	2	3	4	5
1	57.61	58.67	58.47	58.31	58.21
2	24.83	24.44	24.42	24.40	24.39
3	11.25	10.72	10.73	10.76	10.77
4	4.11	3.94	3.99	4.03	4.05
5	1.24	1.23	1.29	1.33	1.36
6	0.49	0.51	0.55	0.57	0.59
7	0.23	0.23	0.26	0.27	0.28
8	0.11	0.12	0.14	0.15	0.15
9	0.05	0.05	0.06	0.06	0.07
10	0.03	0.03	0.04	0.04	0.04
11	0.02	0.02	0.02	0.03	0.03
12	0.01	0.01	0.01	0.02	0.02
13	0.01	0.01	0.01	0.01	0.01
14	0.01	0.01	0.01	0.01	0.01
15	0.00	0.00	0.00	0.00	0.00

TABLE 14.2 Continuation Percentages

intersection of the row labeled 2 and the column labeled 4). The probability that it will decline two or more boxes is 41.69 percent (100 – 58.31).

The continuation percentages may look low since a buy or sell signal has already been generated with a minimum of one continuation box. However, it is not necessary for the price objective to occur in the same column in which the signal is generated. Two, four, or even six columns may occur before the price objective is reached.

OBSERVATIONS

The double top and bottom patterns are two of the simplest price formations to identify. Traders should also calculate existing trend, support, and resistance lines as well as other factors before initiating a new trade based solely on these double pattern signals.

CHAPTER 15

Triple Tops
and Bottoms

OVERVIEW

Essentially triple tops and bottoms are extensions of the double top and bottom formations in the previous chapter.

TRIPLE TOP PATTERN

The triple top pattern consists of three X columns and two O columns. (See Figure 15.1.) The highest Xs in all X columns must be in the same row, thus forming a local (and temporary) line of resistance.

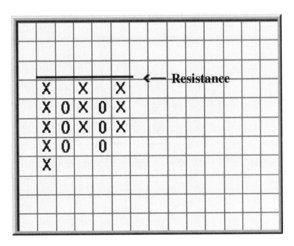

FIGURE 15.1 Triple Top

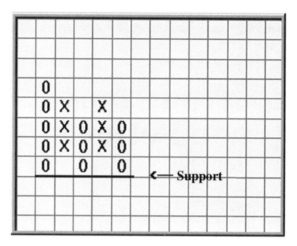

FIGURE 15.2 Triple Bottom

TRIPLE BOTTOM PATTERN

The inverse to the triple top pattern is the triple bottom, which has three O columns and two X columns. (See Figure 15.2.) The lowest Os in all columns must be in the same row, forming a local line of support.

TRIPLE TOP SIGNALS

In the triple top pattern displayed in Figure 15.1, the stage is set for a potential buy or sell market entry signal. If the price can exceed the local line of resistance, then a buy signal is generated. (See Figure 15.3.)

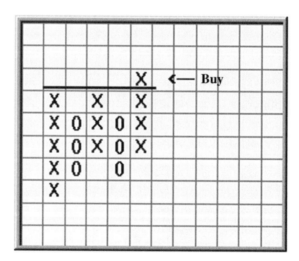

FIGURE 15.3 Triple Top Buy Signal

However, if the price can decline below the lowest O in the previous columns of Os, then a sell market entry signal is triggered. (See Figure 15.4.)

There is a third alternative in which the price does in fact decline but does not go lower than the lowest O in the previous column of Os. (See Figure 15.5.) The pattern does not generate an immediate signal. Note that with the latest price movement the original triple top formation has now become a triple bottom pattern.

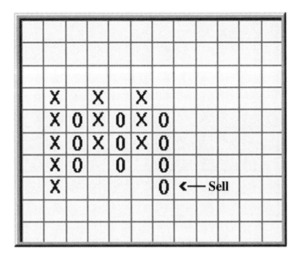

FIGURE 15.4   Triple Top Sell Signal

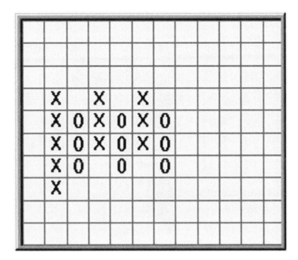

FIGURE 15.5   Triple Top No Signal

TRIPLE BOTTOM SIGNALS

If the price can extend below the local line of support in a triple bottom pattern, then a sell signal is generated, as shown in Figure 15.6.

However, if the price can advance above the highest X in the previous columns of Xs, then a buy market entry signal is triggered. (See Figure 15.7.)

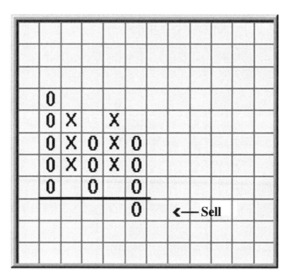

FIGURE 15.6   Triple Bottom Sell Signal

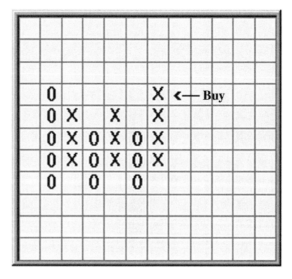

FIGURE 15.7   Triple Bottom Buy Signal

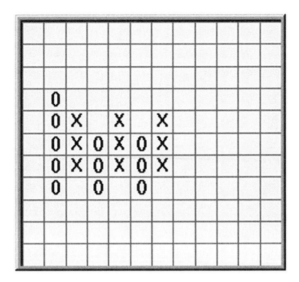

FIGURE 15.8 Triple Bottom No Signal

Analogous to the triple top pattern, there is a third alternative in which the price does in fact advance but does not go higher than the highest X in the previous X column. (See Figure 15.8.) In the diagram, no immediate trading signals have been triggered. The latest price movement has transformed the triple bottom pattern into a triple top formation.

FALSE SIGNALS

All traders are familiar with the concept of false signals, perhaps more intimately than they wish to admit. This undesirable phenomenon involves the following sequence of events: (1) a buy or sell signal is generated by some mechanical means, (2) the trader enters the market at the designated price level, and (3) a breakout in the opposite direction occurs. False signals have also been labeled failures. Regardless of the nomenclature, they can be very disheartening and costly.

Although the effect of false signals can never be completely eliminated, their detrimental impact can be significantly reduced by the use of confirming signals and the proper positioning of stop-loss limit orders.

SIGNAL PERCENTAGES

We will be using Figure 15.9 as the basis for our statistical calculations.

On the left is a triple top pattern and on the right is a triple bottom pattern. Both employ a three-box reversal amount that will remain constant throughout this analysis. We

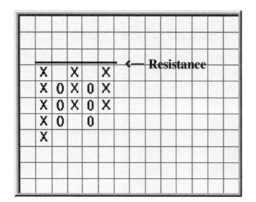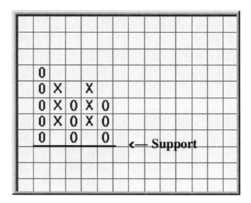

FIGURE 15.9 Statistical Basis

will vary the box size from one pip to five pips. The sample data is our 7,000,000+ quotes in our SQL database, which consists of the streaming tick closes for the calendar year of 2002 in the EURUSD currency pair.

Likelihood of a Reversal

The likelihood of a reversal in price direction after the basic triple top or triple bottom pattern is as shown in Table 15.1.

The results in the table are not particularly impressive since it is a common belief that there is a 50:50 chance that the next price will go either up or down anyway. It is interesting, though, when we consider that a change in price direction must satisfy the minimum reversal amount of three boxes, while a single box is all that is necessary to continue the trend in the most recent column.

Continuation Percentages

In Table 15.2, the leftmost column lists the number of boxes required to continue the existing trend in the current column in either of the two patterns in Figure 15.9. The numbers in the top row indicate the box size for the reversal algorithm.

Box Size	Percentage
1	52.16
2	54.50
3	54.74
4	54.71
5	54.69

TABLE 15.1 Reversal Percentages

Box	1	2	3	4	5
1	59.57	61.32	61.09	60.93	60.87
2	23.57	23.05	23.04	23.05	23.06
3	10.94	10.04	10.07	10.09	10.10
4	4.10	3.77	3.80	3.84	3.85
5	1.06	1.02	1.10	1.12	1.14
6	0.40	0.41	0.45	0.47	0.48
7	0.16	0.17	0.19	0.21	0.21
8	0.10	0.10	0.11	0.13	0.13
9	0.04	0.05	0.06	0.06	0.07
10	0.02	0.02	0.03	0.03	0.03
11	0.01	0.01	0.01	0.02	0.02
12	0.01	0.01	0.01	0.01	0.02

TABLE 15.2 Continuation Percentages

For example, assume a triple bottom pattern with a four-box reversal amount. The likelihood that the price movement will decline exactly two boxes is 23.05 percent (the intersection of the row labeled 2 and the column labeled 4). The probability that it will decline two or more boxes is 39.07 percent (100 – 60.93).

The continuation percentages may look low since a buy or sell signal has already been generated with a minimum of one continuation box. However, it is not necessary for the price objective to occur in the same column in which the signal is generated. Two, four, or even six columns may occur before the price objective is reached.

OBSERVATIONS

The triple top and bottom patterns are two of the simplest price formations to identify. Traders should also calculate existing trend, support, and resistance lines as well as other factors before initiating a new trade based solely on these triple pattern signals.

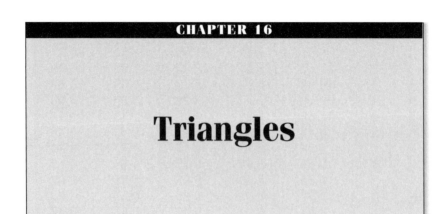

CHAPTER 16

Triangles

OVERVIEW

A triangle pattern occurs when a trend in either direction is in motion and the trading range temporarily diminishes. In the stock market, this is attributed to a retracement phenomenon that allows supply and demand levels to adjust to the recent price changes and is also called accumulation and distribution.

ASCENDING TRIANGLES

An ascending triangle is a point and figure (P&F) pattern that is contained within the line of resistance at the top and a 45-degree upward trend line. (See Figure 16.1.)

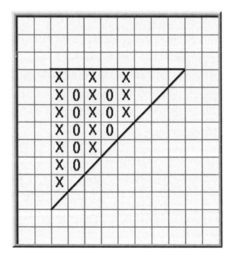

FIGURE 16.1 Ascending Triangle

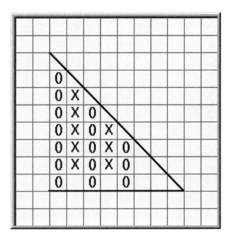

FIGURE 16.2 Descending Triangle

DESCENDING TRIANGLES

A descending triangle is a P&F pattern that is contained within the line of support at the bottom and a 45-degree downward trend line. (See Figure 16.2.)

SYMMETRICAL TRIANGLES

A symmetrical triangle is a P&F pattern in which the trading range decreases equally in both directions and that is contained between a 45-degree downward trend line on the top and a 45-degree upward trend line on the bottom. (See Figure 16.3.)

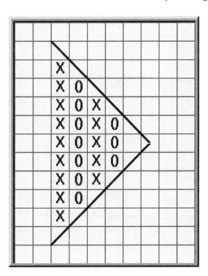

FIGURE 16.3 Symmetrical Triangle

TRIANGLE SIGNALS

Traditionally, triangles have been considered to be continuation patterns. That is, whichever trend was in motion prior to the appearance of a triangle will be the same trend after the conclusion of the triangle.

In the calculations that follow, a one-pip box size and a three-box reversal amount are used with the 7,000,000+ EURUSD database.

ASCENDING AND DESCENDING FREQUENCIES

Since ascending and descending triangles are symmetrical counterparts (inverse patterns rotated about the x-axis), the frequencies of their three-column sequels were calculated together. (See Table 16.1.)

Rank	Pattern	Frequency
1	333	26
2	334	21
3	444	14
4	443	12
5	433	12
6	445	10
7	335	10
8	434	8
9	543	7
10	343	6
11	545	5
12	455	5
13	336	5
14	344	5
15	354	5
16	355	5
17	644	4
18	664	4
19	533	4
20	534	4
21	553	4
22	554	4
23	564	4
24	464	4
25	465	4

TABLE 16.1 Triangle Frequencies

The ascending triangle pattern and its nine most frequent three-column sequels are shown in Figure 16.4.

The descending triangle pattern and its nine most frequent three-column sequels are shown in Figure 16.5.

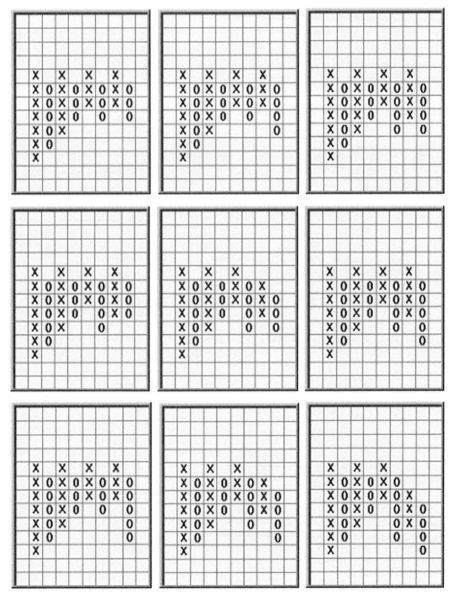

FIGURE 16.4 Ascending Triangle Most Frequent Sequels

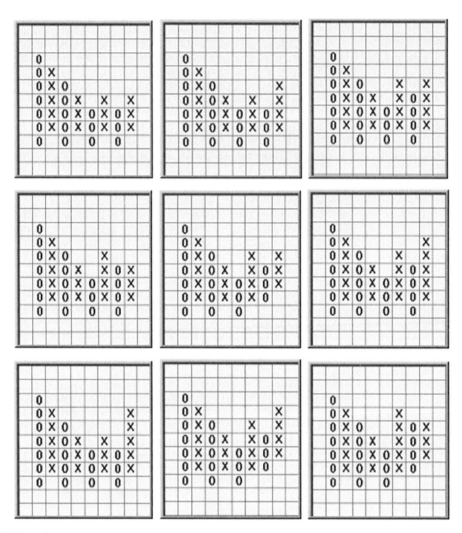

FIGURE 16.5 Descending Triangle Most Frequent Sequels

Rank	Pattern	Frequency
1	333	6
2	334	5
3	443	3
4	353	3
5	343	3
6	554	2
7	544	2
8	336	2
9	434	2
10	344	2
11	345	2
12	354	1
13	356	1
14	357	1
15	358	1
16	363	1
17	365	1
18	366	1
19	375	1
20	438	1
21	444	1
22	453	1
23	464	1
24	475	1
25	494	1

TABLE 16.2 Symmetrical Frequencies

SYMMETRICAL FREQUENCIES

Given the number of Xs and Os in the symmetrical pattern as 9753 (i.e., a sequence of columns consisting of nine, seven, five, and three Xs or Os), the most frequent three-column sequels are listed in Table 16.2.

The symmetrical triangle pattern 9753 and its nine most frequent three-column sequels are shown in Figure 16.6.

OBSERVATION

Readers should be aware that by their very nature all contracting triangles are setting the stage for a major breakout.

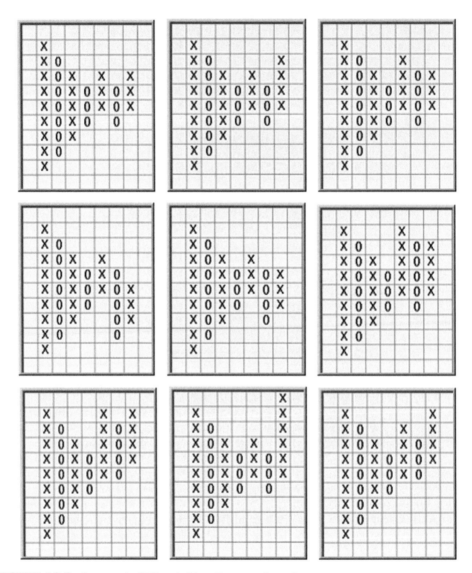

FIGURE 16.6 Symmetrical Triangle Most Frequent Sequels

CHAPTER 17

Pattern Frequencies

OVERVIEW

The ability to identify various point and figure (P&F) patterns and to look up their relative frequencies of occurrence can be advantageous when calculating possible subsequent column values.

Again we will employ our 7,000,000+ closes database as our statistical sample. We will use a reversal amount of three boxes and a seven-column pattern. We will limit the maximum number of figures (Xs or Os) in each column to nine (that is, quantities greater than nine are rounded down to nine). The minimum number of figures in each column is set at three because of the reversal algorithm mechanism. Thus there are seven possibilities for the number of Xs or Os in each column.

Each pattern consists of seven columns. This generates 823,543 possible patterns. In our initial computer tests, we discovered that the lateral congestion patterns like 3333333, 3343333, 3334333, and 3333433 dominated the top of the frequency count. Therefore, we found it necessary to impose a few conditions to filter these lateral patterns.

First, we mandated that the center column have the greatest number of figures among all the columns. This eliminates the redundancy of shifting the pattern one column in either direction. Second, the fourth column must have a minimum of six Xs or Os. These two conditions reduced the number of possible patterns nearly by half to 470,596.

BOX SIZE = ONE PIP

In Table 17.1, patterns are ranked by frequency of occurrence.

Using the one-pip box size, the nine most frequently encountered P&F patterns with seven columns with our filtering constraints are shown in Figure 17.1.

Rank	Pattern	Frequency
1	3346533	85
2	3356433	66
3	3346433	57
4	3356333	53
5	3446533	51
6	3336533	50
7	3346534	49
8	3356533	48
9	3346434	45
10	3356434	45
11	3456333	45
12	4446534	45
13	4456433	45
14	4356433	41
15	4446533	39
16	3356443	38
17	3456334	37
18	3456433	37
19	4346533	37
20	4356333	36
21	4356434	35
22	3346443	35
23	3346543	35
24	4456333	35
25	4356444	34

TABLE 17.1 Pattern Frequencies

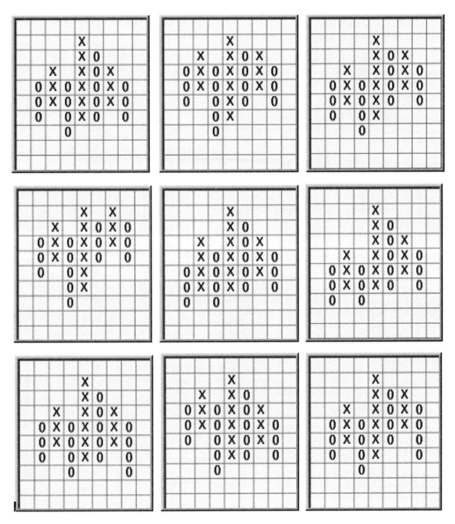

FIGURE 17.1 Patterns with Seven Columns

BOX SIZE = TWO PIPS

A two-pip box size generates the results listed in Table 17.2.

The three most frequent patterns are shown in Figure 17.2.

Rank	Pattern	Frequency
1	3336333	108
2	3336433	74
3	3346333	73
4	3336334	63
5	3346433	56
6	3436333	51
7	3346334	44
8	3356333	44
9	3336343	37
10	4346333	36
11	4436333	36
12	3337333	35
13	3356433	35
14	3336443	34
15	3336344	33
16	3346434	32
17	3446333	32
18	4336333	32
19	3336434	31
20	3336335	31
21	3336533	31
22	3347333	30
23	3436334	30
24	3436433	28
25	4336433	28

TABLE 17.2 Results for Two-Pip Box Size

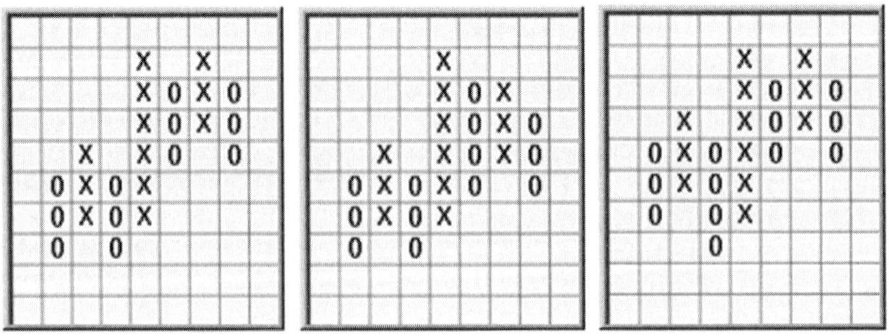

FIGURE 17.2 Most Frequent Two-Pip Patterns

BOX SIZE = THREE PIPS

A three-pip box size produces what is shown in Table 17.3.

The three most common patterns are shown in Figure 17.3.

Rank	Pattern	Frequency
1	3336333	18
2	3346333	18
3	3336334	17
4	3436333	15
5	3337333	14
6	3336533	13
7	3436433	13
8	3336343	10
9	3338333	10
10	3346433	10
11	3336433	9
12	3336344	9
13	3336543	8
14	3337433	8
15	3436443	8
16	5336333	8
17	4336333	7
18	3336443	7
19	3337344	7
20	4336433	6
21	3336353	6
22	3336434	6
23	3338433	6
24	3346343	6
25	3346533	6

TABLE 17.3 Frequencies for Three-Pip Box Size

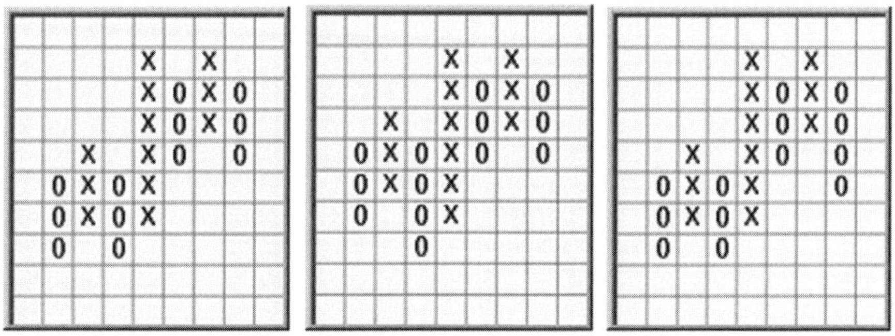

FIGURE 17.3 Most Frequent Three-Pip Patterns

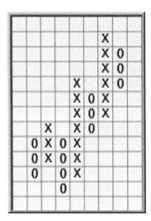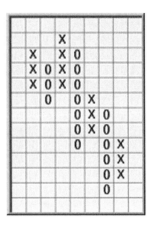

FIGURE 17.4 Inverse Patterns

INVERSE PATTERNS

While compiling these frequency counts, we also combined each unique pattern with its converse pattern (that is, we substituted Os for Xs and vice versa). For example, the two patterns shown in Figure 17.4 are both logged as 3347365.

USAGE

The tables and pattern diagrams in this chapter were compiled more or less as general information. They can, however, be used to estimate the number of Xs or Os in the subsequent columns.

For example, assume we are using a three-pip box size and a three-box reversal amount and we have a five-column pattern that consists of 33363 as in Figure 17.5.

FIGURE 17.5 Pattern 33363

Rank	Pattern	Frequency
1	3336333	18
3	3336334	17
12	3336344	9
21	3336353	6

TABLE 17.4 Frequencies by Rank

Using the third frequency table (Table 17.3), we locate all occurrences of the pattern 33363 in the first five columns. (See Table 17.4.)

By summing the frequencies, we can calculate the percentages of likelihood for each two-column sequel to the 33363 pattern: 33 = 36%, 34 = 34%, 44 = 18%, and 53 = 12%.

CHAPTER 18

Breakout Analysis

OVERVIEW

Breakouts, or very sharp price movements in one direction or the other, appear as elongated vertical columns in P&F charts. For example, in Figure 18.1 there is a 14-box upward breakout in column 5 and a 13-box downward breakout in column 10.

Some P&F analysts have also aptly dubbed these features "walls" or "poles."

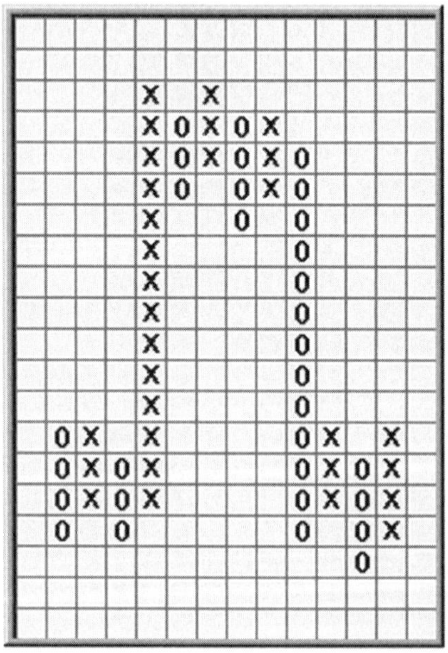

```
            X     X
            X  O  X  O  X
            X  O  X  O  X  O
            X  O        O  X  O
            X           O     O
            X                 O
            X                 O
            X                 O
            X                 O
            X                 O
            X                 O
      O  X     X             O  X        X
      O  X  O  X             O  X  O  X
      O  X  O  X             O  X  O  X
      O     O                O        O  X
                                      O
```

FIGURE 18.1 Breakouts

PRECEDING COLUMNS

Our objective is to catalog which price patterns immediately precede a breakout and to determine their respective percentages of occurrence. In the analysis that follows, we again consult our 7,000,000+ EURUSD database and we employ a three-box reversal amount in all cases.

Specifically, we map the frequencies of occurrence of every four-column pattern preceding the vertical column that contains nine or more boxes of either Xs or Os. Inverse patterns are summed together. For example a sequence of, three Xs, four Os, five Xs, and six Os is represented the same way as three Os, four Xs, five Os, and six Xs except that the succeeding breakout occurs is the opposite direction. (See Figures 18.2 through 18.4.)

Rank	Pattern	Frequency
1	3333	208
2	3334	149
3	3335	165
4	3344	114
5	3336	113
6	4336	105
7	4433	101
8	4334	100
9	3343	89
10	4333	89

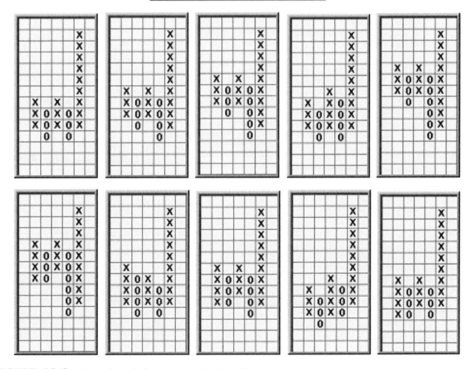

FIGURE 18.2 Preceding Column One-Pip Box Size

Rank	Pattern	Frequency
1	3333	59
2	3433	37
3	3334	33
4	3343	31
5	4333	27
6	4433	24
7	3335	21
8	3344	21
9	5333	18
10	4343	18

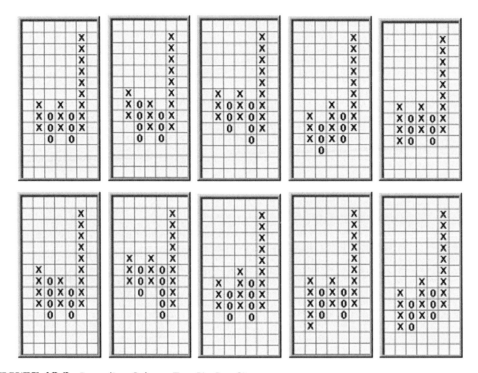

FIGURE 18.3   Preceding Column Two-Pip Box Size

Rank	Pattern	Frequency
1	3333	35
2	3353	22
3	3433	21
4	4333	21
5	3343	19
6	3334	18
7	4343	14
8	3344	14
9	4334	13
10	5333	13

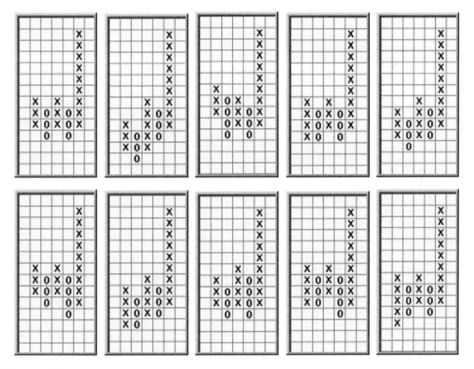

FIGURE 18.4 Preceding Column Three-Pip Box Size

In the remainder of this chapter, we present a table of column patterns with their respective frequencies for each box size along with a graphical representation of each pattern.

SUCCEEDING COLUMNS

Knowing which patterns will most likely follow a breakout can be just as important as knowing its preceding patterns. In the following analysis, we catalog the four-column patterns that immediately follow a nine or more box breakout. In all cases we use a three-box reversal amount for box sizes of one, two, and three pips. (See Figures 18.5 through 18.7.)

Rank	Pattern	Frequency
1	93333	211
2	99333	169
3	99334	143
4	94333	141
5	95333	129
6	94433	120
7	93344	117
8	99433	115
9	93334	114
10	96333	110

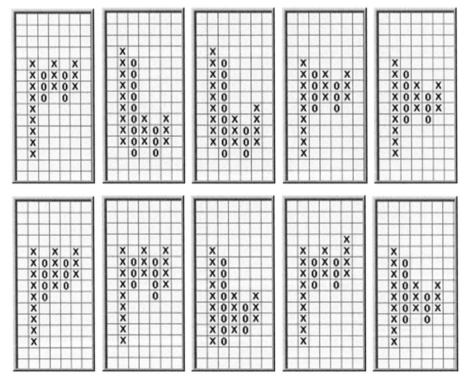

FIGURE 18.5 Succeeding Column One-Pip Box Size

Rank	Pattern	Frequency
1	93333	50
2	93334	30
3	93343	27
4	93433	21
5	94333	20
6	94433	19
7	93443	18
8	94334	15
9	94343	15
10	93434	13

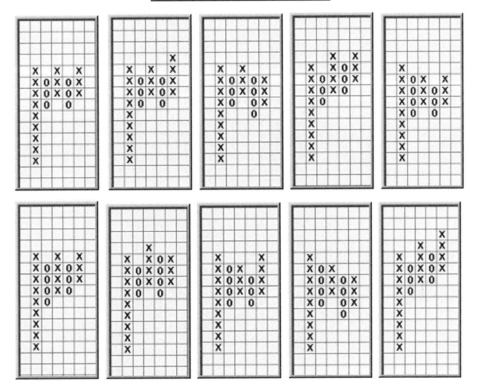

FIGURE 18.6 Succeeding Column Two-Pip Box Size

Rank	Pattern	Frequency
1	93343	30
2	93333	23
3	94333	23
4	93353	14
5	93334	13
6	95343	11
7	93433	11
8	93335	11
9	94334	10
10	93443	10

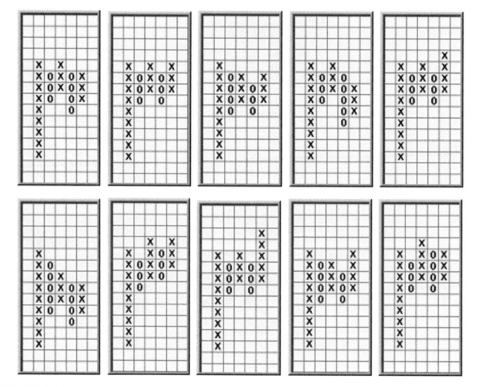

FIGURE 18.7   Succeeding Column Three-Pip Box Size

OBSERVATIONS

While scrutinizing the four-column patterns, we noticed a very high frequency of double tops preceding an upward breakout, as shown in the rightmost column in Table 18.1.

The column headers refer to the highest X in the first column of the predecessor charts and its horizontal relationship with the highest X in the third column of the predecessor charts. Essentially, this study in breakout analysis simply confirms the validity of the buy and sell signals already discussed in Chapter 14, "Double Tops and Bottoms."

Box Size	Column 1 > Column 3	Column 1 < Column 3	Column 1 = Column 3
1	101	203	929
2	61	70	158
3	21	69	190
Total	183	342	1,277
Percent	11.1	20.8	77.7

TABLE 18.1 Percentages

   We also calculated the average number of boxes in each column by multiplying the elements of each pattern by their frequencies, then dividing by the total number of occurrences. The average four-column predecessor pattern was 3344 while the average successor pattern was 3343.

   We intend to continue our analysis of breakouts by using different currency pairs and different time frames. We have only touched the tip of the iceberg in the current introductory study.

CHAPTER 19

Count Methods

OVERVIEW

In the previous chapters we have described numerous techniques that generate buy and sell signals. However, none of these specifies the magnitude of the anticipated price move. This chapter illustrates some common count methods by which many P&F traders calculate their price objectives. In the examples that follow, we assume a one-pip box size and a three-box reversal amount in the EURUSD currency pair (1 pip = 0.0001 USD).

HORIZONTAL COUNT (BUY)

Referring to Figure 19.1, count the number of boxes across the base of the formation that has given a buy signal:

$$4 = \text{Boxes across the base}$$

Multiply that number by 3:

$$4 \times 3 = 12$$

Multiply that product by the pip value of one box:

$$12 \times 0.0001 \text{ USD} = 0.0012 \text{ USD}$$

Add that number to the price corresponding to the lowest X in the rightmost column of Xs:

$$1.3023 + 0.0012 = 1.3035$$

The price objective is 1.3035 USD. (See Figure 19.2.)

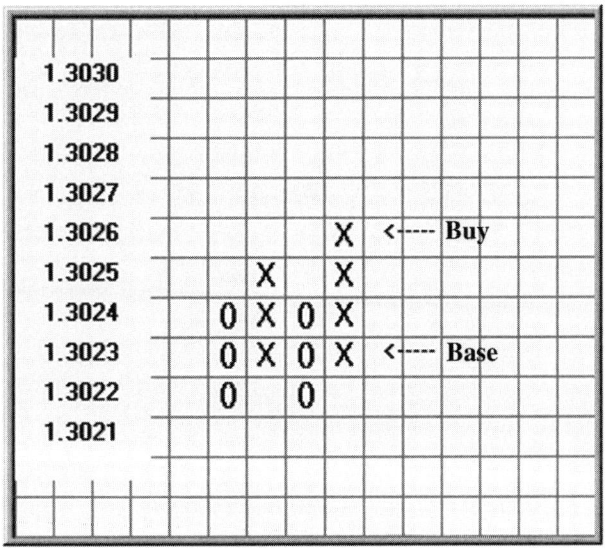

FIGURE 19.1 Horizontal Count (Buy)

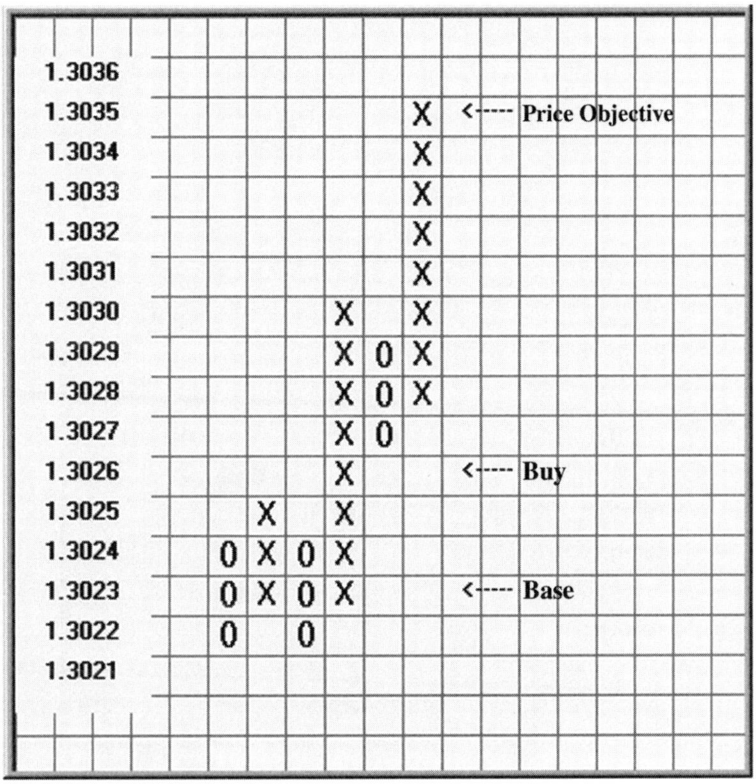

FIGURE 19.2 Price Objective (Buy)

HORIZONTAL COUNT (SELL)

Referring to Figure 19.3, count the number of boxes across the base of the formation that has given a sell signal:

$$4 = \text{Boxes across the base}$$

Multiply that number by 3:

$$4 \times 3 = 12$$

Multiply that product by the pip value of one box:

$$12 \times 0.0001 \text{ USD} = 0.0012 \text{ USD}$$

Subtract that number from the price corresponding to the highest O in the rightmost column of Os:

$$1.3027 - 0.0012 = 1.3015$$

The price objective is 1.3015 USD.

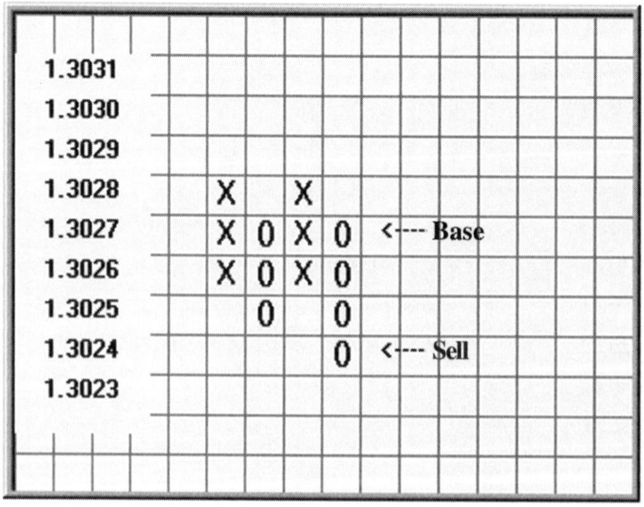

FIGURE 19.3 Horizontal Count (Sell)

VERTICAL COUNT (BUY)

Referring to Figure 19.4, count the number of Xs in the column that produces the buy signal:

$$5 = \text{Boxes in signal column}$$

Multiply this number by 3:

$$5 \times 3 = 15$$

Multiply that product by the pip value of one box:

$$15 \times 0.0001 \text{ USD} = 0.0015 \text{ USD}$$

Add that number to the price corresponding to the lowest X in the rightmost column of Xs:

$$1.3022 + 0.0015 = 1.3037$$

The price objective is 1.3037 USD.

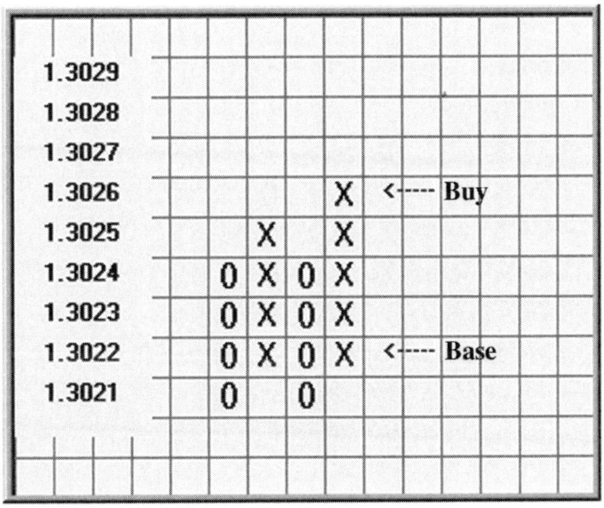

FIGURE 19.4 Vertical Count (Buy)

VERTICAL COUNT (SELL)

Referring to Figure 19.5, count the number of Os in the column that produces the sell signal:

$$5 = \text{Boxes in signal column}$$

Multiply this number by 3:

$$5 \times 3 = 15$$

Multiply that product by the pip value of one box:

$$15 \times 0.0001 \text{ USD} = 0.0015 \text{ USD}$$

Subtract that number from the price corresponding to the highest O in the rightmost column of Os:

$$1.3028 - 0.0015 = 1.3013$$

The price objective is 1.3013 USD.

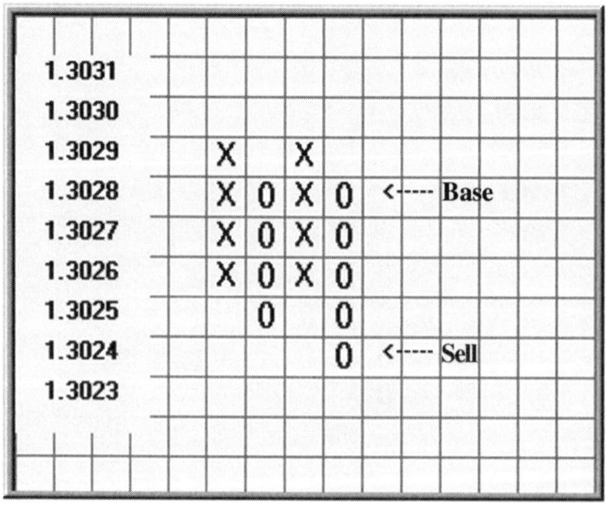

1.3031									
1.3030									
1.3029	X		X						
1.3028	X	0	X	0	<----- Base				
1.3027	X	0	X	0					
1.3026	X	0	X	0					
1.3025		0		0					
1.3024				0	<----- Sell				
1.3023									

FIGURE 19.5 Vertical Count (Sell)

OBSERVATIONS

Currency traders should keep in mind that the methods presented in this chapter are approximating techniques. Martin J. Pring in *Technical Analysis Explained* (McGraw-Hill, 2002) summed it up best when he stated, "No one to my knowledge has thus far satisfactorily explained why this principle appears to work. It seems to be based on the idea that lateral and vertical movements are proportional to each other on a point and figure chart."

Even if the full price objective is not attained, traders can still protect earned profits with trailing stop-loss limit orders. Also, the price objective may not be fulfilled in the same column as the signal column. Two, four, and even six columns may occur before an estimated objective is hit.

CHAPTER 20

Plotting Point and Figure Charts in Real Time

OVERVIEW

Traders who analyze stock market securities are under no severe time pressure to update their charts immediately. The stock market has fixed opening and closing times and traders can update their charts anytime outside market hours at their leisure. Many traders perform this task in the morning with the arrival of the early edition of the newspaper.

This relaxed atmosphere becomes slightly less leisurely when plotting P&F charts of spot currencies in real time, although it is entirely doable. Attention to detail and staying focused are the basic mental requisites.

TOOLS OF THE TRADE

The only equipment necessary to plot P&F charts in real time is a cup of hot coffee, graph paper, a pencil, and an eraser (all the mistakes are there just waiting to be made, but easily correctible). The choice of supplies is very subjective and is determined by whatever you are comfortable with. We prefer a French blend, 11-by-8½-inch graph paper with ¼-inch squares, a No. 2 pencil, and a rubber graphite eraser.

TRADING PLATFORM

Most trading platforms display raw moving tick data as a pip chart that displays prices and the transaction cost. Nearly all platforms allow traders to adjust the time interval within the charting window, typically 5 seconds, 10 seconds, 30 seconds, 1 minute, 5 minutes, 10 minutes, 30 minutes, and so on.

TRADING GOALS

For the time being, we define the investors' trading goals as the number of pips they intend to capture during that trading session. Higher goals and thus greater profits usually infer that traders should employ greater box sizes and/or reversal amounts. Many traders prefer to use the standard three-box reversal amount as a constant and then vary the box size based on the anticipated magnitude of the price objective.

STARTING THE PROCESS

Label the top of the graph paper with the name of the currency pair, the time interval selected, the box size, the reversal amount, the date, and the time of day when your charting session begins. It is a good idea to save the sheets and review them after a week or so to ascertain how significantly your online graphing skills have improved.

Next, check the most recent price displayed in the platform chart window and make this price the median price on the left side of the graph paper. Then fill in the price increments above and below the median price, remembering to add or subtract the box size for each number in the vertical price scale.

When you end the trading/charting session, note the time of day and the number of pips earned or lost.

REAL-TIME EXAMPLE

We begin by labeling the top of the graph paper with the following:

Currency pair:	EURUSD
Date:	Monday, January 31, 2005
Start time	00:05 A.M. MST
End time:	
Box size:	2 pips ($0.0002)
Reversal Amount:	2 boxes

In the chart in Figure 20.1 we can see a distinct downward trend as defined by the diagonal line above the Xs and Os. At 1:50 A.M. we initiated a short trade as a

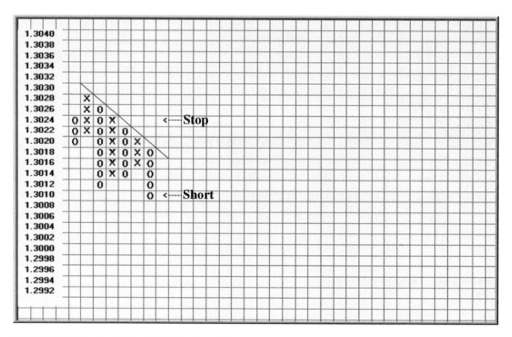

FIGURE 20.1   Real-Time P&F Charting (1)

market order at 1.3010 USD, the first low below all the previous lows. At the same time we placed a stop-loss limit order at 1.3024, the highest X in the previous two X columns.

After a brief period of unavoidable lateral movement, the trend again continued downward. When the price hit 1.3002, we moved the stop-loss down to 1.3016 (again the highest X level in the previous two X columns). (See Figure 20.2.)

We repeated the same method when the price hit 1.2980, and we lowered the stop to 1.2998. (See Figure 20.3.) At this point we have locked in a 12-pip profit.

Another period of lateral movement then developed and no new lows were hit. (See Figure 20.4.) A trend reversal appeared imminent and we manually exited the market at 1.2994 USD, trapping a modest 16 pips. Theoretically, we should have exited slightly sooner, but only hindsight is 20/20. We highly recommend the use of trailing stops to limit losses and protect gains. The selection of the initial stop-loss as the highest X in the two previous X columns was based on this particular pattern and is not a universal rule. Plus our trading objective was essentially a scalping tactic.

A simple caveat here is to not get absorbed in charting for the sake of charting itself. Never neglect the real issue that is occurring on the screen. If violent surges break out, stop charting and adjust your stop-loss, and then take profit limit orders accordingly. Charts can always be updated after the trade is liquidated.

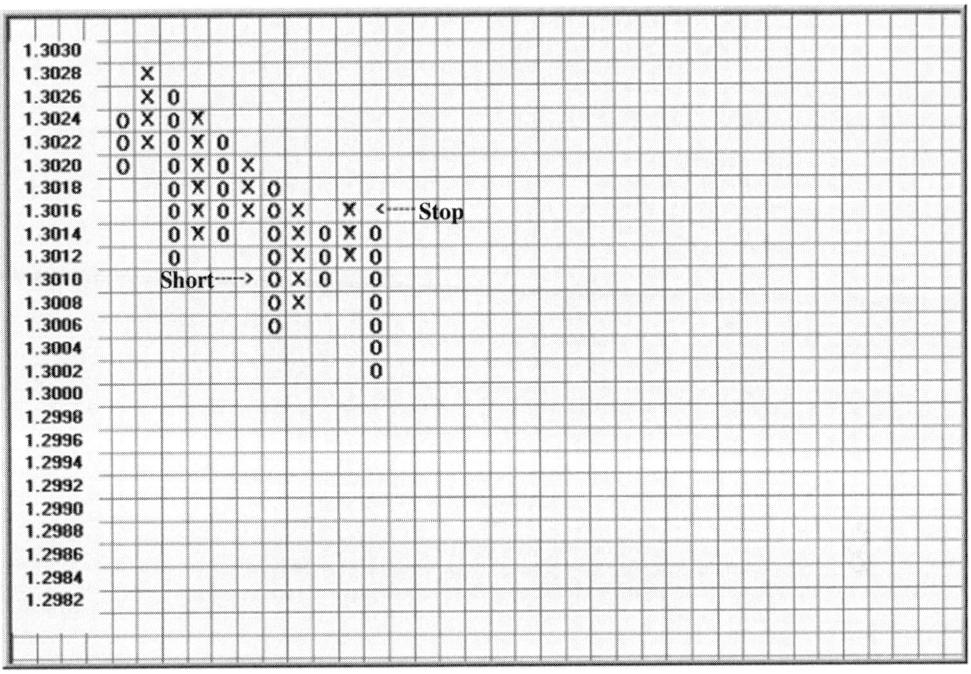

```
1.3030
1.3028       X
1.3026       X  O
1.3024    O  X  O  X
1.3022    O  X  O  X  O
1.3020    O     O  X  O  X
1.3018          O  X  O  X  O
1.3016          O  X  O  X  O  X        X   <---- Stop
1.3014          O  X  O     O  X  O  X  O
1.3012          O           O  X  O  X  O
1.3010 Short--->            O  X  O     O
1.3008                      O  X        O
1.3006                      O           O
1.3004                                  O
1.3002                                  O
1.3000
1.2998
1.2996
1.2994
1.2992
1.2990
1.2988
1.2986
1.2984
1.2982
```

FIGURE 20.2 Real-Time P&F Charting (2)

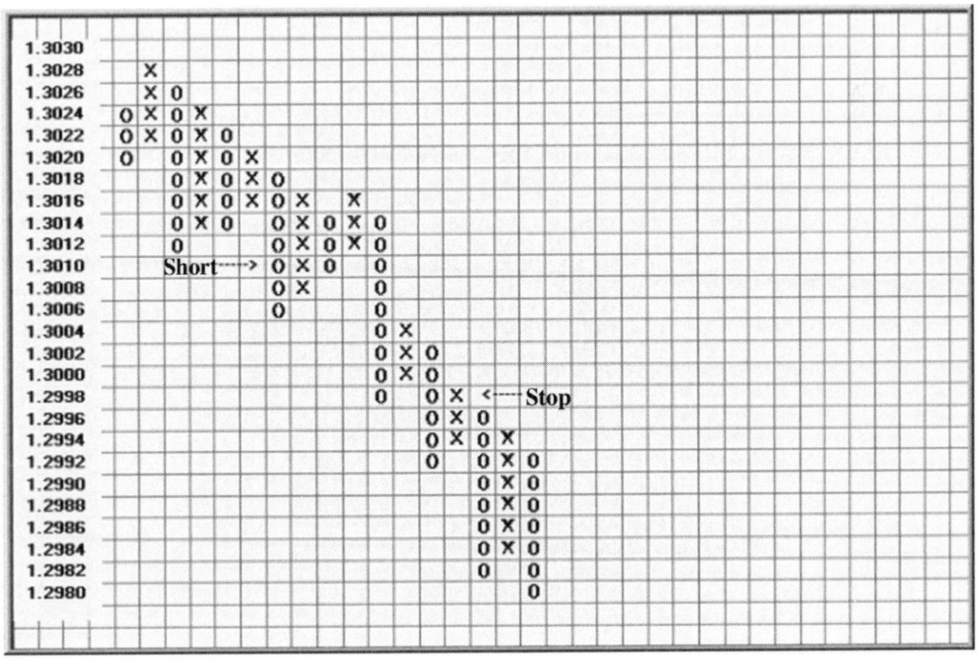

```
1.3030
1.3028       X
1.3026       X  O
1.3024    O  X  O  X
1.3022    O  X  O  X  O
1.3020    O     O  X  O  X
1.3018          O  X  O  X  O
1.3016          O  X  O  X  O  X        X
1.3014          O  X  O     O  X  O  X  O
1.3012          O           O  X  O  X  O
1.3010 Short--->            O  X  O     O
1.3008                      O  X        O
1.3006                      O           O
1.3004                      O  X
1.3002                      O  X  O
1.3000                      O  X  O
1.2998                      O     O  X   <---- Stop
1.2996                            O  X  O
1.2994                            O  X  O  X
1.2992                            O     O  X  O
1.2990                                  O  X  O
1.2988                                  O  X  O
1.2986                                  O  X  O
1.2984                                  O  X  O
1.2982                                  O     O
1.2980                                        O
```

FIGURE 20.3 Real-Time P&F Charting (3)

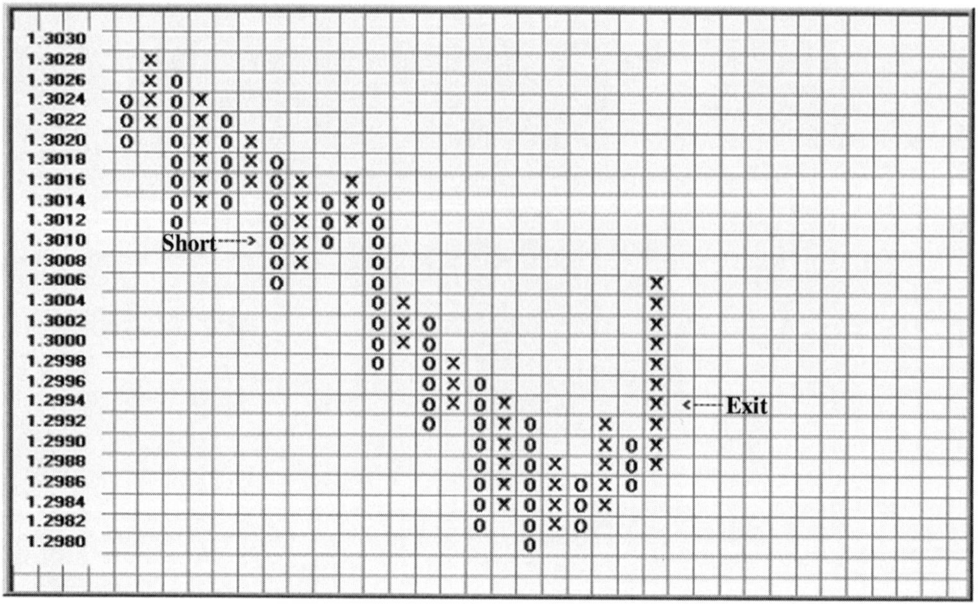

```
1.3030
1.3028        X
1.3026        X  O
1.3024     O  X  O  X
1.3022     O  X  O  X  O
1.3020     O     O  X  O  X
1.3018           O  X  O  X  O
1.3016           O  X  O  X  O  X        X
1.3014           O  X  O        O  X  O  X  O
1.3012           O        O  X  O  X  O
1.3010    Short ---->     O  X  O        O
1.3008                    O  X           O
1.3006                    O              O                          X
1.3004                                   O  X                       X
1.3002                                   O  X  O                    X
1.3000                                   O  X  O                    X
1.2998                                   O     O  X                 X
1.2996                                      O  X  O                 X
1.2994                                      O  X  O  X              X   <----- Exit
1.2992                                      O     O  X  O        X     X
1.2990                                            O  X  O        X  O  X
1.2988                                            O  X  O  X     X  O  X
1.2986                                            O  X  O  X  O  X  O
1.2984                                            O  X  O  X  O  X
1.2982                                            O     O  X  O
1.2980                                                  O
```

FIGURE 20.4   Real-Time P&F Charting (4)

PERFORMANCE EVALUATION

There is an innate tendency to discard the graph papers representing losses. Do not! File *all* the sheets regardless of the outcome (win, lose, or draw). Wait two weeks or so, then retrieve the sheets and make two piles, wins and losses (we treat draws as wins). Scrutinize the sheets in each pile looking for common ingredients and recurring patterns. Try to isolate which factors contributed to losses and which to profits. The clues are all there but some detective work is required. Also, neatness and legibility counts if you intend to review the chart data at a future date.

Real-time P&F charting requires a modicum of discipline (and some patience), which, in turn, develops mental focus, increases familiarity with the personality of a targeted currency pair, and creates an air of forbidden intimacy with the market environment as a whole.

PART III

Forex
Swing Charting

CHAPTER 21

Fibonacci Primer

OVERVIEW

In the original *Currency Trader's Companion: A Visual Approach to Technical Analysis of Forex Markets* (or *CTC* for short) and its sequels, we focused heavily on which currency pairs to trade and when to trade them. Once traders have determined which and when, they are then confronted with yet another major decision: which position to initiate. For that purpose, Chapters 16 through 19 in *CTC* provided a brief introduction to some classical methods in technical analysis for novice traders. In the current chapter, we intend to delve more deeply into science of forecasting price movements, continuations, and reversals. Many famous traders, notably W. D. Gann, Charles L. Lindsay, and Ralph N. Elliott, have based their trading systems on a curious mathematical relationship that exists in nature, the golden mean.

We have therefore decided to open this section with a look at so-called magic numbers, their history and calculation. Our goal is to demystify this esoteric realm in technical analysis. In later chapters, we will refer to possible Fibonacci relationships but, to be quite honest, it is not the motivating force behind the study of swing analysis. Familiarity with Fibonacci numbers is, however, a beneficial and interesting branch of forecasting to be aware of.

FIBONACCI THE MAN

Leonardo Fibonacci was born in Pisa, Italy, around 1170, the son of Guilielmo Bonacci, a secretary of the Republic of Pisa who was responsible for directing the Pisan trading colony in Algeria. Sometime after 1192, Bonacci brought his son with him to Algeria. The father intended for Leonardo to become a merchant and so arranged for his instruction in calculational techniques, especially those involving the Hindu-Arabic numerals, which had not yet been introduced into Europe. Eventually, Bonacci enlisted his son's help in carrying out business for the Pisan republic and sent him on trips to Egypt, Syria, Greece, Sicily, and Provence. Leonardo took the opportunity offered by his travel abroad to study and learn the mathematical techniques employed in these various regions.

Around 1200, Leonardo Fibonacci returned to Pisa, where, for at least the next 25 years, he worked on his own mathematical compositions. The five works from this period that have come down to us are: the *Liber abbaci* (1202, 1228); the *Practica geometriae* (1220/1221); an undated letter to Theodorus, the imperial philosopher to the court of the Hohenstaufen Emperor Frederick II; *Flos* (1225), a collection of solutions to problems posed in the presence of Frederick II; and the *Liber quadratorum* (1225), a number-theoretic book concerned with the simultaneous solution of equations quadratic in two or more variables.

So great was Leonardo Fibonacci's reputation as a mathematician as a result of his early works that Frederick summoned him for an audience when he was in Pisa around 1225. Fibonacci died sometime after 1240, presumably in Pisa. He is recognized as the mathematician who introduced the decimal system and the Arabic numeral system to Europeans. He has also been acclaimed as the greatest European mathematician of the Middle Ages. More of Fibonacci's accomplishments are documented in his biographical entry at the web page www-groups.dcs.st-and.ac.uk/~history/Mathematicians/Fibonacci.html.

FIBONACCI THE SERIES

Leonardo Fibonacci is best remembered for the numerical series that he discovered. Each Fibonacci number is the sum of the previous two Fibonacci numbers. (See Figure 21.1.)

The first two Fibonacci numbers are defined as $Fib_1 = 1$ and $Fib_2 = 1$. Table 21.1 lists the first 50 numbers in the series.

$$Fib_n = Fib_{n-1} + Fib_{n-2}$$

FIGURE 21.1   Fibonacci Series

n	Fibn	n	Fibn	n	Fibn	n	Fibn	n	Fibn
1	1	11	89	21	10,946	31	1,346,269	41	165,580,141
2	1	12	144	22	17,711	32	2,178,309	42	267,914,296
3	2	13	233	23	28,657	33	3,524,578	43	433,494,437
4	3	14	377	24	46,368	34	5,702,887	44	701,408,733
5	5	15	610	25	75,025	35	9,227,465	45	1,134,903,170
6	8	16	987	26	121,393	36	14,930,352	46	1,836,311,903
7	13	17	1,597	27	196,418	37	24,157,817	47	2,971,215,073
8	21	18	2,584	28	317,811	38	39,088,169	48	4,807,526,976
9	34	19	4,181	29	514,229	39	63,245,986	49	7,778,742,049
10	55	20	6,765	30	832,040	40	102,334,155	50	12,586,269,025

TABLE 21.1 The First 50 Fibonacci Numbers

FIBONACCI THE RATIOS

The major significance of Fibonacci numbers is its role in the calculation of the golden mean. The following series, which uses Fib_n/Fib_{n-1} as the criterion, has as its limit the golden ratio (1.618 . . .). (See Table 21.2.)

1/1 2/1 3/2 5/3 8/5 13/8 21/13 34/21 55/34 89/55 144/89

Ratio	Approximation
1/1	1.0000000000
2/1	2.0000000000
3/2	1.5000000000
5/3	1.6666666667
8/5	1.6000000000
13/8	1.6250000000
21/13	1.6153846154
34/21	1.6190476190
55/34	1.6176470588
89/55	1.6181818182
144/89	1.6179775281
233/144	1.6180555556
377/233	1.6180257511
610/377	1.6180371353
987/610	1.6180327869

TABLE 21.2 The Golden Mean as a Ratio

The golden mean (or ratio) expresses itself throughout nature, such as in the spiral compartments in a nautilus shell, the population growth of rabbits, the location of colored tiles on a turtle shell, seed patterns in sunflowers, the arrangement of bumps on a pineapple, the ratio of bone lengths in human anatomy, and numerous other phenomena. The Fibonacci series has also been observed in phyllotaxis (the study of the ordered position of leaves on a stem) and extensively studied in three different spiral arrangements.

FIBONACCI THE EQUATIONS

The golden mean can be solved by applying the quadratic formula to the following equation:

$$x^2 - x - 1 = 0$$

which yields:

$$x = \frac{1 \pm \sqrt{5}}{2}$$

The two roots of the quadratic are conventionally designated as:

Phi = +1.61803 39887 49894 84820 45868 34366

And

phi = −0.61803 39887 49894 84820 45868 34366

where

$$\sqrt{5} = 2.23606\ 79774\ 99789\ 69640\ 91736\ 68731$$

Please note the use of upper- and lower-case letters to identify the different roots. The upper- and lower-case Greek equivalents are also used to denote the golden ratio: Φ for Phi and φ for phi.

Other ratios that we will examine when scrutinizing currency price movements are:

$$\frac{\text{Fib}(n)}{\text{Fib}(n+1)} = 0.61803398874989 = -\text{phi}$$

$$\frac{\text{Fib}(n)}{\text{Fib}(n-1)} = 1.61803398874989 = \text{Phi}$$

$$\frac{\text{Fib}(n)}{\text{Fib}(n-2)} = 2.61803398874989 = \text{Phi}+1$$

$$\frac{\text{Fib}(n)}{\text{Fib}(n-3)} = 4.23606797749979 = \sqrt{5}+2$$

$$\frac{\text{Fib}(n)}{\text{Fib}(n-4)} = 6.85410196624969 = \left(\sqrt{5}+2\right) \times \text{Phi}$$

$$\frac{\text{Fib}(n)}{\text{Fib}(n-5)} = 11.0901699437494 = \left(\sqrt{5}+2\right) \times \text{Phi}^2$$

Powers of the golden mean Phi are:

$$
\begin{aligned}
\text{Phi} &= 1.61803398874989 \\
\text{Phi}^2 &= 2.61803398874989 \\
\text{Phi}^3 &= 4.23606797749979 \\
\text{Phi}^4 &= 6.85410196624969 \\
\text{Phi}^5 &= 11.0901699437495
\end{aligned}
$$

Powers of phi are:

$$
\begin{aligned}
\text{phi} &= -0.61803398874989 \\
\text{phi}^2 &= 0.38196601125011 \\
\text{phi}^3 &= -0.23606797749979 \\
\text{phi}^4 &= 0.14589803375032 \\
\text{phi}^5 &= -0.09016994374947
\end{aligned}
$$

Some special arithmetic relationships between Phi and phi are:

$$
\begin{aligned}
\text{Phi} + \text{phi} &= 1 \\
\text{Phi} - \text{phi} &= 2.23606797749979 \\
\text{Phi} \times \text{phi} &= -1 \\
\frac{\text{Phi}}{\text{phi}} &= -2.61803398874989 \\
\frac{\text{phi}}{\text{Phi}} &= -0.38196601125011 \\
\text{Phi}^5 + \text{phi}^5 &= 11
\end{aligned}
$$

$$\text{Fib}_n = \frac{\text{Phi}^n - \text{phi}^n}{\sqrt{5}}$$

FIGURE 21.2 Binet's Formula

BINET'S FORMULA

In 1843, the French mathematician Philippe Marie Binet discovered a method to calculate the nth term in the Fibonacci series. (See Figure 21.2.)

Despite the floating-point operations involved, Binet's formula always produces an integer result when n is also a positive integer.

INTERPRETATION

Many technical analysts use Fibonacci numbers when trying to determine support and resistance, and frequently use 38.2 percent, 50 percent, 61.8 percent retracements.

- *38.2 percent retracement.* It is commonly thought that a 38.2 percent retracement from a trend move will tend to imply a continuation of the original trend. (See Figure 21.3.)
- *61.8 percent retracement.* A 61.8 percent retracement implies that a trend change may be in the making. (See Figure 21.4.)

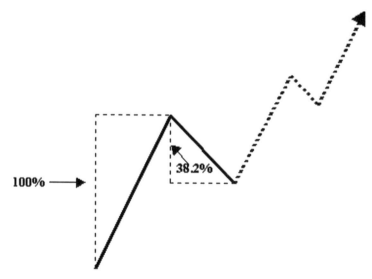

FIGURE 21.3 Example of 38.2 Percent Retracement

- *50% Retracement.* A 50 percent retracement shows indecision and may be followed by a lateral movement of prices. (See Figure 21.5.)

Many such rules have been adopted by technicians. The steps involved when looking for a continuation of a trend after a retracement are:

1. Calculate the total value of a significant price move (high to low or vice versa).
2. Calculate a Fibonacci retracement (in this case 38.2 percent) of the previous move.
3. Look for price to confirm by resistance (or support in an up move) near that predicted retracement area.

Other technicians have devised very complex systems involving Fibonacci fans, arcs, spirals, squares, zones, and other geometric motifs. Traders are advised to review the works of W. D. Gann and his followers for more information. As usual, we recom-

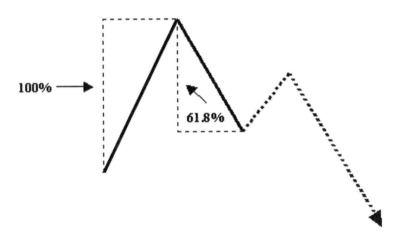

FIGURE 21.4   Example of 61.8 Percent Retracement

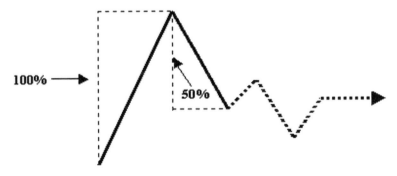

FIGURE 21.5   Example of 50 Percent Retracement

mend thorough testing via paper trading before traders incorporate such techniques into their overall trading systems. We admit that the preceding examples are somewhat simplistic in nature. In later chapters, we examine the retracement phenomena in much greater detail.

RESOURCES

Traders who are interested in more detailed information on Fibonacci numbers will be pleased to know that there is even an official Fibonacci Association, incorporated in 1963, which focuses on numbers and related mathematics, research proposals, challenging problems, and new proofs of old ideas (http://mscs.dal.ca/Fibonacci). Some other interesting Fibonacci web sites and web pages are:

http://www.mcs.surrey.ac.uk/Personal/R.Knott/Fibonacci/fib.html

http://ulcar.uml.edu/~iag/CS/Fibonacci.html

http://math.holycross.edu/~davids/fibonacci/course.html

http://ccins.camosun.bc.ca/~jbritton/fibslide/jbfibslide.htm

http://www.thinkquest.org/library/site_sum.html?tname=27890&url=27890/main Index.html

CHAPTER 22

Swing Charts

OVERVIEW

A swing chart is a member of a genre of charts normally referred to as reversal charts. The most commonly used reversal chart is the point and figure (P&F) chart, which dates back to the last decade of the nineteenth century and is usually credited to legendary trader James R. Keene. Other members in the reversal family are the exotic Japanese charts: renko, kagi, and three-line break charts.

DEFINITIONS

A reversal chart is any chart that filters the raw data in order to accentuate significant points of interest while ignoring points of less interest. All technical analysts find peaks and valleys of great interest, while areas of lateral price movements are less interesting. Peaks and valleys are those points of inflection where price directions reverse and the slope of an existing trend changes its arithmetic sign (minus to plus and plus to minus). (See Figure 22.1.)

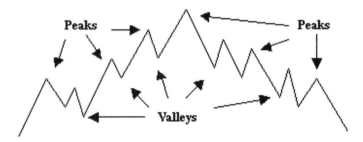

FIGURE 22.1 Peaks and Valleys

In this study, we prefer to use Ralph N. Elliott's original terms to avoid any unnecessary confusion with terms used by other swing analysts.

A *wave* is a single straight diagonal line in the swing chart. Waves are always diagonal lines with positive or negative slope, never perfectly horizontal or vertical.

A *peak* is the point of intersection between an upward wave on the left and a downward wave on the right. This represents a local maximum in the raw data.

A *valley* (or trough) is the point of intersection between a downward wave on the left and an upward wave on the right. This represents a local minimum in the raw data.

A *cycle* is a series of adjacent interconnected waves depicting specific price formations.

To convert a sequence of raw tick data or open, high, low, close (OHLC) interval data to its corresponding swing data, a swing reversal algorithm is employed in which two user-supplied variables must be initialized: the box size and the reversal amount.

BOX SIZE

Traditionally, the minimum price unit is the smallest fractional price increment by which the quote currency (or underlying security) can change. In the currency markets, this increment is a single pip. For example, if the EURUSD currency pair is currently trading at 1.2451, a single pip is 0.0001 USD.

There are three cases where a box size greater than one pip might be used. The first is when the parity rate between two currencies is very wide and causes a very large bid/ask spread. For example, if the bid/ask spread (transaction cost) for the EURCZK currency pair is 350 koruny, then a one-pip box size will have very negligible filtering power.

A second reason for using a box size greater than one pip occurs when performing historical analysis and a longer time frame is being analyzed. In this case, the analyst will probably be scrutinizing major reversals and may have little interest in minor reversals. This pertains more to position traders than session or day traders.

Lastly, a larger box size may be used in order to align peaks and valleys with the grid lines of the chart. This is purely a display preference, though.

REVERSAL AMOUNT

The reversal amount is the number of boxes necessary to plot a reversal in price direction. For instance, if the current trend is upward and the reversal amount is set at three boxes, then a decline of three box units must be reached before the downward movement is plotted. If, instead, a new price continues in the direction of the existing trend, then single boxes are automatically added to the last extreme.

It is the mutual interaction between the box size and the reversal amount that triggers the reversal mechanism in the swing algorithm necessary to plot peaks and valleys while ignoring lateral price movements.

There is one final case for increasing the box size. If an analyst, for whatever reason, has become very partial to one specific reversal amount, it is possible to increase the box size instead of the reversal amount when market conditions change.

For example, a three-box reversal amount is favored by many traders. If traders wish to filter out some of the minor swings, they can increase either the reversal amount or the box size. However, keep in mind that although a two-pip box size with a three-box reversal amount algorithm will generate results very similar to a one-pip box size with a six-box reversal amount algorithm, they will not be identical. This requires some reflection. The reason is that, when plotting a continuation of an existing trend, smaller distances can be plotted when a smaller box size is used.

SWING REVERSAL ALGORITHM

Given this information and these user-supplied variables, we now define the swing reversal algorithm as follows (this algorithm assumes we are using daily OHLC quotes as the input data rather than simply the closing prices):

```
Step 1: Initialize BoxSize and ReversalAmount variables.
Step 2: Create a new variable called Direction.
Step 3: Create two array variables called Price and Time to hold the swing data.
Step 4: Set Price(1) = Close(1) and Time(1) = 1.
Step 5: If High(2) – Price(1) > BoxSize * ReversalAmount Then
        Set Price(2) = High(2)
        Set Time(2) = 2
        Set Direction = UP
    ElseIf Price(1) – Low(2) > BoxSize * ReversalAmount Then
        Set Price(2) = Low(2)
        Set Time(2) = 2
        Set Direction = DOWN
    Else
        Increment day number and repeat Step 5
    End If
Step 6: Increment DayNo
    If DayNo = Number of OHLC quotes Then
        Go to Step 9
```

```
    If Direction = DOWN Then
          Go to Step 8
    End If
Step 7:  If High(DayNo) – Price(Idx) > BoxSize Then
          Set Price(Idx) = High(DayNo)
          Set Time(Idx) = DayNo
    ElseIf Price(Idx) – Low(DayNo) > BoxSize * ReversalAmount Then
          Increment Swing Idx
          Set Price(Idx) = Low(DayNo)
          Set Time(Idx) = DayNo
          Set Direction = DOWN
    End If
    Go to Step 6
Step 8:  If High(DayNo) – Price(Idx) > BoxSize * ReversalAmount Then
          Increment Swing Idx
          Set Price(Idx) = High(DayNo)
          Set Time(Idx) = DayNo
          Set Direction = UP
    ElseIf Price(Idx) – Low(DayNo) > BoxSize Then
          Set Price(Idx) = Low(DayNo)
          Set Time(Idx) = DayNo
    End If
    Go to Step 6
Step 9:  Set Number of Swings = Swing Idx
    Exit
```

At this point the two swing arrays Price() and Time() have been populated with corresponding pairs of swing data. The complete code for this algorithm written in Microsoft Visual Basic 6.0 is provided in Appendix P.

TIME ALIGNMENT

Adherents of the point and figure charting method believe that the compression of time along the x-axis is an advantage since the trader can then focus solely on price movements. Proponents of swing charts, by contrast, are more comfortable viewing the points of inflection (peaks and valleys) as they occur in real time. When a swing chart is displayed directly below an OHLC bar chart, the respective peaks and valleys align vertically with the corresponding bar above. Swing charts also display the *velocity* of the market; that is, the slope of each wave determines how quickly the market is moving.

The P&F chart versus swing chart debate is, in the final analysis, a matter of preference. Any swing chart can be readily massaged into a P&F chart by simply converting the straight lines to columns of Xs and Os. The converse, however, is not possible since P&F charts do not normally record the day numbers at the reversal vertices. We prefer the swing chart because in later chapters the number of time units in each wave will be used in numerous mathematical calculations.

PRACTICAL EXAMPLES

In the four swing charts shown in Figures 22.2 through 22.5, the box size is set to one pip while four different reversal amounts (3, 6, 9, and 12 boxes) are employed.

As stated earlier, the number of waves generated by the swing algorithm has an inverse relationship with the reversal amount (that is, as the reversal amount increases, the number of waves decreases and vice versa). Using the EURUSD currency pair for the time frame specified above, this equates to what is shown in Table 22.1.

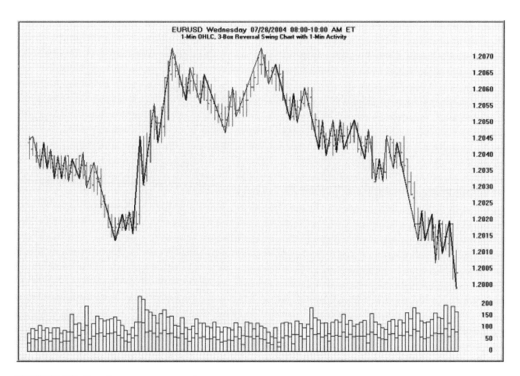

FIGURE 22.2 Three-Box Reversal

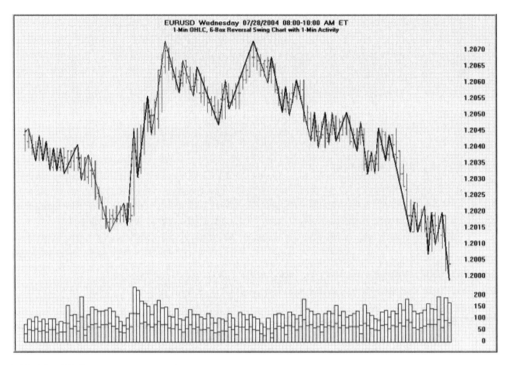

FIGURE 22.3   Six-Box Reversal

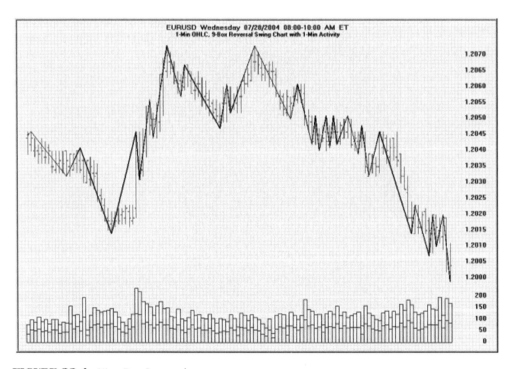

FIGURE 22.4   Nine-Box Reversal

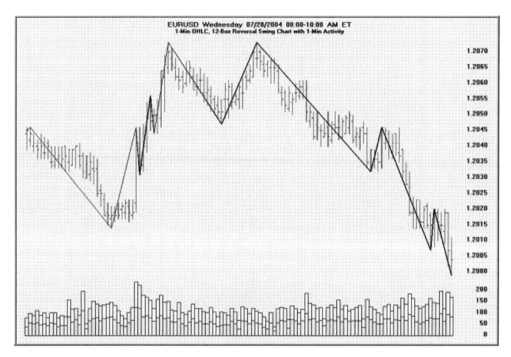

FIGURE 22.5 Twelve-Box Reversal

Reversal Amount	Swing
3	65
4	65
5	65
6	61
7	59
8	49
9	37
10	23
11	19
12	15
13	11
14	9
15	7

TABLE 22.1 Inverse Relationship

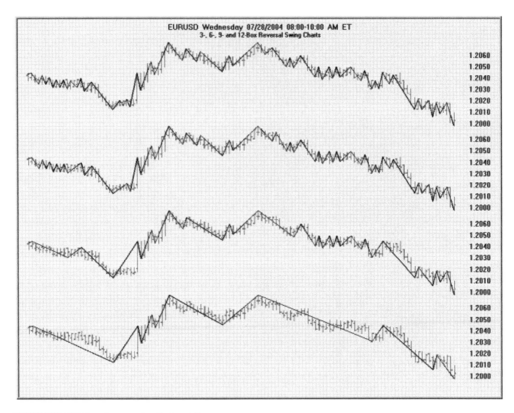

FIGURE 22.6 Composite Swing Chart

COMPOSITE SWING CHARTS

Figure 22.6, an aggregate of the previous four swing charts, is included here so traders can conceptually scrutinize the effect of different reversal amounts when using the same OHLC data.

USAGE

The advantage of comparing identical raw data time frames using different reversal amounts in twofold. Any time traders view a single data set from different perspectives, there is a greater likelihood of discovering one particular nuance in one of the charts that may not be readily apparent in the sibling charts (more is better).

Additionally, several trading systems are based on specific swing patterns, such as Elliott cycles and others in later chapters in this book. Many of these systems generate a discrete price estimate or at least predict price direction. Systematically varying the reversal amount allows traders to compare and log the forecasts at different levels, which adds an additional tier of reliability in the signal confirmation mechanism.

For those traders who home-brew their own trading programs, we have included the Microsoft Visual Basic source code for the swing reversal algorithm in Appendix P. This source code converts OHLC interval data to swing data. It is a relatively simple process to create an analogous function that converts raw tick data (close only) to swing data.

CHAPTER 23

The Measured Move

OVERVIEW

The concept of a measured move is simple in theory. Essentially, it is the estimate of the length of a price movement in one direction following a specific price pattern or chart event. However, in practice numerous factors influence this phenomenon: the underlying financial security being analyzed, the box size and reversal amount used to generate the swing data, the chart pattern, the number of waves in the pattern, and the location of the key inflection points in the swing data.

In Figure 23.1, we see a bull wave of 11 pips followed by a bear wave of 7 pips and then another (incomplete) bull wave.

The goal of the measured move principle is to estimate the height of the third wave

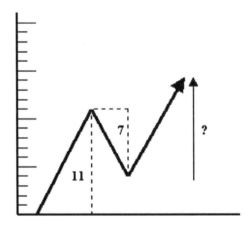

FIGURE 23.1 Three-Wave Swing Cycle

based on the percentage of retracement between the first and second waves or some other mathematical relationship. The measured move concept can also be applied to more complex price formations and multiwave cycles (which we will examine later).

TESTING APPROACH

In this study, we take a purely statistical approach to estimate the measured move, drawing from the 7,000,000+ quotes in our historical currency database. Raw streaming tick data was converted to swing data using our standard reversal algorithm with a constant box size of one pip in the EURUSD currency pair.

In the initial run of this analysis, we limit ourselves to three input variables:

1. Reversal amount in the swing algorithm.
2. Height of the bull wave.
3. Height of the bear wave.

CLUSTER CHARTS

Our first step is to examine the data by displaying it in its most pristine form using cluster charts. In Figures 23.2, 23.3, and 23.4, the x-axis (the independent variable) represents the percent of retracement between wave 1 and wave 2, or

$$\text{X-Axis Retracement Percent} = 100 \times \frac{\text{Height of Wave 2}}{\text{Height of Wave 1}}$$

The y-axis represents the dependent variable and is calculated as the percent of retracement between wave 3 and wave 1.

$$\text{Y-Axis Retracement Percent} = 100 \times \frac{\text{Height of Wave 3}}{\text{Height of Wave 1}}$$

To the untrained eye, cluster diagrams may appear confusing. This is true also to the trained eye sometimes. There appears to be no clear linear relationship between the dependent and independent variables. However, the crucial point in the three cluster charts is to note how the cluster patterns change when the reversal amount is increased (the examples use three-, five-, and nine-box reversal amounts).

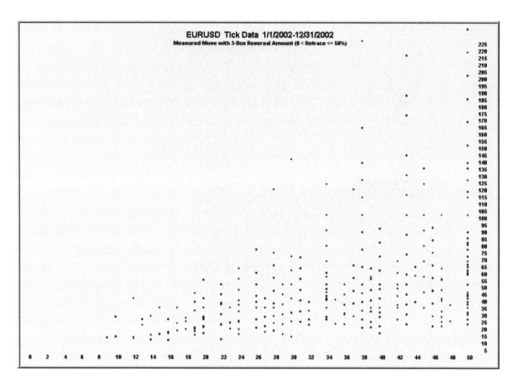

FIGURE 23.2 Cluster Chart Using Three-Box Reversal

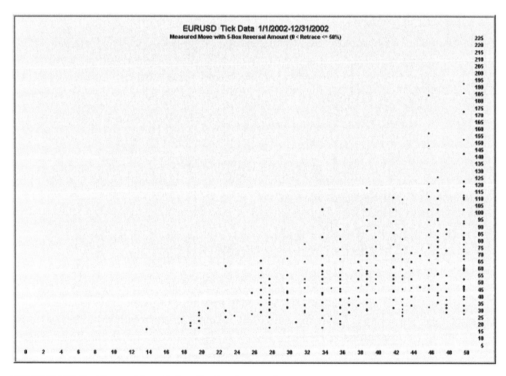

FIGURE 23.3 Cluster Chart Using Six-Box Reversal

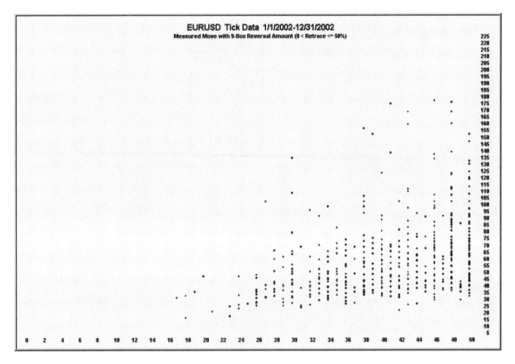

FIGURE 23.4   Cluster Chart Using Nine-Box Reversal

AVERAGE RETRACEMENT

To coerce the cluster charts into displaying more revealing information, we average the y-axis values for each corresponding integer x-axis value. (See Figures 23.5 through 23.7.)

By plotting only the y-axis mean values, we have eliminated the original confusion displayed in the corresponding cluster charts. The straight diagonal line in each line chart represents the results of an ordinary least squares (OLS) linear regression. (See Table 23.1.)

To forecast the height of the third wave with this information, we use the following linear formula:

$$y = Ax + B$$

where x = wave 2/wave 1
y = wave 3/wave 1
A = slope
B = intercept

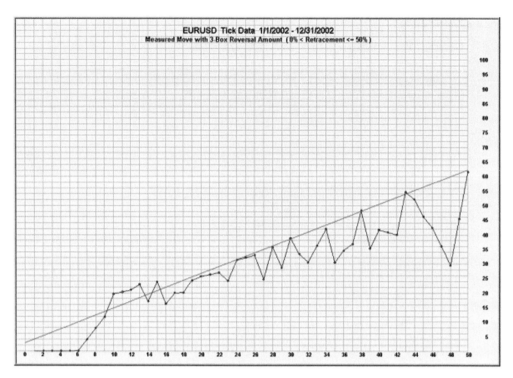

FIGURE 23.5 Measured Move with Three-Box Reversal

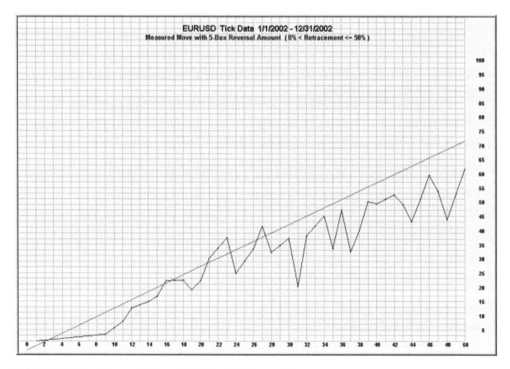

FIGURE 23.6 Measured Move with Five-Box Reversal

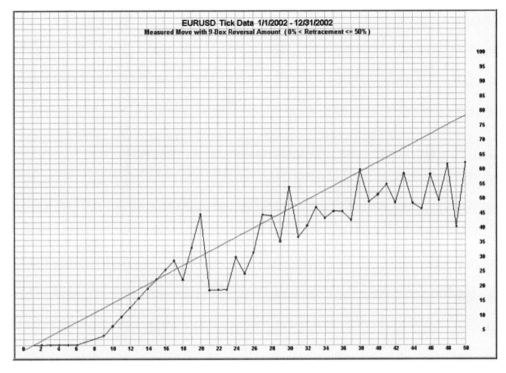

FIGURE 23.7 Measured Move with Nine-Box Reversal

Reversal Amount	Slope	Intercept	Correlation
3-Box	0.9652	2.8638	91.75
5-Box	1.2153	-3.1934	95.57
9-Box	1.2891	1.7301	93.10

TABLE 23.1 Wave Correlations

There is one drawback to using the average y-axis mean values as opposed to using all the data points (as in the cluster diagrams). When using all the cluster data points, the coefficient of correlation drops below 50 percent in all three cases, although the estimated slopes and intercepts are extremely close to those in the table using just the average values.

DECILE DIVISIONS

Tables 23.2, 23.3, and 23.4 were calculated in order to enhance the validity of the forecast of the measured move by a statistical method referred to as partitioning or

X-Value	Y-Value	Std Dev	Matches
10	16.98	8.40	3
20	22.19	8.98	61
30	35.51	12.36	644
40	44.79	14.94	2,705
50	59.19	18.97	18,217
60	73.34	23.42	32,782
70	65.33	20.53	17,922
80	89.97	29.18	109,341
90	69.49	22.80	25,818
100	59.08	27.86	264

TABLE 23.2 Standard Deviation for Three-Box Reversal

X-Value	Y-Value	Std Dev	Matches
10	0.00	0.00	0
20	19.20	3.77	10
30	35.51	12.36	63
40	45.86	13.54	508
50	57.69	16.77	2,828
60	65.98	18.94	4,637
70	73.21	20.11	9,378
80	82.86	22.19	18,845
90	64.68	25.24	35,250
100	70.70	21.84	531

TABLE 23.3 Standard Deviation for Five-Box Reversal

X-Value	Y-Value	Std Dev	Matches
10	0.00	0.00	0
20	30.25	10.98	5
30	41.45	20.98	64
40	49.29	24.27	233
50	58.48	22.82	624
60	71.34	26.36	1,016
70	81.59	31.28	1,555
80	87.14	31.02	2,057
90	103.40	36.81	3,319
100	98.66	33.51	1,847

TABLE 23.4 Standard Deviation for Nine-Box Reversal

grouping. Each table corresponds to a different reversal amount. The x-axis (wave 2/wave 1) has been divided into 10 partitions called deciles. For example, the fourth decile (40 percent) means that the partition includes x-axis values ranging from 30% < x-axis <= 40% retracement.

The column headers in Table 23.2 (and the following two tables) are defined as:

X-Value is $100 \times$ wave 2/wave 1.

Y-Value is $100 \times$ wave 3/wave 1.

Std Dev is the standard deviation of the dependent variables (y-values).

Matches defines the number of times that the x-axis retracement percentage occurred in the swing data.

PRACTICAL EXAMPLES

Example 1: Three-Box Reversal Amount, 11-Pip Bull Wave, 7-Pip Bear Wave

In this example, a three-box reversal amount was used to create the swing data and we have isolated an 11-pip bull wave (the impulse wave) followed by a 7-pip bear wave (the corrective or retracement wave). Our objective is to estimate the height of the third wave and its likelihood of occurrence. (See Figure 23.8.)

Step 1: Divide the height of wave 2 by the height of wave 1:

$$\frac{7}{11} = 0.63636363\ldots$$

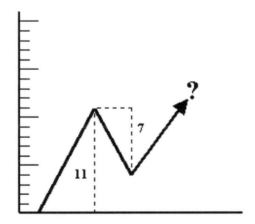

FIGURE 23.8 Example 1

Step 2: Multiply by 100:

$$0.6363 \times 100 = 63.63\%$$

Step 3: Round up to the nearest multiple of 10:

$$63.63 \text{ becomes } 70$$

Step 4: Locate the corresponding row (70) in the appropriate reversal amount table (Table 23.2, three-box):

$$\text{Row 70} \qquad 65.33 \qquad 20.53 \qquad 17{,}922$$

Step 5: Multiply the height of wave 1 by the measured move percentage in that row (y-value, column 2):

$$11 \text{ pips} \times 65.33\% = 7.1863 \text{ pips}$$

The estimated length of wave 3 (the measured move) is 7.19 pips.

Given these input parameters, we estimate that the third wave will rally to a point of 11.19 pips. (See Figure 23.9.)

Next we must calculate the level of confidence that this point will be reached.

Step 6: Locate the standard deviation table, the third column in the corresponding row, or:

$$20.53\%$$

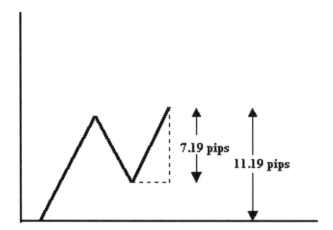

FIGURE 23.9   Example 1 Estimate

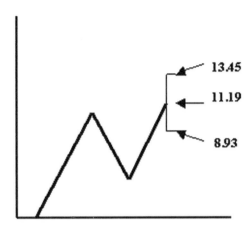

FIGURE 23.10 Example 1 Estimate with Confidence Boundaries

Step 7: Multiply the height of wave 1 times the percentage of standard deviation:

$$11 \text{ pips} \times 20.53\% = 2.2583 \text{ pips}$$

Step 8: Add the calculated deviation value to the forecast estimate to obtain the upper confidence boundary:

$$\text{Upper confidence boundary} = 11.19 \text{ pips} + 2.26 \text{ pips} = 13.45 \text{ pips}$$

Step 9: Subtract the calculated deviation value from the forecast estimate to obtain the lower confidence boundary:

$$\text{Lower confidence boundary} = 11.19 \text{ pips} - 2.26 \text{ pips} = 8.93 \text{ pips}$$

Placing upper and lower boundaries above and below the forecast estimate as shown in Figure 23.10 allows us to make the following statement about this particular measured move:

There is a 68 percent likelihood using a normal distribution that the peak of the third wave will fall between 13.45 pips and 8.93 pips.

Example 2: Five-Box Reversal Amount, 16-Pip Bull Wave, 8-Pip Bear Wave

Calculate retracement of wave 2:

$$\frac{8}{16} = 0.50$$

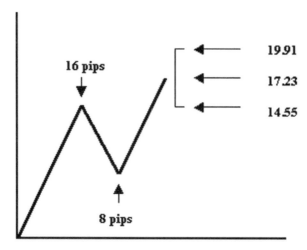

FIGURE 23.11   Example 2 Estimate with Confidence Boundaries

Retrieve corresponding row for 50 percent from the five-box reversal table:

$$\text{Row 50} \qquad 57.69 \qquad 16.77 \qquad 2{,}828$$

Multiply height of wave 1 times measured move percentage:

$$16 \text{ pips} \times 57.69\% = 9.2304 \text{ pips}$$

Multiply height of wave 1 times standard deviation percentage:

$$16 \text{ pips} \times 16.77\% = 2.6832 \text{ pips}$$

The results are shown in Figure 23.11.

There is a 68 percent likelihood that the peak of the third wave will fall between 19.91 pips and 14.55 pips.

Example 3: Nine-Box Reversal Amount, 14-Pip Bull Wave, 10-Pip Bear Wave

Calculate retracement of wave 2:

$$\frac{10}{14} = 0.7142$$

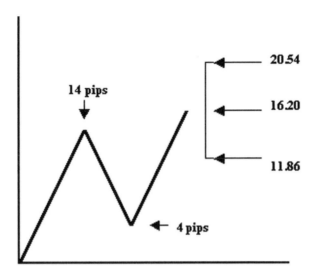

FIGURE 23.12 Example 3 Estimate with Confidence Boundaries

Round up (71.42 percent becomes 80 percent) and retrieve corresponding row from appropriate table:

Row 80   87.14   31.02   2,057

Multiply height of wave 1 times measured move percentage:

14 pips × 87.14% = 12.1996 pips

Multiply height of wave 1 times standard deviation percentage:

14 pips × 31.02% = 4.3428 pips

The results are shown in Figure 23.12.

There is a 68 percent likelihood that the peak of the third wave will fall between 20.54 pips and 11.86 pips.

CONCLUSION

From this initial study of the measured move, we have learned that it is possible to estimate the height of the third wave in a three-wave cycle when the heights of the first two waves are known. However, the magnitude of the standard deviation of the estimate often lessens the value of a discrete forecast. In subsequent chapters, we attempt to isolate chart patterns and multiple-wave formations where the magnitude of the standard deviation is noticeably less, thus enhancing the efficiency of a discrete forecast.

CHAPTER 24

The Fifty Percent Principle

OVERVIEW

Many trading systems are based on special numbers, like certain integers, Fibonacci numbers, prime numbers, trigonometric relationships, and the like. It comes as no surprise that a 50 percent retracement holds a tantalizing fascination with many traders.

This special case is called the 50 percent retracement principle and implies but does not adamantly state that when the second wave retraces the first wave by exactly 50 percent, then the height of the third wave will approximate the height of the first wave.

The ideal 50 percent retracement is depicted in Figure 24.1.

However the 50 percent principle is not a proven theory, merely a principle. If the 50 percent principle could be trusted with a very high degree of certainty, the impact on the currency markets (all markets, for that matter) would of course be cataclysmic.

TESTING APPROACH

We are interested in knowing just how much faith traders can put into the 50 percent principle and if it should be incorporated as an integral part of any profitable trading system. This study is a continuation of the analysis performed in the previous chapter on measured moves but focuses solely on the specialized case of 50 percent retracement. Our approach is again statistical in nature and will involve the 7,000,000+ EURUSD currency pair database. In the reversal algorithm, we maintain the box size as constant (1 pip = 0.0001 USD).

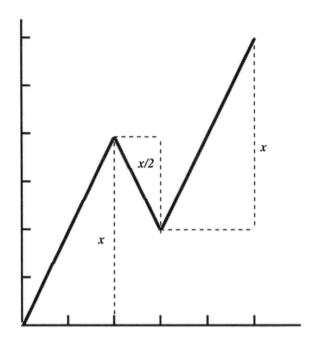

FIGURE 24.1 Ideal 50 Percent Retracement

INITIAL RESULTS

Our initial computer run generated the table in Table 24.1. The column headers are defined as:

Rev Amt is the reversal amount for the swing algorithm.

Y-Value is $100 \times$ wave 3/wave 1.

Std Dev is the standard deviation of the dependent variables (y-values).

Swings is the number of peaks and valleys in the swing data created by the reversal algorithm.

Matches defines the number of 50 percent retracements that occurred in that set of swing data.

The bottom-line statistics for the 50 percent principle using the current database are:

Average Retracement of Third Wave = 74.83%
Average Standard Deviation for Third Wave = 30.15%

Given a bull wave of 20 pips followed by a bear wave of 10 pips, this information can be represented graphically as shown in Figure 24.2.

Rev Amt	Y-Value	Std Dev	Swings	Matches
2	64.64	25.75	2,333,017	122,587
3	60.80	18.54	1,309,727	29,991
4	60.81	17.34	725,775	8,333
5	60.61	16.67	404,597	3,045
6	61.25	18.29	237,927	1,554
7	62.68	21.86	139,499	960
8	62.42	23.91	82,347	622
9	61.54	21.98	51,107	499
10	64.18	24.75	33,687	435
11	64.94	27.81	23,023	338
12	66.31	32.29	16,311	234
13	66.61	34.77	12,145	164
14	67.98	34.02	9,375	134
15	70.94	38.75	7,585	110
16	75.20	45.65	6,171	101
17	73.34	38.05	5,169	84
18	74.31	41.20	4,405	73
19	76.89	35.67	3,737	67
20	76.41	36.05	3,213	47
21	78.39	38.47	2,773	44
22	76.23	37.36	2,451	40
23	71.53	35.65	2,207	38
24	67.54	32.42	1,977	30
25	67.10	26.47	1,797	25

TABLE 24.1 Reversal Amount versus Number of Waves

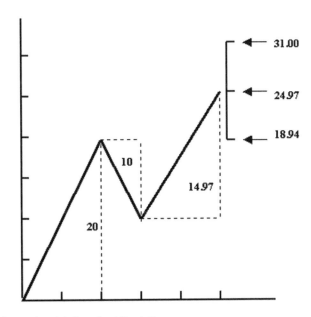

FIGURE 24.2 Example with Standard Deviations

Thus, there is a 68 percent likelihood the peak of wave 3 will fall between 18.94 pips and 31.00 pips. In this particular case (20-pip bull wave and 10-pip bear wave), the 50 percent retracement principle implies that the peak (or valley) of the third wave may reach 30 pips (20 − 10 + 20 = 30).

Given that we allow the 50 percent principle to include the range of one standard deviation on either side of the forecast value (24.97 pips), then the principle holds true. However, if we enforce a strict single-point discrete forecast, then the retracement of the third wave is only 74.83 percent of the first wave and the principle falls short of its expectation.

Also interesting to note in Figure 24.2 is that the highest percentage of retracement, 78.39 percent, occurred when the reversal amount was set to 21 boxes. This may be a unique property of the EURUSD pair during the 2002 calendar year, though.

INCREASING TOLERANCE

The study required that the retracement percent be a perfect 50 percent. Since technical analysis is not an exact science, we feel that an exact 50 percent retracement constraint is too mathematically rigorous, particularly as the reversal amount in the swing algorithm increases. Therefore, some tolerance should be permitted. We will increase our zone of acceptable candidates to encompass the range 47.5% <= retracement percentage <= 52.5% instead of a strict 50 percent. The additional 5 percent leeway increases the number of matches, which may help stabilize the percentages and standard deviations. (See Table 24.2.)

Average Retracement of Third Wave = 67.35%
Average Standard Deviation for Third Wave = 28.61%

We need only to add these two numbers together to determine if the height of the third wave will equal the height of the first wave:

67.35% + 28.61% = 95.96%

The result of adding a ±2.5 percent tolerance range did not improve the case for the 50 percent retracement principle.

We increased the tolerance percentage one final time to 45% <= retracement percent <= 55% and produced the following averages:

Average Retracement of Third Wave = 66.63%
Average Standard Deviation for Third Wave = 28.24%

Rev Amt	Y-Value	Std Dev	Swings	Matches
2	64.64	25.75	2,333,017	122,587
3	60.80	18.54	1,309,727	29,991
4	60.80	17.35	725,775	8,335
5	60.61	16.68	404,597	3,047
6	61.18	18.36	237,927	1,562
7	62.32	21.91	139,499	984
8	61.24	23.44	82,347	691
9	60.51	21.64	51,107	625
10	64.02	24.59	33,687	613
11	65.28	26.65	23,023	494
12	66.46	29.75	16,311	354
13	67.34	34.21	12,145	243
14	67.93	31.75	9,375	192
15	68.13	35.34	7,585	164
16	71.05	41.27	6,171	141
17	70.25	34.45	5,169	119
18	71.46	36.48	4,405	109
19	72.95	31.71	3,737	104
20	72.32	32.25	3,213	71
21	76.50	35.10	2,773	66
22	76.27	35.61	2,451	58
23	72.66	33.94	2,207	58
24	70.07	31.70	1,977	48
25	71.62	28.09	1,797	41

TABLE 24.2 Results of Increased Tolerance

A ±5% tolerance range produces the following maximum retracement sum:

$$66.63\% + 28.24\% = 94.87\%$$

Again the result falls short of the basic premise of the 50 percent principle. In defense of the 50 percent principle, though, we admit that it was originally applied to stock prices nearly a century ago and we are applying it to one specific currency pair for one specific time frame (1/1/2002 to 12/31/2002). Future studies in the 50 percent principle will involve different time frames in the EURUSD pair and even different currency pairs.

CHAPTER 25

Improving The Third Wave Forecast

OVERVIEW

Prior to our endeavors to improve the forecast for the height of third wave in a three-wave cycle, we wish to examine some characteristics about the first two waves. In this chapter we use 3 to 15 boxes as the reversal amounts in the swing algorithm. Again we rely on our EURUSD database with 7,000,000+ raw tick currency prices.

A very fundamental question is: what percentage of the time do the heights of the first and second wave equal each other in swing data? (See Table 25.1.)

Reversal Amount	Swings	Matches	Percent
3	1,309,727	453,041	34.59
4	725,775	226,441	31.20
5	404,597	111,205	27.49
6	237,927	60,426	25.40
7	139,499	31,487	22.57
8	82,347	15,914	19.33
9	51,107	8,406	16.45
10	33,687	4,767	14.15
11	23,023	2,691	11.69
12	16,311	1,540	9.44
13	12,145	972	8.00
14	9,375	615	6.56
15	7,585	450	5.93
Total	3,053,105	917,955	Average 30.07

TABLE 25.1 Matching Percentages

First, we observe the unexpectedly high percentage of matches that occurred signifying that the heights of the first two waves are equal. This is explainable by the fact that we are dealing with discrete price differentials that have been converted to integer pip values and is in part due to the intrinsic filtering mechanism of the swing reversal algorithm.

Also, we note an inverse relationship between reversal amounts in the swing algorithm and the percentage of matches. But this, too, appears logical after a brief period of reflection.

Next is another logical conclusion: The percentage of matches when the height of the first wave is greater than the height of the second wave is equal to the percentage of matches when the height of the first wave is less than the height of the second wave.

For instance, in the table, the percentage of matches for a reversal amount of six boxes is 25.40 percent. The percentage in this case where the height of the first wave is greater than the height of the second wave is (100% – 25.40%)/2 or 37.30 percent. The percentage for the case where the height of the first wave is less than the height of the second wave is also 37.30 percent. This is because we are comparing adjacent waves iteratively.

METHODOLOGY

In the previous two chapters, we estimated the height of the third wave by using a simple linear regression model of the form shown in Figure 25.1, where:

x = independent variable (wave 2/wave 1)
y = dependent variable (wave 3/wave 1)
A = slope
B = intercept

The linear regression model was employed because of its simplicity in calculations and because its concept is easy to grasp. Its functionality is based on the retracement relationship of all three waves. This has the drawback of hiding the actual magnitudes of each wave since the dependent and independent variables are actually ratios.

In this section, we intend to enhance the forecast for the height of third wave by using the actual integer pip magnitudes instead of retracement ratios. To accomplish this, we must regrettably incorporate an extra order of complexity into the forecasting model.

$$y = Ax + B$$

FIGURE 25.1 Linear Regression Model

$$z = Ax + By + C$$

FIGURE 25.2 Multiple Regression Model

MULTIPLE REGRESSION

A multiple regression is an extension of the linear regression in which the number of independent variables has been increased. See Figure 25.2, where:

x = first independent variable (height of first wave)
y = second independent variable (height of second wave)
z = dependent variable (height of third wave)
A = first partial coefficient of regression
B = second partial coefficient of regression
C = intercept or error factor

Note that there are now three regression coefficients (A, B, and C) instead of two (A and B) as in the linear regression. This, in itself, adds a tweaking factor to the validity of the forecast.

In plain English, this formula states that the height of one wave is dependent upon the heights of the two preceding waves. An inexpensive beginning text on the importance of regression operations and how they work is *Statistics* by Murray R. Spiegel in the Schaum's Outline series (McGraw-Hill, 1998).

QUARTILES

In our efforts to estimate the height of the third wave that follow, we limit ourselves to the single condition that the height of the second wave must be less than the height of the first wave.

Height of wave 2 < Height of wave 1

We will, however, divide the analysis into four equal parts called quartiles. Each quartile division will examine the retracement percentage between 0 percent and 25 percent, between 25 percent and 50 percent, between 50 percent and 75 percent, or between 75 percent and 100 percent.

In Tables 25.2 through 25.5, the column headers are defined as:

Rev Amt is the number of boxes in the swing reversal algorithm.

Swings is the number of waves in the swing data created by the reversal amount in column 1.

Matches defines the number of occurrences that satisfied the quartile conditions.

Coef A is the first partial coefficient of correlation (factor for wave 1).

Coef B is the second partial coefficient of correlation (factor for wave 2).

Coef C is the intercept or error factor.

Std Dev is the standard deviation of the dependent variable (the third wave).

Coef Cor is the coefficient of correlation between the dependent variable and the estimate.

Rev Amt	Swings	Matches	Coef A	Coef B	Coef C	Std Dev	Coef Cor
3	1,309,727	279	0.0365	-1.0848	-0.1669	2.8020	84.08
4	725,775	87	-0.0516	-1.5082	0.5199	2.8170	89.18
5	404,597	36	-0.0322	-1.3688	-0.4681	2.0815	96.08
6	237,927	27	-0.1641	-2.0314	-1.1301	3.4422	91.96
7	139,499	37	-0.0306	-1.4330	-0.4164	2.9299	96.02
8	82,347	30	-0.0757	-1.8030	-0.9634	4.0099	96.31
9	51,107	30	0.1300	-0.7399	-1.2414	4.2030	94.96
10	33,687	36	0.1223	-0.8021	-1.1931	4.4965	94.92
11	23,023	31	0.1409	-0.8244	-4.1070	5.9438	95.55
12	16,311	27	-0.3852	-2.9494	0.1900	5.8195	94.30
13	12,145	22	-0.2614	-2.5380	0.4648	5.5440	96.05
14	9,375	22	-0.3125	-2.9298	-2.2315	7.3268	96.41
15	7,585	19	-0.1665	-2.1727	-1.2080	8.4147	96.30

TABLE 25.2   First Quartile: 0 Percent of Wave 1 < Wave 2 < 25 Percent of Wave 1

Rev Amt	Swings	Matches	Coef A	Coef B	Coef C	Std Dev	Coef Cor
3	1,309,727	17,981	0.0773	-0.9883	0.0076	1.2723	94.69
4	725,775	6,226	0.0864	-0.9762	0.0013	1.6119	95.29
5	404,597	3,597	0.0565	-1.0627	0.0073	2.0466	95.16
6	237,927	2,563	0.0926	-1.0078	0.0133	2.6537	94.66
7	139,499	1,991	0.0794	-1.0547	0.0319	3.1102	94.61
8	82,347	1,622	0.0674	-1.0820	-0.1010	4.1434	93.23
9	51,107	1,326	0.1428	-0.9028	0.0416	5.2773	91.90
10	33,687	1,115	0.1197	-0.9721	-0.0594	5.8822	91.82
11	23,023	935	0.1024	-1.0178	-0.2182	6.9108	91.19
12	16,311	784	0.0366	-1.1945	-0.2565	7.8587	90.87
13	12,145	672	0.0278	-1.2140	-0.2761	8.7057	91.04
14	9,375	578	0.1752	-0.9003	0.0988	9.7683	90.92
15	7,585	506	0.1434	-0.9582	0.2806	10.4580	90.82

TABLE 25.3   Second Quartile: 25 Percent of Wave 1 < Wave 2 < 50 Percent of Wave 1

Rev Amt	Swings	Matches	Coef A	Coef B	Coef C	Std Dev	Coef Cor
3	1,309,727	123,352	0.7119	0.0871	0.0110	1.2479	94.95
4	725,775	90,099	0.2441	-0.7226	0.0035	1.3825	95.99
5	404,597	49,477	0.0140	-1.1137	0.0047	1.6877	96.10
6	237,927	23,040	0.3126	-0.6283	-0.0009	2.1668	95.77
7	139,499	16,261	0.1248	-0.9494	0.0015	2.7484	95.11
8	82,347	10,367	0.1145	-0.9830	0.0009	3.4437	94.38
9	51,107	6,336	0.2167	-0.8128	-0.0011	4.1850	93.66
10	33,687	4,769	0.0994	-1.0097	0.1053	5.0327	92.95
11	23,023	3,467	0.0431	-1.1109	0.1282	6.0319	91.92
12	16,311	2,504	0.1252	-0.9855	-0.1395	7.1486	91.14
13	12,145	1,989	0.2972	-0.7202	-0.2050	8.0629	90.66
14	9,375	1,582	0.2662	-0.7708	-0.0999	9.2946	89.74
15	7,585	1,263	0.1771	-0.9077	-0.1901	10.2599	89.36

TABLE 25.4 Third Quartile: 50 Percent of Wave 1 < Wave 2 < 75 Percent of Wave 1

Rev Amt	Swings	Matches	Coef A	Coef B	Coef C	Std Dev	Coef Cor
3	1,309,727	120,743	2.1297	1.6818	-0.0287	1.4905	94.92
4	725,775	136,424	2.6342	2.1432	0.0175	1.4917	95.91
5	404,597	78,868	1.0141	0.1687	0.0072	1.7016	96.00
6	237,927	50,093	0.4759	-0.4822	0.0073	2.0254	96.07
7	139,499	33,796	0.7277	-0.2133	0.0147	2.4770	95.69
8	82,347	19,578	0.4007	-0.6042	0.0231	3.1706	94.81
9	51,107	12,208	0.3565	-0.6614	0.0766	3.9841	93.84
10	33,687	8,260	0.4286	-0.5964	-0.0158	4.9298	92.78
11	23,023	5,470	0.3027	-0.7346	-0.0126	5.7517	92.01
12	16,311	3,826	0.3370	-0.7026	-0.0925	6.5676	91.80
13	12,145	2,838	0.4820	-0.5544	0.0310	7.6737	91.23
14	9,375	2,107	0.2959	-0.7534	0.2235	8.2550	91.12
15	7,585	1,705	0.3505	-0.6973	0.1905	9.1763	90.52

TABLE 25.5 Fourth Quartile: 75 Percent of Wave 1 < Wave 2 < 100 Percent of Wave 1

Before presenting some practical examples, let's first examine the four quartile tables. The greatest number of matches with the swing data occurs when the retracement of the first wave by the second wave (that is, wave 2/wave 1) is between 50 percent and 75 percent.

When using a three-box reversal amount, this equates to what is summarized in Table 25.6.

We can credit the low showing of the less than 25 percent quartile to the intrinsic nature of the swing reversal algorithm. Lower percentages are filtered out by the mini-

Retracement	Matches	Likelihood
0 to 25%	279	1.06%
25 to 50%	17,981	6.85%
50 to 75%	123,352	47.02%
75 to 100%	120,743	46.02%
Total	262,355	100.00%

TABLE 25.6 Quartile Summary

mum reversal mechanism. If we had used a one-box or two-box reversal amount, the percentage of frequency of the first quartile would be higher.

Also interesting to note is the fact that a retracement of less than 50 percent occurred only 7.91 percent of the time while a retracement of 50 percent to 100 percent occurred 93.04 percent of the time. Another interesting characteristic to the four quartile tables is the relationship between the reversal amount and the standard deviation. As the reversal amount increases, the standard deviation increases proportionally.

Lastly, we should note that the coefficient of correlation ranges from 84.08 percent to 96.41 percent with an average value of 94 percent. A high coefficient of correlation confirms that the selected forecasting model (in this case, a multiple regression with two independent variables) is a valid representation of the real-world data.

PRACTICAL EXAMPLES

The multiple regression model is symmetrical about the x-axis. That is, it works regardless of whether the first wave is a bull wave or a bear wave. In the examples that follow, the height of bull waves must be entered as positive integers and the height of bear waves as negative integers.

Example No. 1

Reversal amount   = 3
Height of first wave   = 10
Height of second wave = –4

First we must determine which table to use by calculating the retracement percentage: 4/10 = 40 percent or the second quartile table spanning 25 percent to 50 percent. Next locate the row containing that reversal amount:

Rev Amt	Swings	Matches	A	B	C	Std Dev	Cor
3	1,309,727	17,981	0.0773	–0.9883	0.0076	1.2723	94.69

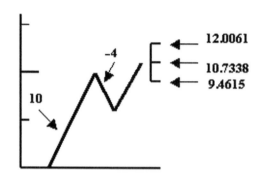

FIGURE 25.3 Example No. 1

The estimate for the height of the third wave is calculated as:

$$z = Ax + By + C$$
$$\text{wave } 3 = A(\text{wave } 1) + B (\text{wave } 2) + C$$
$$= (0.0773)(10) + (-0.9883)(-4) + (0.0076)$$
$$= 0.7730 + 3.9532 + 0.0076$$
$$= 4.7338$$

Thus the estimate for the height of the third wave is 4.7338 pips. To compute a confidence level of 68 percent likelihood, we must calculate the upper and lower confidence levels by adding and subtracting one standard deviation from the estimate respectively:

$$\text{Upper confidence level} = 4.7338 + 1.2723 = 6.0061 \text{ pips}$$
$$\text{Lower confidence level} = 4.7338 - 1.2723 = 3.4615 \text{ pips}$$

Example No. 2

Reversal amount   = 6
Height of first wave   = –8
Height of second wave   = 7

Retrieve the corresponding reversal amount row from the appropriate table (7/8 = 87.50% = fourth quartile):

Rev Amt	Swings	Matches	A	B	C	Std Dev	Cor
6	237,927	50,093	0.4759	–0.4822	0.0073	2.0254	96.07

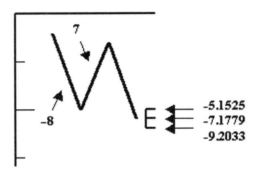

FIGURE 25.4 Example No. 2

$$z = Ax + By + C$$
$$\text{wave } 3 = A(\text{wave } 1) + B\,(\text{wave } 2) + C$$
$$= (0.4759)\,(-8) + (-0.4822)\,(7) + (0.0073)$$
$$= -3.8072 + -3.3754 + 0.0047$$
$$= -7.1779$$
Upper confidence level $= -7.1779 + 2.0254 = -5.1525$ pips
Lower confidence level $= -7.1779 - 2.0254 = -9.2033$ pips

(See Figure 25.4.)

Example No. 3

Reversal amount   = 5
Height of first wave   = 12
Height of second wave   = −7

Retrieve the corresponding reversal amount row from the appropriate table ($7/12 = 58.33\% =$ third quartile):

Rev Amt	Swings	Matches	A	B	C	Std Dev	Cor
5	404,597	49,477	0.0140	−1.1137	0.0047	1.6877	96.10

$$z = Ax + By + C$$
$$\text{wave } 3 = A(\text{wave } 1) + B(\text{wave } 2) + C$$
$$= (0.0140)(12) + (-1.1137)(-7) + (0.0047)$$
$$= 0.1680 + 7.7959 + 0.0047$$
$$= 7.9686$$
Upper confidence level $= 7.9686 + 1.6877 = 9.6563$ pips
Lower confidence level $= 7.9686 - 1.6877 = 6.2809$ pips

Rev Amt	Swings	Matches	Coef A	Coef B	Coef C	Std Dev	Coef Cor
3	1,309,727	30,650	0.2733	-0.6152	0.0209	1.1717	95.08
4	725,775	9,750	0.3991	-0.3403	0.0136	1.4788	95.71
5	404,597	6,258	0.4556	-0.2433	-0.0058	1.9548	95.63
6	237,927	5,241	0.0036	-1.1971	0.0234	2.3483	95.41
7	139,499	2,892	0.0977	-1.0253	0.0204	3.1765	94.20
8	82,347	1,836	0.0247	-1.1611	0.2868	3.9261	93.46
9	51,107	1,299	0.1481	-0.8928	-0.0366	4.3597	93.53
10	33,687	1,037	0.4298	-0.3410	-0.0405	5.0384	93.22
11	23,023	800	0.0974	-0.9947	0.3420	6.1030	91.71
12	16,311	643	-0.0514	-1.3591	0.4699	8.0308	90.25
13	12,145	488	0.1364	-0.9969	0.1779	9.6277	89.24
14	9,375	410	0.4379	-0.3691	0.1042	9.2926	90.49
15	7,585	333	0.3022	-0.6341	1.1514	10.6011	89.77

TABLE 25.7   Quartiles Using 50 Percent Principle

FIFTY PERCENT PRINCIPLE

We will also reexamine the 50 percent principle using the multiple regression model. We performed the same analysis as used previously on the quartiles with the following condition:

$$47.5\% \text{ of Wave 1} < \text{Wave 2} < 52.5\% \text{ of Wave 1}$$

and obtained the results shown in Table 25.7.

Amazingly, a 50 percent retracement occurred only about 2 percent of the time in our 2002 EURUSD database for reversal amounts ranging from 3 to 15 boxes (a total of 61,637 matches occurred). This may appear inordinately low at first glance, but in a volatile, news-driven market the unexpected is to be expected.

FIFTY PERCENT EXAMPLES

In Table 25.8, we set the first wave to +14 pips and the second wave to –7 pips. Column headers are:

Estimate—the regression forecast for the height of the third wave.

Upper—the upper confidence level (estimate + one standard deviation).

Lower—the lower confidence level (estimate – one standard deviation).

Rev Amt	Coef A	Coef B	Coef C	Std Dev	Estimate	Upper	Lower
3	0.2733	-0.6152	0.0209	1.1717	8.1326	9.3043	6.4156
4	0.3991	-0.3403	0.0136	1.4788	7.9695	9.7575	6.4907
5	0.4556	-0.2433	-0.0058	1.9548	8.0815	10.0363	6.1267
6	0.0036	-1.1971	0.0234	2.3483	8.4301	10.7784	6.0818
7	0.0977	-1.0253	0.0204	3.1765	8.5449	11.7214	5.3684

TABLE 25.8 Examples Using 50 Percent Principle

Reversal amounts greater than 7 are not included in this table since the swing reversal algorithm would automatically filter out the second wave (–7 pips).

In the table, we observe that as the reversal amount grows, the standard deviation and the regressed estimate also grow. From this data, given a 50 percent retracement (wave 2/wave 1), we can conclude that on *average* the third wave will have a height of 58.80 percent of the height of the first wave; ergo:

Average retracement for third wave = 58.80%

CHAPTER 26

Forecasting The Fourth Wave

OVERVIEW

In the preceding chapters, we analyzed some concepts on how to estimate the height of the third wave in a three-wave cycle when the heights of the first two waves are known. In the current chapter, we will extend this idea one logical step further and attempt to estimate the height of the fourth wave based on the known heights of the first three waves.

TESTING APPROACH

We will again employ an ordinary least squares (OLS) multiple regression, this time using the model with three independent variables. See Figure 26.1, where

w = the first independent variable (height of first wave)
x = the second independent variable (height of second wave)
y = the third independent variable (height of third wave)
z = the dependent variable (height of fourth wave)
A = the first partial coefficient of regression
B = the second partial coefficient of regression
C = the third partial coefficient of regression
D = intercept or error term

$$z = Aw + Bx + Cy + D$$

FIGURE 26.1 Multiple Regression Model with Three Independent Variables

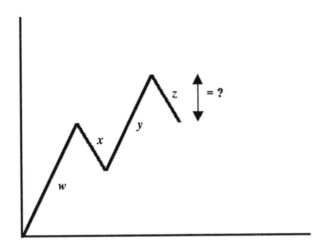

FIGURE 26.2 Fourth Wave Unknown

Note that we are now dealing with four regression coefficients (*A*, *B*, *C*, and *D*), which definitely increases the complexity of the mathematical operations involved (specifically, the solution to simultaneous equations).

Given a known three-wave bull cycle, we label the four heights as *w*, *x*, *y*, *z* with the objective of estimating the height *z*. (See Figure 26.2.)

In Table 26.1, we have calculated the values of the four regression coefficients based on *any* possible three-wave cycle. That is, there are no constraints on retracement percentages between any two adjacent waves. We scanned the EURUSD database sequentially for every four-wave combination.

Rev Amt	Coef A	Coef B	Coef C	Coef D
3	-0.3700	-0.0786	-0.6785	-0.0008
4	-0.3377	0.0362	-0.6031	-0.0013
5	-0.3104	0.1445	-0.5251	-0.0021
6	-0.2961	0.2327	-0.4518	-0.0042
7	-0.2985	0.2674	-0.4125	-0.0072
8	-0.3229	0.2864	-0.3665	-0.0123
9	-0.3052	0.3080	-0.3584	-0.0198
10	-0.3184	0.3163	-0.3329	-0.0286
11	-0.3283	0.2890	-0.3443	-0.0447
12	-0.3292	0.3051	-0.3245	-0.0603
13	-0.3255	0.3145	-0.3164	-0.0793
14	-0.3178	0.3212	-0.3168	-0.1338
15	-0.3096	0.3053	-0.3358	-0.1663

TABLE 26.1 Partial Regression Coefficients

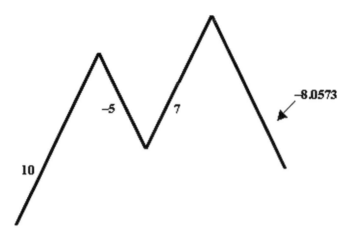

FIGURE 26.3 Example No. 1

PRACTICAL EXAMPLES

Example 1: Three-Box Reversal Amount, Wave 1 = 10, Wave 2 = −5, Wave 3 = 7

$$
\begin{aligned}
\text{Wave 4} &= A(\text{Wave 1}) + B(\text{Wave 2}) + C(\text{Wave 3}) + D \\
&= (-0.3700)(10) + (-0.0786)(-5) + (-0.6785)(7) + (-0.0008) \\
&= -3.7000 + 0.3930 - 4.7495 - 0.0008 \\
&= -8.0573
\end{aligned}
$$

(See Figure 26.3.)

Example 2: Five-Box Reversal Amount, Wave 1 = −8, Wave 2 = 3, Wave 3 = −6

$$
\begin{aligned}
\text{Wave 4} &= A(\text{Wave 1}) + B(\text{Wave 2}) + C(\text{Wave 3}) + D \\
&= (-0.3104)(-8) + (0.1445)(3) + (-0.5251)(-6) + (-0.0021) \\
&= 2.4832 + 0.4335 + 3.1506 - 0.0021 \\
&= 6.0640
\end{aligned}
$$

IMPROVING THE FORECAST

As stated previously, the coefficients in the preceding table can be applied to *any* three-wave cycle to forecast the height of the fourth wave. The disadvantage to such a generic approach is that, even though the forecasts are intrinsically accurate, the standard deviation is very high, which widens the channel of confidence too much to be of serious practical use. In other words, the further the upper confidence level and the lower confidence level are from the estimate, the less reliable the forecast.

For that purpose, we decided to analyze two basic and distinct three-wave patterns with the premise that their common characteristics will generate similar forecasts for the fourth wave with a smaller standard deviation. The patterns are a three-wave *trending cycle* and a three-wave *nontrending cycle*.

THREE-WAVE TRENDING CYCLES

This cycle consists of two complementary patterns, which are displayed in Figure 26.4. In the case of the bull cycle on the left, the inequality constraints are:

$$A < C < B < D$$

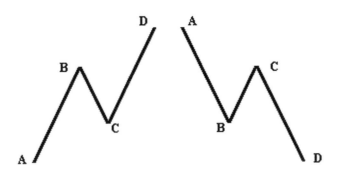

FIGURE 26.4 Complementary Patterns

Rev Amt	Coef A	Coef B	Coef C	Coef D
3	-0.2861	-0.0917	-0.7396	-0.0414
4	-0.2014	0.2190	-0.5782	-0.0209
5	-0.1716	0.5042	-0.3715	0.0177
6	-0.0778	0.7645	-0.2542	0.0049
7	-0.0517	0.8506	-0.2068	0.0401
8	-0.0708	0.9516	-0.1236	0.0569
9	-0.0537	0.9912	-0.1190	-0.0439
10	-0.0648	1.0312	-0.0907	0.1153
11	-0.0585	1.0430	-0.1040	0.0393
12	-0.0925	0.9872	-0.1053	0.2064
13	-0.0313	1.2619	-0.0079	0.5029
14	-0.0513	1.1247	-0.0725	0.4260
15	-0.0552	1.1116	-0.0750	0.4366

TABLE 26.2 Fourth Wave Partial Regression Coefficients

The bear cycle on the right has the following constraints:

$$A > C > B > D$$

The coefficients of regression for the height of the fourth wave for *both* bull and bear trending patterns are calculated in Table 26.2.

TRENDING EXAMPLE

As noted previously, the heights of bull waves must be entered as positive integers, while the heights of bear waves must be entered as negative integers.

Reversal Amount= 4 Boxes, Wave 1 = +9, Wave 2 = − 4, Wave 3 = +7

$$\begin{aligned}
\text{Wave 4} &= A(\text{Wave 1}) + B(\text{Wave 2}) + C(\text{Wave 3}) + D \\
&= (-0.2014)(9) + (0.2190)(-4) + (-0.5782)(7) + (-0.0209) \\
&= -1.8126 - 0.8760 - 4.0474 - 0.0209 \\
&= -6.7151
\end{aligned}$$

THREE-WAVE NONTRENDING CYCLES

These cycles (known as contracting triangles) consist of two symmetrical patterns, which are displayed in Figure 26.5.

In the case of the contracting triangle on the left, the inequality constraints are:

$$A < C < D < B$$

The contracting triangle on the right has the following constraints:

$$A > C > D > B$$

The coefficients of regression for the height of the fourth wave for both contracting triangle patterns are calculated in Table 26.3.

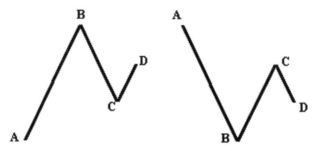

FIGURE 26.5 Nontrending Cycles

Rev Amt	Coef A	Coef B	Coef C	Coef D
3	-0.3387	-0.1737	-0.7909	0.0084
4	-0.2715	-0.1317	-0.8698	0.0139
5	-0.1916	-0.0396	-0.8880	0.0203
6	-0.1823	-0.0522	-0.9188	0.0664
7	-0.1756	-0.1007	-1.0075	-0.0776
8	-0.1822	-0.0656	-0.9714	-0.0850
9	-0.0546	0.1120	-0.9726	-0.0517
10	-0.0474	0.2170	-0.9068	0.0636
11	0.0037	0.3234	-0.8785	0.1872
12	-0.0963	0.2950	-0.7394	-0.6050
13	-0.1823	0.0633	-0.8598	-0.2648
14	-0.2633	0.0031	-0.7748	-0.7746
15	0.2538	-0.0781	-0.9301	-1.1264

TABLE 26.3 Nontrending Regression Coefficients

NONTRENDING EXAMPLE

Reversal Amount = 3 Boxes, Wave 1 = –10, Wave 2 = +8, Wave 3 = –5

Wave 4 = A(Wave 1) + B(Wave 2) + C(Wave 3) + D
   = (–0.3387)(–10) + (–0.1737)(8) + (–0.7909) (–5) + (0.0084)
   = –0.3387 – 1.3896 + 3.9545 + 0.0084
   = 2.2346

EXTENDING THE FORECAST

It is possible to forecast the height of the fifth wave from a three-wave cycle using the information in this chapter. Simply follow the preceding procedure to estimate the height of the fourth wave. Next make the following substitutions:

Let new wave 1 = old wave 2.

Let new wave 2 = old wave 3.

Let new wave 3 = estimate for wave 4.

Then repeat the procedure. However, the disadvantage to this method is that the standard deviation of the estimate increases with each new iteration and the reliability of each new forecast decreases significantly.

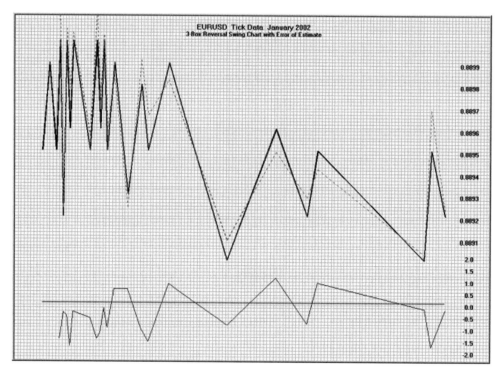

FIGURE 26.6   Estimate Chart No. 1

ESTIMATE CHARTS

In Figure 26.6, the bold solid line represents swing data using a three-box reversal amount for the EURUSD currency pair during January of 2002. The lighter dotted line represents the estimate of the fourth wave using the regression analysis described in this chapter. The zero-mean oscillator at the bottom of the chart represents the error of the estimate (the swing data value minus the corresponding fourth wave estimate).

In Figure 26.7, the reversal amount has been increased to seven boxes for comparison.

One simple observation about these two swing charts is that as the reversal amount increases, the error of the estimate increases proportionately. Increasing the reversal amount also generates fewer waves for the same time frame, although this was to be expected in retrospect.

Many traders are probably curious about the effect of large reversal amounts on the error of the estimate. For that purpose, we present one more swing chart in Figure 26.8, this time with a 15-box reversal amount.

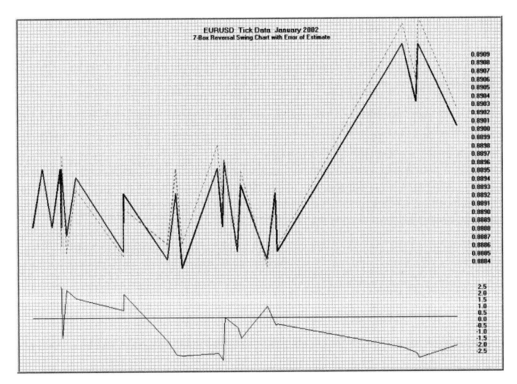

FIGURE 26.7 Estimate Chart No. 2

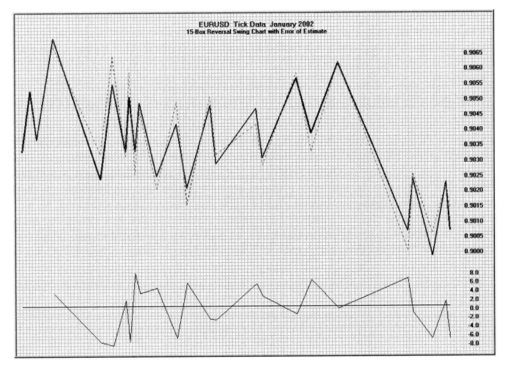

FIGURE 26.8 Estimate Chart No. 3

LIVE USAGE

Traders will note that there is a wealth of information in this chapter and will probably wonder just how to apply these new concepts to an actual trading session inside the currency dealer's online trading platform.

First, a pencil and a sheet of graph paper are required. Some traders may find a six-inch transparent ruler helpful when measuring price movements directly on the monitor. Traders familiar with point and figure charting methods should have no problem. We recommend the following initial steps:

1. Display the EURUSD currency pair in the trading platform window.
2. Set the time interval in the window to a minimum, such as 5, 10, 15, or 30 seconds.
3. Mentally set the box size to one pip.
4. Set the reversal amount to three boxes (again mentally).
5. Begin plotting the Xs and Os in the point and figure chart.
6. If a distinguishable match between the P&F pattern and either a three-wave trending pattern or a contracting triangle occurs, then refer to the corresponding table in this chapter and perform the necessary arithmetic to calculate the height of the subsequent wave. Mark the estimate on the graph paper and set up an imaginary stop-loss limit order and an imaginary take-profit limit order.
7. Continue plotting Xs and Os until the objective is attained or a stop-loss level is encountered.

Note that this method might take numerous paper trades before traders are comfortable with this form of trading. Also, we chose a box size of one pip and a three-box reversal amount simply as a beginning exercise. Traders should base their choices on the magnitude of the bid/ask spread of the underlying currency pair, the current volatility of that pair, familiarity with P&F techniques, and individual trading goals.

Traders should save each completed sheet of graph paper for subsequent scrutiny. Date, time, currency pair, box size, reversal amount, arithmetic calculations, the estimate, and the actual outcome should all be logged directly on the graph sheet.

CHAPTER 27

Cycle Frequencies

OVERVIEW

In this chapter we examine some very fundamental characteristics about cycles: how frequently they recur and in what percentages. The identification criteria that distinguish one cycle from the others will be the inequality constraints between the vertices (peaks and valleys) of each cycle. The lower-case letters, a, b, c, d, and so on, represent discrete prices and not the heights of individual waves. The upper-case letters, A, B, C, D, and so on, will be used to identify the different cycle patterns within a family of cycles. (See Figure 27.1.)

TWO-WAVE CYCLES

When scrutinizing two-wave cycles, we see in Figure 27.2 that there are only six permutations if we use the mathematical operators <, > and =.

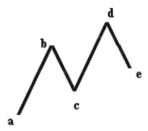

FIGURE 27.1 Lower-Case Letters Indicate Price Levels

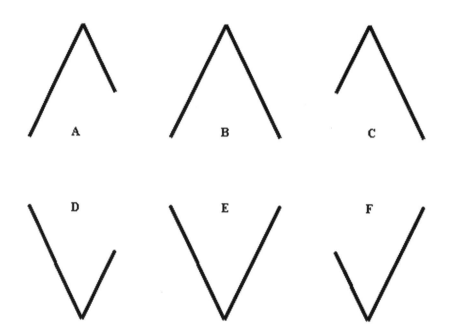

FIGURE 27.2 The Six Possible Two-Wave Cycles

The identifying criteria for the two-wave bull cycles are:

Cycle A $a < c < b$
Cycle B $a = c < b$
Cycle C $c < a < b$

The identifying criteria for the two-wave bear cycles are:

Cycle D $a > c > b$
Cycle E $a = c > b$
Cycle F $c > a > b$

Using the 7,000,000+ EURUSD tick database, the results were calculated as shown in Table 27.1.

The columns labeled A through F represent the percentage of occurrences for the corresponding cycle. Thus, summing these columns in each row will equal 100 percent. The salient feature about this table is that the two symmetrical cycles, B and E, decrease in frequency as the reversal amount increases. The remaining cycles occur with nearly identical frequencies, which is to be expected since they are bull-bear inverse cycles.

Rev Amt	Matches	A	B	C	D	E	F
3	1,309,204	15.86	18.37	15.77	16.74	16.22	17.04
4	725,462	16.75	16.53	16.72	17.59	14.67	17.74
5	404,422	17.81	14.44	17.75	18.39	13.05	18.56
6	237,822	18.41	13.23	18.35	18.88	12.17	18.96
7	139,438	19.22	11.65	19.12	19.58	10.92	19.50
8	82,312	20.18	10.00	19.82	20.51	9.33	20.16
9	51,082	20.97	8.44	20.59	21.31	8.02	20.67
10	33,668	21.68	7.24	21.08	21.90	6.92	21.18
11	23,010	22.30	5.93	21.77	22.59	5.77	21.64
12	16,300	23.02	4.71	22.28	22.99	4.74	22.26
13	12,136	23.45	4.03	22.52	23.33	3.98	22.68
14	9,370	23.87	3.31	22.82	23.46	3.25	23.28
15	7,580	24.07	2.94	22.99	23.57	2.98	23.44
16	6,166	24.53	2.61	22.86	23.75	2.55	23.69
17	5,164	24.98	2.37	22.67	23.64	2.33	24.03
18	4,400	24.97	2.23	22.81	24.13	1.98	23.88
19	3,732	25.10	1.85	23.06	24.03	1.72	24.24
20	3,208	25.12	1.81	23.09	24.12	1.72	24.15
21	2,768	24.74	1.67	23.61	24.34	1.56	24.09
22	2,446	24.89	1.64	23.49	24.48	1.56	23.94
23	2,202	24.56	1.69	23.78	24.87	1.41	23.69
24	1,974	24.30	1.53	24.20	24.76	1.32	23.89
25	1,794	24.45	1.57	24.01	24.68	1.34	23.95

TABLE 27.1 Frequencies Based on Reversal Amounts

THREE-WAVE CYCLES

When analyzing cycles with three or more waves, it is more expedient to ignore cycles in which two vertices are equal. We focus solely on the "greater than" and "less than" conditions. Therefore, we examine only the three-wave cycles shown in Figure 27.3.

The inequality constraints for the cycles are:

Cycle A $a < c < b < d$ Cycle F $a > c > b > d$
Cycle B $a < c < d < b$ Cycle G $c > a > b > d$
Cycle C $c < d < a < b$ Cycle H $c > d > a > b$

| Cycle D | c < a < d < b | Cycle I | c > a > d > b |
| Cycle E | c < a < b < d | Cycle J | a > c > d > b |

The first noteworthy feature in Table 27.2 is the very low frequencies for cycles C and H, although they do increase geometrically as the reversal amount increases linearly. Cycles D and I are the table leaders, although both are components of longer lateral movement cycles. Erroneously, we expected the ideal bull cycle (A) and the ideal bear cycle (F) to exhibit slightly higher table frequencies, but intuition is not always correct.

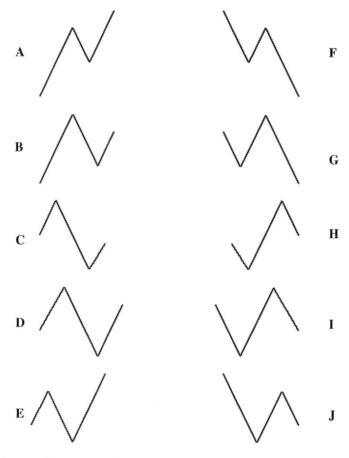

FIGURE 27.3   Ten Three-Wave Cycles

Rev Amt	Matches	A	B	C	D	E	F	G	H	I	J
3	564,264	14.35	8.69	0.28	18.25	8.34	13.94	8.32	0.27	18.46	9.10
4	347,772	14.74	8.12	0.29	19.07	7.71	14.63	7.65	0.30	19.19	8.29
5	214,803	15.37	7.69	0.39	19.13	7.41	15.20	7.35	0.42	19.23	7.81
6	133,914	15.59	7.48	0.55	19.18	7.18	15.56	7.19	0.62	19.14	7.49
7	84,586	15.83	7.47	0.78	18.86	7.09	15.91	7.22	0.88	18.79	7.16
8	54,050	15.98	7.79	1.06	18.00	7.17	16.20	7.40	1.21	18.06	7.12
9	35,964	16.15	7.89	1.33	17.54	7.10	16.28	7.71	1.62	17.14	7.24
10	24,974	16.28	8.04	1.63	16.93	7.10	16.45	7.84	1.96	16.60	7.17
11	17,989	15.97	8.38	1.95	16.19	7.44	16.74	8.02	2.22	16.02	7.08
12	13,351	16.22	8.56	2.17	15.31	7.65	16.93	7.92	2.55	15.67	7.02
13	10,257	16.48	8.63	2.39	14.99	7.59	16.80	7.96	2.80	15.16	7.20
14	8,143	16.71	8.55	2.62	14.42	7.75	16.52	8.02	3.02	14.90	7.50
15	6,696	17.04	8.32	2.55	14.67	7.54	16.43	8.05	3.38	14.37	7.66
16	5,531	16.94	8.64	2.71	14.07	7.67	16.33	8.21	3.44	14.61	7.39
17	4,668	17.25	8.72	3.15	13.32	7.63	16.05	8.31	3.45	14.70	7.43
18	4,020	17.24	8.71	3.16	13.56	7.36	16.32	8.51	3.73	14.13	7.29
19	3,455	17.71	8.31	3.10	13.63	7.29	15.95	8.60	3.70	14.04	7.67
20	2,977	17.43	8.53	3.36	13.40	7.46	15.99	8.60	3.83	13.71	7.69
21	2,584	16.99	8.51	3.44	13.43	7.74	16.56	8.32	4.26	13.00	7.74
22	2,286	17.15	8.49	3.63	13.56	7.35	16.40	8.57	4.37	12.69	7.79
23	2,061	17.08	8.35	3.40	14.26	7.13	16.89	8.39	4.51	12.42	7.57
24	1,860	17.04	8.01	3.60	14.19	7.31	17.10	8.06	4.78	12.20	7.69
25	1,688	17.06	8.12	3.55	14.04	7.41	16.77	8.35	5.15	11.73	7.82

TABLE 27.2 Frequencies for Three-Wave Cycles

FOUR-WAVE BULL CYCLES

In order to limit the number of cycles examined, we again ignore cycles where any two vertices are equal. Also we confine our analysis to bull formations only in this section. Bear cycles are examined in the following section.

The first seven four-wave cycles that we examine are bull cycles in which the height of the first wave is greater than the height of the second wave. (See Figure 27.4.)

The inequality constraints are:

Cycle A $a < c < b < e < d$
Cycle B $a < c < e < b < d$
Cycle C $a < e < c < b < d$
Cycle D $e < a < c < b < d$

Cycle E   a < c < e < d < b
Cycle F   a < e < c < d < b
Cycle G   e < a < c < d < b

Examination of Table 27.3 reveals that the ideal bull cycle (cycle A) has a rather low percentage of occurrences. Trend followers are happiest when the trend in which they have invested continues for more than three cycles. The obvious winner is cycle B, a bull cycle in which the last wave has dipped slightly below vertex b. However, this is not an omen of any sort, particularly if the first three waves are treated as a single bull wave. The distribution of the remaining cycles is somewhat unimpressive. One key observation, though, is the effect of reversal amount on individual columns.

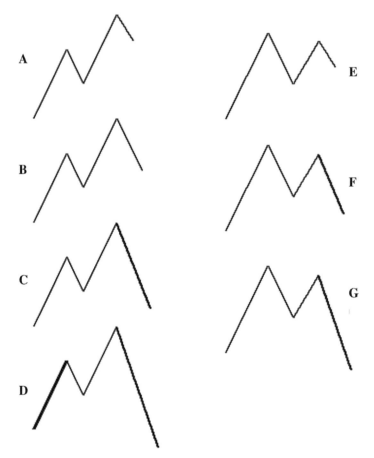

FIGURE 27.4 Four-Wave Bull Cycles

Rev Amt	Matches	A	B	C	D	E	F	G
3	65,291	0.96	48.44	11.29	9.92	7.82	10.58	11.00
4	45,048	1.03	52.68	10.64	9.35	6.96	9.11	10.24
5	30,589	1.45	54.03	10.48	8.74	6.52	8.88	9.90
6	20,477	2.10	53.74	10.35	8.81	6.54	8.96	9.49
7	13,920	2.69	52.68	10.48	8.97	6.54	9.33	9.32
8	9,617	3.30	49.94	10.53	9.71	7.03	9.49	9.99
9	6,782	4.04	48.04	10.09	10.01	6.96	10.35	10.51
10	4,951	4.85	46.21	9.84	10.73	7.53	10.46	10.38
11	3,755	5.54	43.46	10.81	11.00	7.59	10.84	10.76
12	2,892	6.19	41.70	10.41	11.58	8.09	11.69	10.34
13	2,256	6.38	40.38	10.55	12.01	8.07	11.04	11.57
14	1,790	6.87	37.65	11.23	12.51	8.10	11.73	11.90
15	1,514	6.80	38.11	10.57	12.22	7.93	12.42	11.96
16	1,256	7.80	37.26	10.67	11.86	8.20	11.94	12.26
17	1,051	9.04	35.97	10.75	11.32	9.42	11.42	12.08
18	936	9.08	35.68	9.40	11.97	8.76	12.07	13.03
19	798	8.65	35.71	10.03	10.65	7.64	12.66	14.66
20	702	9.40	34.62	10.97	10.26	8.12	12.82	13.82
21	619	10.02	33.76	11.95	10.99	7.92	12.28	13.09
22	547	10.24	34.19	9.87	11.52	9.32	11.88	12.98
23	503	9.54	36.78	9.15	11.33	8.35	10.34	14.51
24	452	9.73	36.73	9.96	11.50	7.52	10.40	14.16
25	411	9.49	35.04	10.46	11.92	7.54	10.71	14.84

TABLE 27.3 Frequencies for Four-Wave Bull Cycles

FOUR-WAVE BEAR CYCLES

Again we will limit the number of cycles to examine by ignoring cycles where any two vertices are equal. The first seven four-wave cycles that we examine are bear cycles in which the height of the first wave is greater than the height of the second wave. (See Figure 27.5.)

The inequality constraints are:

Cycle A $a > c > b > e > d$
Cycle B $a > c > e > b > d$
Cycle C $a > e > c > b > d$
Cycle D $e > a > c > b > d$
Cycle E $a > c > e > d > b$
Cycle F $a > e > c > d > b$
Cycle G $e > a > c > d > b$

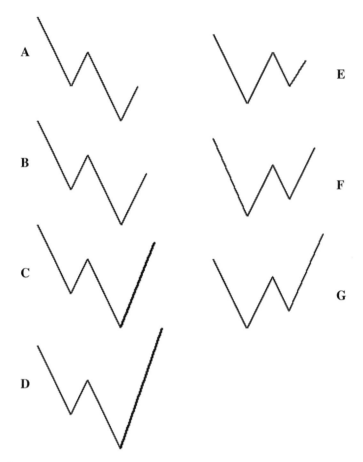

FIGURE 27.5 Four-Wave Bear Cycles

The observations with regard to the four-wave bull cycle table (Table 27.3) apply in Table 27.4 too; simply keep in mind the effect of the bull-bear inverse relationship. Statistically, the two tables are very similar.

USAGE

Cycle frequencies analysis should not be employed as a trading system unto itself since it is purely a mechanical percentage technique. Nonetheless, knowledge of these percentages of likelihood may assist traders in the decision-making process when coupled with other signal-generation systems.

Also, we must note that the tables in this chapter pertain specifically to the raw tick data for the EURUSD currency pair during the 2002 calendar year. However, they do exhibit a sort of generic quality that may be used as a template for other currency pairs.

Rev Amt	Matches	A	B	C	D	E	F	G
3	63,168	0.84	48.89	11.03	10.45	8.27	9.90	10.63
4	43,835	1.06	52.83	10.21	9.37	7.12	9.33	10.08
5	30,092	1.44	54.19	10.25	8.89	6.45	9.13	9.66
6	20,156	2.11	54.10	9.85	9.13	6.42	9.27	9.10
7	13,773	2.93	52.70	10.01	8.80	6.43	9.79	9.34
8	9,539	3.84	50.01	9.58	9.30	6.85	10.73	9.70
9	6,729	4.77	47.26	10.16	9.64	7.25	10.69	10.22
10	4,955	5.85	44.20	10.03	10.11	7.47	11.73	10.62
11	3,696	6.49	40.96	10.52	10.12	8.28	12.31	11.31
12	2,876	7.13	39.78	10.40	10.01	7.79	12.69	12.20
13	2,284	7.22	39.58	10.60	10.16	7.44	12.96	12.04
14	1,854	8.14	38.24	11.17	10.41	8.25	12.51	11.27
15	1,556	8.87	37.47	11.63	10.67	8.03	12.72	10.60
16	1,301	9.61	36.59	10.76	10.53	8.92	11.22	12.38
17	1,121	10.08	36.66	9.63	11.24	9.01	10.62	12.76
18	979	10.52	36.36	8.78	11.75	9.19	11.24	12.16
19	853	10.43	36.58	9.85	12.19	9.14	10.32	11.49
20	736	11.01	34.78	10.33	11.68	9.24	10.60	12.36
21	629	12.56	31.96	10.97	11.13	8.74	12.40	12.24
22	554	13.18	31.59	12.09	10.47	8.30	12.09	12.27
23	499	13.43	31.46	12.02	10.82	8.62	12.22	11.42
24	449	15.14	30.51	12.92	9.80	8.69	12.25	10.69
25	406	15.76	29.80	12.81	9.85	8.87	11.82	11.08

TABLE 27.4 Frequencies for Four-Wave Bear Cycles

CHAPTER 28

Bull Cycles

OVERVIEW

One of the most fascinating and complex disciplines within the realm of forecasting security prices is the Elliott wave principle. This is the brainchild of author/analyst Ralph N. Elliott, who developed his system during the 1930s and 1940s along with an accompanying philosophy about cycles in nature. Elliotticians are quite adamant about Elliott's system even after three-quarters of a century due to its diversity and subjectivity. We recommend that novice traders visit the following web sites for details: www.elliott wave.com and www.acrotec.com/ewt.htm.

IDEAL BULL CYCLE

Analysts have identified and cataloged a plethora of unique price patterns like head-and-shoulders formations, pennants, flags, and wedges. In this current study, we intend to focus our research and analysis specifically on the ideal bull cycle. (See Figure 28.1.)

This cycle consists of five waves, three upward and two downward. The upward waves in a bull cycle are called *impulse waves* and the downward waves are called *corrective waves* (Elliott's terms). The ideal bull cycle has the following mathematical constraints given that the letters "a" through "f" represent discrete prices (and not wave lengths).

First, the length of each corrective wave must be less than the length of its preceding impulse wave:

$$b - c < b - a$$
$$d - e < d - c$$

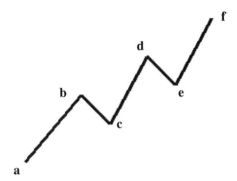

FIGURE 28.1   Ideal Bull Cycle

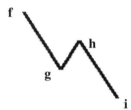

FIGURE 28.2   Elliott's Postulation

Second, no valley in a five-wave bull cycle may dip below any preceding peak:

$$b < e$$

Elliott's theory now postulates that a well-behaved five-wave bull cycle will be followed by a three-wave bear cycle (See Figure 28.2) with the following price constraints:

$$i < g < h < f$$

Note that price "f" is the junction point between the known bull cycle and the estimated bear cycle.

OBJECTIVE

The purpose of this study is to determine the percentage of retracement that the three-wave bear cycle covers in relation to the height of the preceding five-wave bull cycle. In the first testing pass to achieve this objective we have selected the streaming tick data for the EURUSD currency pair over the time period of 1/1/2002 through 12/31/2002. This amounts to 7,079,300 closing prices.

Tick data was selected in this initial study because this is how session and day traders view the live streaming data as it is displayed in their forex dealer's trading platform. Thus, this study focuses on very short-term trading goals.

INITIAL RESULTS

In the current study, we set the box size to one pip (0.0001 USD) and vary the reversal amounts from 2 boxes to 25 boxes. A reversal amount of one box has no filtering potential and is therefore omitted. (See Table 28.1.)

Rev Amt	Swings	Matches	Ratio	Retrace
2	2,333,017	391	1.219	0.491
3	1,309,727	215	1.195	0.456
4	725,777	240	1.161	0.403
5	404,597	222	1.162	0.403
6	237,927	229	1.160	0.396
7	139,499	221	1.178	0.378
8	82,347	202	1.180	0.359
9	51,107	177	1.216	0.348
10	33,687	165	1.194	0.371
11	23,023	135	1.185	0.363
12	13,311	111	1.175	0.326
13	12,145	93	1.194	0.390
14	9,375	90	1.219	0.348
15	7,585	88	1.211	0.366
16	6,171	86	1.247	0.310
17	5,169	77	1.272	0.347
18	4,405	63	1.265	0.486
19	3,737	56	1.214	0.511
20	3,213	48	1.251	0.530
21	2,773	46	1.267	0.393
22	2,451	52	1.206	0.366
23	2,207	47	1.183	0.416
24	1,977	47	1.193	0.421
25	1,797	45	1.171	0.396
Average			1.205	0.399

TABLE 28.1 Retracement Results

Rev Amt is the reversal amount, the number of boxes required to trigger a reversal in price direction.

Swings is the number of waves in the swing data or the sum of the peaks and valleys less 1. As the reversal amount increases, the number of peaks and valleys decreases due to the filtering process.

Matches defines the number of occurrences where the test pattern (the ideal bull cycle) matches a sequence in the swing data.

Ratio is the average ratio between the height of all five waves in the bull cycle divided by the height of the first three waves in the bull cycle:

$$\frac{f-a}{d-a}$$

Retrace is the average retracement of the three-wave bear cycle in relation to the five-wave bull cycle, defined mathematically as:

$$\frac{f-i}{f-a}$$

PRAXIS

Many traders will now ask: How can this information be used as a trading mechanism? A practical example follows.

Given that the price formation in Figure 28.3 has already occurred with the following prices:

a	1.0000
b	1.0010
c	1.0005
d	1.0015
e	1.0012

we can now estimate the market entry point "f" for a short trade to trap the length of the three-wave bear cycle by first computing the height of the first three waves "a" to "d" in the bull cycle:

$$\text{Length} = d - a$$
$$0.0015 = 1.0015 - 1.000$$

Next we must project the price of f, the height of the fifth and final wave in the bull cycle:

$$f = 1.205 \times (d - a) + a$$
$$1.0018 = 0.0018 + 1.0000$$

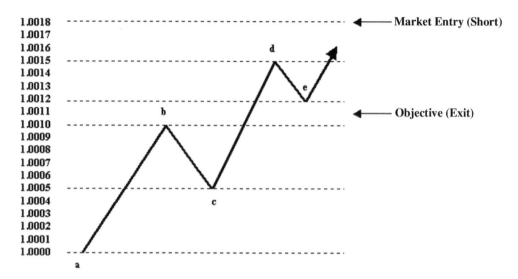

FIGURE 28.3 Trading Praxis

To calculate the objective price (the market exit price), we multiply the average retracement percentage (39.9 percent) times the height of the five waves in the bull cycle:

$$
\begin{aligned}
\text{Height} &= f - a \\
&= .0018 \\
\text{Exit Price} &= f - (\text{Percent} \times \text{Height}) \\
&= 1.0018 - (0.399 \times 0.0018) \\
&= 1.0018 - 0.00072 \\
&= 1.0011
\end{aligned}
$$

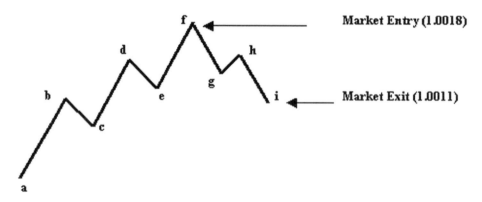

FIGURE 28.4 Market Entry and Exit Signals

Ideally, the trade will occur as show in Figure 28.4, with the following projected prices:

f   1.0018
g   1.0013
h   1.0016
i   1.0011

CAVEAT

As usual, any new trading mechanism has to be thoroughly tested via paper trading before incorporating it into one's overall trading system. One drawback in the bull cycle trading mechanism example is that the standard deviation of the average retracement percentage is slightly high at 4.9 percent. This means that there is a 68 percent likelihood that the exit price will fall between 35.0 percent and 44.8 percent retracement of the height of the bull cycle (39.9 – 4.9 and .39.9 + 4.9).

FURTHER STUDIES

In the present cycle study, we have only touched the tip of the iceberg. We intend to delve much deeper into the predictive value of swing data, varying the dependent variables of box size, underlying currency pair, raw data intervals, and unique cycle formations.

We were astonished to see how closely the average retracement ratio 39.9 percent aligned itself with the primary Fibonacci ratio 38.2 percent. This is no coincidence since many Fibonacci analysts believe that a 38.2 percent retracement indicates that the three-wave corrective cycle will be followed by a new five-wave impulse cycle in the same direction of the first impulse cycle.

However, it is these same analysts who believe that if the retracement percentage of the three-wave corrective cycle reaches 61.8 percent, then a new five-wave impulse cycle is developing in the opposite direction of the original five-wave impulse cycle.

Lastly, we should point out that the ratio of the height of the five waves in the bull cycle divided by the height of the first three waves in the bull cycle is 1.205. This, too, is extremely close to the primary Fibonacci number 0.618 multiplied by 2 (that is, $0.618 \times 2 = 1.236$).

This initial study is in no way complete, nor is it intended as an affirmation or a refutation of Elliott's works. Instead it is intended as an unbiased independent analysis based solely on rigorous statistical methods, although resulting ratios and averages tend to align with Fibonacci numbers with an accuracy greater than mere coincidence. We may attribute the slight deviations to simple round-off error. As we increase the size of the raw quotes in our historical currency database, we will be able to more accurately determine critical inflection points in the cyclical data.

CHAPTER 29

Bear Cycles

OVERVIEW

The current study is identical to the study of bull cycles in the previous chapter except, of course, the trend is moving downward. The terminology and the testing approach are also the same as in the previous chapter.

IDEAL BEAR CYCLE

The ideal bear cycle is the arithmetic inverse complement to the ideal bull cycle. (See Figure 29.1.)

This cycle consists of five waves, three downward and two upward. The downward waves in a bear cycle are called *impulse waves* and the upward waves are called *correc-*

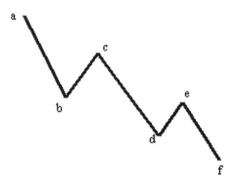

FIGURE 29.1 Ideal Bear Cycle

tive waves. The ideal bear cycle has the following mathematical constraints given that the letters "a" through "f" represent prices.

First, the length of each corrective wave must be less than the length of its preceding impulse wave:

$$c - b < a - b$$
$$e - d < c - d$$

Second, no peak in a five-wave bear cycle may advance above any preceding valley:

$$e < b$$

OBJECTIVE

Our goal is this study is to determine if the same levels of retracement occur in bear cycles that occur in bull cycles and how closely they align.

INITIAL RESULTS

The column headers in Table 29.1 are defined as:

Rev Amt is the reversal amount, the number of boxes required to trigger a reversal in price direction.

Swings is the number of waves in the swing data or the sum of the peaks and valleys less 1. As the reversal amount increases, the number of peaks and valleys decreases due to the filtering process.

Matches defines the number of occurrences where the test pattern (the ideal bear cycle) matches a sequence in the swing data.

Ratio is the average ratio between the height of all five waves in the bear cycle divided by the height of the first three waves in the bear cycle.

$$\frac{a - f}{a - d}$$

Retrace is the average retracement of the three-wave bull cycle in relation to the five-wave bear cycle; defined mathematically as:

$$\frac{i - f}{a - f}$$

Rev Amt	Swings	Matches	Ratio	Retrace
2	2,333,017	391	1.219	0.491
3	1,309,727	215	1.195	0.456
4	725,777	240	1.161	0.403
5	404,597	222	1.162	0.403
6	237,927	229	1.160	0.396
7	139,499	221	1.178	0.378
8	82,347	202	1.180	0.359
9	51,107	177	1.216	0.348
10	33,687	165	1.194	0.371
11	23,023	135	1.185	0.363
12	13,311	111	1.175	0.326
13	12,145	93	1.194	0.390
14	9,375	90	1.219	0.348
15	7,585	88	1.211	0.366
16	6,171	86	1.247	0.310
17	5,169	77	1.272	0.347
18	4,405	63	1.265	0.486
19	3,737	56	1.214	0.511
20	3,213	48	1.251	0.530
21	2,773	46	1.267	0.393
22	2,451	52	1.206	0.366
23	2,207	47	1.183	0.416
24	1,977	47	1.193	0.421
25	1,797	45	1.171	0.396
Average			1.205	0.399

TABLE 29.1 Retracement Results

PRAXIS

A practical example follows. (See Figure 29.2.)

Given that the price formation has already occurred with the following prices:

a   1.0018
b   1.0008
c   1.0013
d   1.0003
e   1.0006

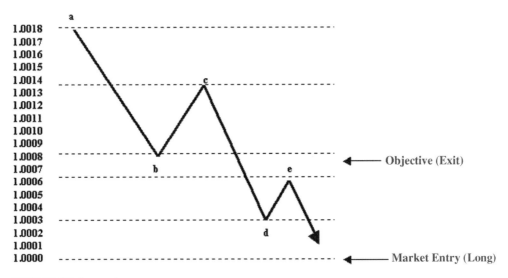

FIGURE 29.2 Trading Praxis

we can now estimate the market entry point "f" for a long trade to trap the length of the following three-wave bull cycle by first computing the height of the first three waves "a" to "d" in the bear cycle:

$$\text{Length} = a - d$$
$$.0015 = 1.0018 - 1.0003$$

Next we must project the price of f, the height of the fifth and final wave in the bear cycle:

$$f = a - 1.205 \times (a - d)$$
$$1.0000 = 1.0018 - 0.0018$$

To calculate the objective price (the market exit price), we multiply the average retracement percentage (39.9 percent) times the height of the five waves in the bear cycle:

$$\text{Height} = a - f$$
$$= 0.0018$$
$$\text{Exit price} = f + (\text{Percent} \times \text{Height})$$
$$= 1.0000 + (0.399 \times 0.0018)$$
$$= 1.0000 + 0.00072$$
$$= 1.0007$$

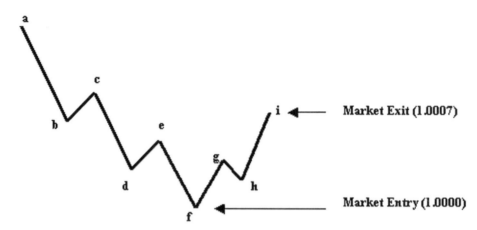

FIGURE 29.3   Market Entry and Exit Signals

Ideally, the trade will occur as shown in Figure 29.3, with the following projected prices:

f	1.0000
g	1.0005
h	1.0002
i	1.0007

In this example and the analogous example in the previous chapter, we used a three-pip box size to create the swing data and forecast a return of seven pips. Using this system, the projected profit will always be at least the size of the reversal amount times the box size. In this case, it was 2.3333 times the minimum swing threshold.

CAVEAT

As usual, any new trading mechanism has to be thoroughly tested via paper trading before incorporating it into one's overall trading system. One drawback in the bear cycle trading mechanism is that the standard deviation of the average retracement percentage was slightly high at 4.9 percent. This means that there is a 68 percent likelihood that the exit price will fall between 35.0 percent and 44.8 percent retracement of the height of the bull cycle (39.9 − 4.9 and .39.9 + 4.9).

CHAPTER 30

Swing Properties

OVERVIEW

We mentioned earlier that swing data is bivariate data; that is, it is represented in pairs: a price member and a time member. It is true that univariate data like daily closing prices also has a time element, but since the time elements are all equally spaced, the data is normally presented as an ordered set of prices only.

WAVE ANATOMY

The height of a wave is the number of pips it spans along the y-axis (the current price minus the previous price). The width of a wave is the number of time units along the x-axis that it spans. (See Figure 30.1.) The distance of each wave is calculated using the Pythagorean theorem:

$$Distance = \sqrt{Height^2 + Width^2}$$

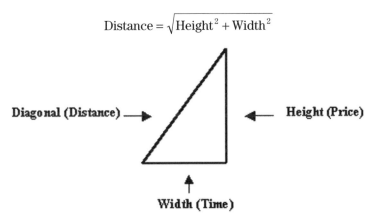

FIGURE 30.1 Wave Anatomy

SIMPLE RATIOS

The three ratios of each wave with its predecessor are then calculated and logged as:

$$\text{Height ratio} = \frac{\text{Height of wave}_n}{\text{Height of wave}_{n-1}}$$

$$\text{Width ratio} = \frac{\text{Width of wave}_n}{\text{Width of wave}_{n-1}}$$

$$\text{Distance ratio} = \frac{\text{Distance of wave}_n}{\text{Distance of wave}_{n-1}}$$

We have already used the height ratio in earlier chapters, where we referred to it as retracement.

SWING AVERAGES

Table 30.1 displays averages for heights, widths, and distances for both bull waves and bear waves using EURUSD tick data (7,000,000+ closing quotes). A box size of one pip is used, while reversal amounts range from 3 to 25 boxes.

The column definitions for the table are:

Rev Amt is the reversal amount of the swing algorithm using a box size of one pip.

Swings is the number of peaks and valleys in the swing data. The number of waves equals swings minus 1.

+X is the average number of time units (ticks) in each bull wave.

–X is the average number of time units (ticks) in each bear wave.

+Y is the average number of pips in each bull wave.

–Y is the average number of pips in each bear wave.

+Z is the average diagonal distance in each bull wave.

– Z is the average diagonal distance in each bear wave.

One obvious feature about the table is that the averages for the bull values are slightly higher than the averages for the bear values. This implies some sort of statistical bias. However, this is not the case. The opening price of the EURUSD currency pair on 1/1/2002 was 0.8896 while the closing price on 12/31/2002 was 1.0489. This discrepancy of 1,593 pips accounts for the slight (and negligible) skew in the averages. (Coincidently, January 1, 2002, was the day that the euro currency became the legal tender of the member countries in the European Monetary Union.)

Another peculiarity in the table is how rapidly the X values grow in relation to the Y

Rev Amt	Swings	+ X	- X	+ Y	- Y	+ Z	- Z
3	1,309,727	5.7	5.1	4.4	4.4	7.8	7.3
4	725,775	10.5	9.0	5.5	5.5	12.7	11.4
5	404,597	18.8	16.2	6.7	6.7	21.2	18.7
6	237,927	31.7	27.8	7.9	7.9	34.1	30.3
7	139,499	53.6	47.9	9.2	9.2	55.9	50.4
8	82,347	89.9	82.0	10.7	10.7	92.1	84.3
9	51,107	143.9	133.1	12.4	12.3	146.0	135.2
10	33,687	218.4	201.9	14.1	14.0	220.3	203.7
11	23,023	319.3	295.6	16.0	15.9	321.0	297.4
12	16,311	448.1	419.9	18.1	17.9	449.7	421.4
13	12,145	598.2	567.6	20.1	19.9	599.6	569.1
14	9,375	773.5	736.7	22.3	21.9	774.9	738.1
15	7,585	959.3	907.2	24.2	23.8	960.6	908.6
16	6,171	1,179.8	1,114.4	26.3	25.8	1,181.1	1,115.7
17	5,169	1,409.2	1,329.8	28.3	27.7	1,410.4	1,331.0
18	4,405	1,657.1	1,556.8	30.3	29.6	1,658.4	1,558.1
19	3,737	1,947.6	1,840.9	32.5	31.6	1,948.8	1,842.2
20	3,213	2,265.1	2,141.2	34.7	33.7	2,266.3	2,142.4
21	2,773	2,643.7	2,461.9	37.0	35.8	2,644.8	2,463.0
22	2,451	2,985.1	2,791.2	39.1	37.8	2,986.3	2,792.2
23	2,207	3,309.1	3,105.8	41.0	39.5	3,310.2	3,106.9
24	1,977	3,698.2	3,463.0	43.1	41.5	3,699.4	3,464.1
25	1,797	4,093.3	3,785.2	45.0	43.2	4,094.5	3,786.4

TABLE 30.1 Averages Based on Reversal Amounts

values. But this is easily explained by the fact that the X values share an inverse proportional relationship with the number of swings. Keep in mind that there are 7,000,000+ closing quotes in the EURUSD 2002 database. Fewer swings mean longer X values.

In Table 30.2 we have combined the + and − columns of Table 30.1 for each parameter X, Y, and Z.

This table should not be used to forecast market entry or exit timing because the standard deviation on 7,000,000+ quotes is too high, thus creating a confidence band too wide to use in a discrete forecast.

It is, however, a good guideline to estimate the *average* price movement (Y) and its corresponding *average* time duration (X). For example, assume for some external reason that a reversal amount of 12 boxes was selected where each box equals one pip. Also assume that we know that we have just hit a vertex (either a peak or a valley) and price direction will reverse. *On average* the following wave will reach 18 pips. *On average* the following wave will require 434 ticks of time. All traders will now ask, "How long is 434 ticks?" During periods of high activity, as many as 200 ticks have been

Rev Amt	Swings	Avg X	Avg Y	Avg Z
3	1,309,727	5.4	4.4	7.5
4	725,775	9.8	5.5	12.1
5	404,597	17.5	6.7	19.9
6	237,927	29.8	7.9	32.2
7	139,499	50.7	9.2	53.1
8	82,347	86.0	10.7	88.2
9	51,107	138.5	12.3	140.6
10	33,687	2,10.1	14.1	212.0
11	23,023	307.5	15.9	309.2
12	16,311	434.0	18.0	435.5
13	12,145	582.9	20.0	584.3
14	9,375	755.1	22.1	756.5
15	7,585	933.3	24.0	934.6
16	6,171	1,147.1	26.1	1,148.4
17	5,169	1,369.5	28.0	1,370.7
18	4,405	1,607.0	29.9	1,608.3
19	3,737	1,894.3	32.0	1,895.5
20	3,213	2,203.2	34.2	2,204.3
21	2,773	2,552.8	36.4	2,553.9
22	2,451	2,888.1	38.5	2,889.3
23	2,207	3,207.4	40.3	3,208.5
24	1,977	3,580.6	42.3	3,581.7
25	1,797	3,939.2	44.1	3,940.4

TABLE 30.2   Combined Averages

recorded in one minute. During low activity periods, zero ticks have been recorded. Thus, it depends on the time of day, the day of the week, the preceding chart pattern, and what form of intervention is lurking in the shadows.

SWING DATA PRELIMINARIES

Prior to delving deeper, we must explain some of the tools we use when analyzing swing data. In Figure 30.2 , we use the following data to illustrate swing concepts using a simple three-wave cycle. The letters A–D define discrete prices:

A   1.0000
B   1.0020
C   1.0010
D   1.0030

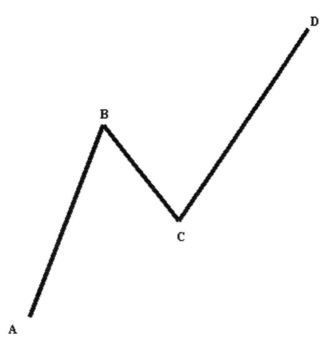

FIGURE 30.2 Three-Wave Cycle

BIVARIATE DATA

We now need to devise some new statistical tools that pertain specifically to swing data. The first characteristic of swing data that we must emphasize is that it is bivariate in nature. That is, for each peak or valley price there is a corresponding time value. This is the sequence number of that price in the raw data time series.

Thus, the peaks and valley in Figure 30.2 are more accurately displayed as shown in Table 30.3.

To capitalize on the bivariate nature of swing data, we must infuse a little more complexity into the diagram in Figure 30.2, although it consists entirely of simple algebraic operations. (See Figure 30.3.)

Point	Price	Time Index
A	1.0000	1
B	1.0020	9
C	1.0010	17
D	1.0030	31

TABLE 30.3 Bivariate Data

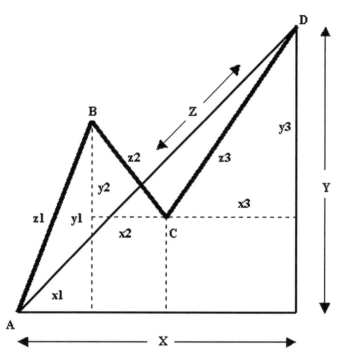

FIGURE 30.3 Cycle Properties

Our first step is to convert the discrete prices to price differentials expressed as pips (multiply by 10,000 for the EURUSD) for the y-axis values:

$$y1 = B - A = 1.0020 - 1.0000 = 20 \text{ pips}$$
$$y2 = C - B = 1.0000 - 1.0010 = -10 \text{ pips}$$
$$y3 = D - C = 1.0030 - 1.0020 = 10 \text{ pips}$$

Next we will convert the raw tick numbers to time differentials:

$$x1 = \text{tick } 2 - \text{tick } 1 = 9 - 1 = 8 \text{ ticks}$$
$$x2 = \text{tick } 3 - \text{tick } 2 = 17 - 9 = 8 \text{ ticks}$$
$$x3 = \text{tick } 4 - \text{tick } 3 = 31 - 17 = 14 \text{ ticks}$$

To calculate the diagonal distances between consecutive peaks and valleys, we simply employ the Pythagorean theorem:

$$z1 = \sqrt{(x1^2 + y1^2)} = \sqrt{(8^2 + 20^2)} = \sqrt{464} = 21.54$$
$$z2 = \sqrt{(x2^2 + y2^2)} = \sqrt{(8^2 + (-10)^2)} = \sqrt{164} = 12.81$$
$$z3 = \sqrt{(x3^2 + y3^2)} = \sqrt{(14^2 + 20^2)} = \sqrt{596} = 24.41$$

Note that the sum z1 + z2 + z3 now represents that total distance that the chart pattern travels when the time element is added to the mix.

If we increase reversal amount in the swing reversal algorithm to filter out the downward wave (z2), then the chart pattern collapses to a single wave. A reversal amount of 11 will accomplish this since wave z2 consists of only 10 pips. We now have a right triangle to describe the diagonal distance traveled:

$$X = x1 + x2 + x3 = 30 \text{ ticks}$$
$$Y = y1 + y2 + y3 = 30 \text{ pips}$$
$$Z = \sqrt{X^2 + Y^2} = \sqrt{30^2 + 30^2} = \sqrt{1,800} = 42.43$$

SWING VOLATILITY

It is common practice for traders to use the standard deviation of a data set to describe the volatility of an underlying security. However, the conventional standard deviation from descriptive statistics normally applies to a univriate set of data, in which the closing price is almost always chosen as the dependent variable. We have devised an alternative method to describe deviations when bivariate swing data is involved.

First, we must sum the total diagonal distance traveled using only the absolute values (waves with downward slopes are treated as positive):

$$\text{Sum} = \text{Abs}(z1) + \text{Abs}(z2) + \text{Abs}(z3)$$

Next, divide this result into the diagonal distance Z generated from the single wave representation of the data after increasing the reversal amount:

$$\text{Swing volatility} = 100 \times \frac{Z}{\text{Sum}}$$
$$= 100 \times \frac{42.43}{21.54 + 12.81 + 24.41}$$
$$= 100 \times \frac{42.43}{58.76}$$
$$= 72.21$$

Thus, by using the diagram in Figure 30.3, we can calculate just how much the three waves z1, z2, and z3 deviate from the single wave Z. First, we note that the mathematical lower limit of swing volatility approaches zero. The upper limit approaches +100, which can be attained only if both cycles have only one identical wave.

One interesting feature of swing volatility is its ability to confirm how closely a given data set follows a linear trend. In this respect, swing volatility is similar to the coefficient of correlation from an ordinary least squares (OLS) linear regression.

More importantly, swing volatility provides us with a tool by which we can compare a single set of raw data that has been converted to multiple sets of swing data using different reversal amounts.

Our next example uses the following swing data in Table 30.4 to generate a five-wave cycle.

The swing volatility for the cycle shown in Figure 30.4 is 66.04. The illustrious trader may confirm this using the math formulas given earlier.

Point	Price	Time Index
A	1.0000	1
B	1.0020	7
C	1.0013	12
D	1.0027	19
E	1.0017	30
F	1.0039	41

TABLE 30.4 Five-Wave Bivariate Data

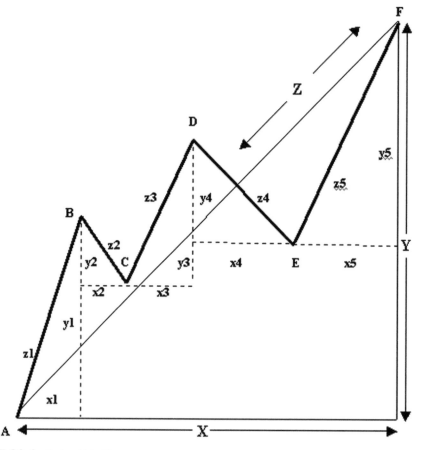

FIGURE 30.4 Swing Volatility

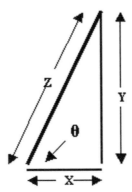

FIGURE 30.5 Swing Velocity

SWING VELOCITY

Swing velocity is another tool we developed in order to measure the magnitude or certainty of a trend. For this purpose, it was necessary to borrow an inverse function from trigonometry, the arc sine.

The simplest case is best illustrated in the diagram in Figure 30.5, which consists of a single wave with the following values: X = 5 ticks and Y = 10 pips. Using the Pythagorean theorem, we can calculate Z as the square root of 125 or 11.18. We now define swing velocity as follows:

$$\text{Swing velocity} = 200 \, \text{Arcsin} \frac{Y/Z}{\pi}$$

$$= 200 \, \text{Arcsin} \frac{10/11.18}{3.14159}$$

$$= 200 \, \text{Arcsin} \frac{0.8945}{3.14159}$$

$$= 200 \frac{1.1072}{3.14159}$$

$$= 70.49$$

Most computer languages express the values returned from trigonometric functions in terms of radians, a convention to which we have also adhered. The return value above, however, has been rescaled to range from +100 to –100, where +100 represents abnormally high upward trending, –100 represents violent downward trending, and a value of 0 indicates that prices are moving horizontally. Essentially, it is the magnitude of the angle q that determines how quickly a single wave or a composite wave approaches its destination in relation to the distance traveled diagonally.

CHAPTER 31

Swing Summary

OVERVIEW

We have introduced quite a lot of new and technical information in the preceding chapters. Our goal in this chapter is to unify the salient estimating routines into a viable tool that traders may incorporate into their existing trading systems.

SELECTING SWING PARAMETERS

In his very informative book, *Point and Figure: Commodity and Stock Trading Techniques* (Traders Press, 1997), author and trader Kermit C. Zieg Jr. suggests the use of a constant reversal amount, which he sets at three boxes. He prefers to vary the box size according to the underlying security. Table 31.1 is our recommendation based loosely on Mr. Zieg's idea.

An alternative method of setting swing reversal parameters is the converse of Zieg's suggestion; that is, set the box size to the constant minimum price fluctuation (one pip in currency markets), then vary the reversal amounts according to the influence of the parity rates of the individual currency pairs. We recommend that the transaction cost (the bid/ask spread) multiplied by 3 be used to initialize the swing reversal algorithm. The second column in Table 31.2 is the average transaction cost of several major currency dealers.

However, if Zieg's method is preferred, then set the box size to the transaction cost, and a constant three-box reversal amount can be used. Essentially, we recommend that currency traders experiment with different combinations based on their different trading objectives.

The advantage to our alternative method is that the plotting of an existing trend is

Underlying Security	Price Range	Box Size
Common and Preferred Stocks	$0 < price < $5	¼ point
	$5 <= price < $20	½ point
	$20 <= price < $100	1 point
	$100 <= price	2 points
Corporate Bonds	$0 < price < $50	¼ point
	$50 <= price < $200	½ point
	$200 <= price < $1000	1 point
	$1000 <= price	2 points
Commodity Futures	Grains	1 cent
	Soybeans	2 cents
	Sugar	5 points
	Crude oil	10 points
	Copper	50 points
	Silver	100 points
	Gold	$2

TABLE 31.1 Reversal Amount Based on Underlying Security
Source: Kermit C. Zieg Jr., *Point and Figure: Commodity and Stock Trading Techniques* (Traders Press, 1997).

Currency Pair	Transaction Cost	Reversal Amount
EURUSD	3	9
EURGBP	3	9
EURCHF	3	9
USDJPY	3	9
AUDUSD	3	9
EURJPY	4	12
NZDUSD	4	12
USDCHF	4	12
GBPUSD	5	15
USDCAD	5	15
GBPJPY	6	18
GBPCHF	7	21
EURSEK	50	150

TABLE 31.2 Reversal Amount Based on Currency Pair

allowed to continue because an increment of a single box is all that is necessary to move to the next possible price level. Also, broader reversal amounts are frequently favored by position traders, who are primarily interested in major price movements. Smaller reversal amounts are traditionally employed by session and day traders, who are content to reap modest profits from minor price movements.

COMPOSITE AVERAGE ESTIMATES

The idea here is very simple and direct: to generate multiple discrete estimates using the different methods described in earlier chapters and combine them to create one average forecast. In all instances we use one pip as the box size and three-, five-, and nine-box reversal amounts. We also use a three-wave cycle where the heights of the last three waves in the swing data are 15, –12, and 9 (see Figure 31.1):

$$A = 1.0002 \qquad B = 1.0017 \qquad C = 1.0005 \qquad D = 1.0014$$

Retracement Percentage Method

First we calculate the retracement percent between the second and third wave:

$$100 \times \frac{\text{Wave 3}}{\text{Wave 2}} = 100 \times \frac{9}{12} = 75\%$$

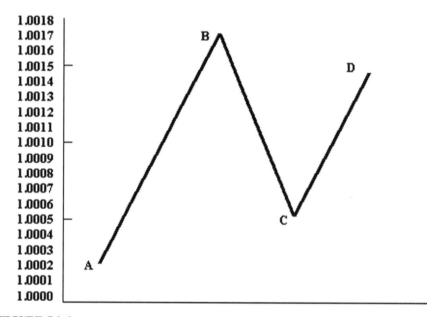

FIGURE 31.1 Composite Average Estimate (1)

Using the corresponding decile table in Chapter 23, "The Measured Move," we find:

Reversal Amount	Wave 4/Wave 2
3	89.97
5	82.86
9	87.14

Multiply retracement percentages by height of second wave:

$$89.97\% \times 12 = 10.7964$$
$$82.86\% \times 12 = 9.8568$$
$$87.14\% \times 12 = 10.4568$$

Convert pips to discrete prices and subtract from last vertex D:

$$1.0014 - 0.00108 = 1.00032$$
$$1.0014 - 0.00099 = 1.00041$$
$$1.0014 - 0.00105 = 1.00035$$

Retracement Percentage Forecasts are shown in Figure 31.2.

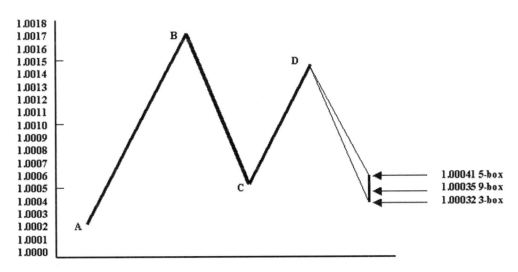

FIGURE 31.2 Composite Average Estimate Average Estimate (2)

Linear Regression Method

In this section, we apply an ordinary least squares (OLS) linear regression to the same three waves with heights 15, –12 and 9. Technically, the regression method requires only the final two waves and our model becomes:

$$\text{Wave 4} = (A \times \text{Wave 2}) + (B \times \text{Wave 3}) + C$$

Using the third quartile table in Chapter 25, "Improving the Third Wave Forecast," we locate the following partial regression coefficients:

Reversal Amount	A	B	C
3	0.7119	0.0871	0.0110
5	0.0140	–1.1137	0.0047
9	0.2167	–0.8128	4.1850

The estimate for the three-box reversal amount is:

$$\text{Wave 4} = 0.7119(12) + 0.0871(-9) + 0.0110$$
$$\text{Wave 4} = 8.5428 - 0.7839 + 0.0110$$
$$\text{Wave 4} = 7.7699$$

A five-box reversal amount produces:

$$\text{Wave 4} = 0.0140(12) - 1.1137(-9) + 0.0047$$
$$\text{Wave 4} = 0.1680 + 7.8863 + 0.0047$$
$$\text{Wave 4} = 8.0590$$

The estimated height using a nine-box reversal amount is:

$$\text{Wave 4} = 0.2167(12) - 0.8128\,(-9) + 4.1850$$
$$\text{Wave 4} = 2.6004 + 7.3152 + 4.1850$$
$$\text{Wave 4} = 14.1006$$

Convert pips to discrete prices and subtract from last vertex D:

$$1.0014 - 0.00078 = 1.00062$$
$$1.0014 - 0.00081 = 1.00059$$
$$1.0014 - 0.00141 = 0.99999$$

Linear regression forecasts are shown in Figure 31.3.

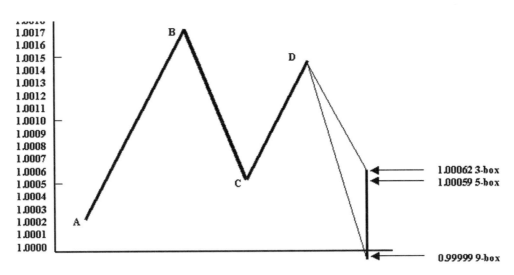

FIGURE 31.3 Composite Average Estimate (3)

Multiple Regression Method

The multiple regression method, illustrated is Chapter 26, "Forecasting the Fourth Wave," requires the height of all three sample waves and uses the following regression model:

$$\text{Wave } 4 = (\text{A} \times \text{Wave } 1) + (\text{B} \times \text{Wave } 2) + (\text{C} \times \text{Wave } 3) + \text{D}$$

Locate the corresponding partial regression coefficients in the nontrending table in Chapter 6:

Reversal Amount	A	B	C	D
3	−0.3387	−0.1737	−0.7909	0.0084
5	−0.1916	−0.0396	−0.8880	0.0203
9	−0.0546	0.1120	−0.9726	−0.0517

Three-box estimate:

$$\text{Wave } 4 = (\text{A} \times 15) + (\text{B} \times -12) + (\text{C} \times 9) + \text{D}$$
$$\text{Wave } 4 = -0.3387(15) - 0.1737(-12) - 0.7909(9) + 0.0084$$
$$\text{Wave } 4 = -5.0805 + 2.0844 - 7.1181 + 0.0084$$
$$\text{Wave } 4 = -10.1058$$

Five-box estimate:

$$\text{Wave } 4 = -0.1916(15) -0.0396(-12) -0.8880(9) + 0.0203$$
$$\text{Wave } 4 = -2.8740 + 0.4752 - 7.9920 + 0.0203$$
$$\text{Wave } 4 = -10.3705$$

Nine-box estimate:

$$\text{Wave } 4 = -0.0546(15) + 0.1120(-12) -0.9726(9) -0.0517$$
$$\text{Wave } 4 = -0.8190 - 1.3440 - 8.7534 - 0.0517$$
$$\text{Wave } 4 = -10.9681$$

Convert pips to discrete prices and subtract from last vertex D

$$1.0014 - 0.00101 = 1.00039$$
$$1.0014 - 0.00104 = 1.00036$$
$$1.0014 - 0.00110 = 1.00030$$

Multiple Regression Forecasts are shown in Figure 31.4.

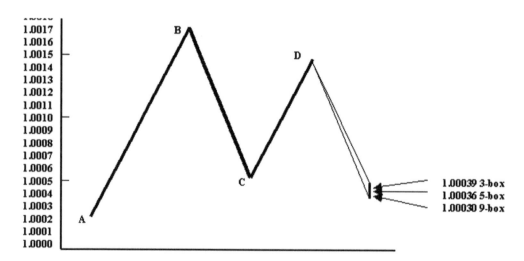

FIGURE 31.4 Composite Average Estimate (4)

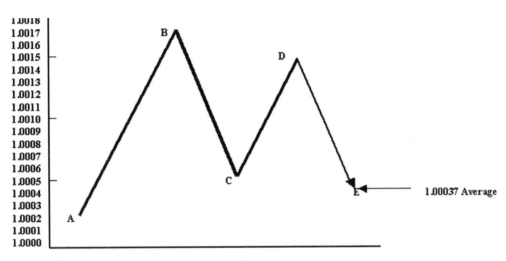

FIGURE 31.5 Composite Average Estimate (5)

Summary

Composite average estimates are summarized as follows (see Figure 31.5):

Method	Reversal Amount	Price Estimate
Retracement percentage	3-box	1.00032
Retracement percentage	5-box	1.00041
Retracement percentage	9-box	1.00035
Linear regression	3-box	1.00062
Linear regression	5-box	1.00059
Linear regression	9-Box	0.99999
Multiple regression	3-box	1.00039
Multiple regression	5-box	1.00036
Multiple regression	9-box	1.00030
Composite average estimate	1.00037	

CAVEAT

The various mathematic and statistical approaches illustrated in this book are, to our knowledge, new and therefore experimental. The rationale behind averaging multiple discrete forecasts (nine in the example in this chapter) is very logical, though, and should theoretically enhance the validity of the desired output. Nonetheless, the authors would like to emphasize that a thorough testing period and ample paper trading are advisable before traders incorporate any one method into their existing trading systems.

PART IV

Other Reversal Charts

CHAPTER 32

Western
Reversal Charts

OVERVIEW

All reversal charts share a common functionality: to filter out insignificant price movements below a user-selected range. The most popular is the point and figure (P&F) chart. In this chapter and the following chapter, we explore the other variations within the reversal chart family so that traders may gain a modest acquaintance with alternative methods to P&F and diagonal swing charting.

GEOMETRIC CHART

The earliest reference to the geometric chart that we were able to locate is in the very informative book *Point and Figure Method of Anticipating Stock Market Price Movements* by Victor De Villiers and Owen Taylor (Traders Library, 1934).

This chart in theory displays the same information as a standard P&F chart except that the columns of Xs and Os have been converted to vertical lines with interconnecting horizontal lines at the reversal points. Some traders may say the advantage of the geometric chart is that it has a cleaner, simpler visual presentation of the data, while an advantage of the standard P&F chart is that its component elements (Xs and Os) are readily countable. We emphasize that traders should use the method with which they feel most comfortable. In Figures 32.1 through 32.3 are examples of the geometric charts using different box sizes and reversal amounts.

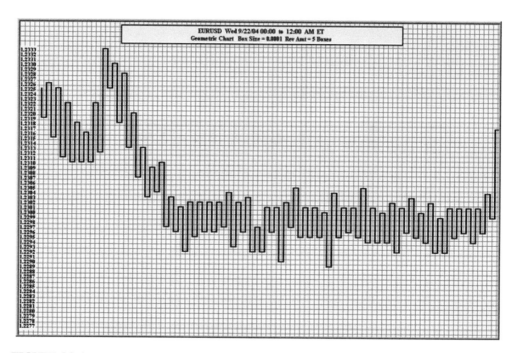

FIGURE 32.1 Geometric Chart with Box Size = 1 and Reversal Amount = 5

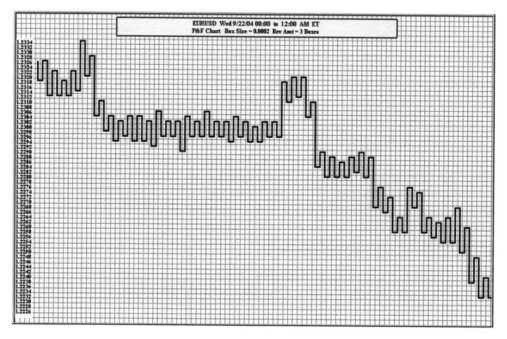

FIGURE 32.2 Geometric Chart with Box Size = 2 and Reversal Amount = 3

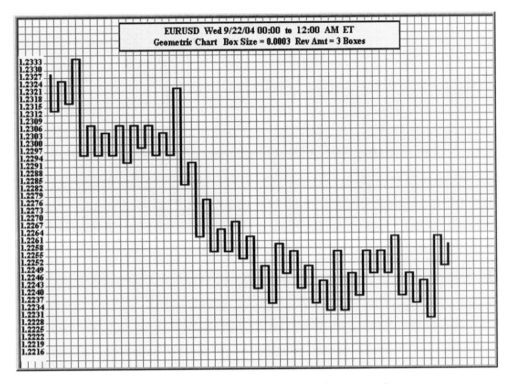

FIGURE 32.3 Geometric Chart with Box Size = 3 and Reversal Amount = 3

TREND OUTLINE CHART

The trend outline chart can also be attributed to De Villiers and Taylor in the same book cited earlier. One diagonal line in the trend outline chart represents two straight lines in the geometric chart (one vertical and an adjacent horizontal line). Examples of the trend outline chart are provided in Figures 32.4, 32.5, and 32.6.

Readers will note the similarities between the trend outline chart and the swing chart described in Part 3. The difference is that each subsequent vertex (either a peak or a valley) is equally spaced along the x-axis in the trend outline chart while peaks and valleys in a swing chart represent the actual time elapsed in the corresponding OHLC bar chart.

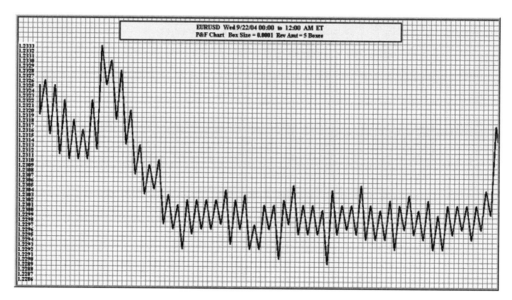

FIGURE 32.4   Trend Outline Chart with Box Size = 1 and Reversal Amount = 3

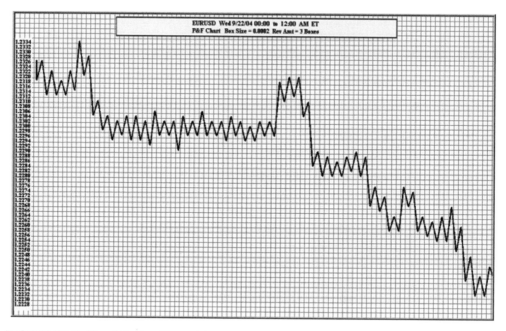

FIGURE 32.5   Trend Outline Chart with Box Size = 2 and Reversal Amount = 3

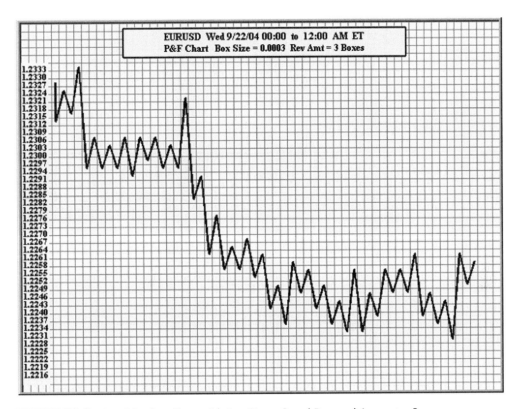

FIGURE 32.6   Trend Outline Chart with Box Size = 3 and Reversal Amount = 3

PIVOT CHART

The pivot chart (shown in Figure 32.7) is unique among reversal charts in that it requires no user-supplied parameters. This chart uses the interval high and low only, so that converting OHLC data to its equivalent closes-only time series is not necessary.

The underlying premise of the pivot chart is that once a trend is in motion then the pivot algorithm favors the continuation of that trend. A reversal in direction is possible only when a continuation increment does not occur. For example, assume an upward trend has been established. The following rules apply:

- If the current high is greater than the previous high regardless of magnitude, then the trend continues.
- If the current high is equal to the previous high, nothing is plotted.
- If the current high is less than the previous high, then the trend reverses and the current low is plotted.
- The converse is true when the original trend is downward.

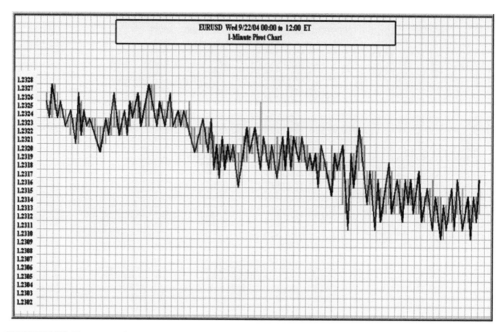

FIGURE 32.7 Pivot Chart

Technically there is a method by which the trader can increase or decrease the sensitivity of the pivot reversal mechanism: change the time interval of the underlying data. As the time interval increases (say from 1-minute-interval data to 10-minute-interval data), the sensitivity decreases in terms of minimum fluctuation units. This phenomenon occurs because the percentage of overlapping range between adjacent bars decreases as the time interval grows.

It may appear at first sight that a pivot chart is equivalent to a swing chart of the same OHLC data using a single minimum price fluctuation as the box size and a reversal amount of one unit. However, they do differ since the pivot chart shows a stronger bias toward showing continuation of an existing trend.

OBSERVATION

As long as creative technical analysts pursue the quest to display raw and processed data in innovative and revealing methods, no matter how bizarre or esoteric, charting theory will never become stagnant.

CHAPTER 33

Japanese Reversal Charts

OVERVIEW

The Japanese reversal charts described in this chapter are a relatively new addition to the realm of technical analysis. Their introduction to Western traders is primarily due to the efforts of trader and author Steven Nison.

RENKO CHART

The renko charting method is thought to have acquired its name from *renga*, the Japanese word for bricks. Renko charts are similar to three-line break charts except that in a renko chart, a line (or "brick" as they are called) is drawn in the direction of the prior move only if prices move by a minimum amount (i.e., the box size). The bricks are always equal in size. For example, in a 3-unit ("3-brick") renko chart, a 12-point rally is displayed as four 3-unit-tall renko bricks. (See Figures 33.1 through 33.4.)

Basic trend reversals are signaled with the emergence of a new white or black brick. A new white brick indicates the beginning of a new uptrend. A new black brick indicates the beginning of a new downtrend. Since the renko chart is a trend-following technique, there are times when renko charts produce whipsaws, giving signals near the end of short-lived trends. However, the expectation with a trend-following technique is that it allows you to ride the major portion of significant trends. Since a renko chart isolates the underlying price trend by filtering out the minor price changes, renko charts can also be very helpful when determining support and resistance levels.

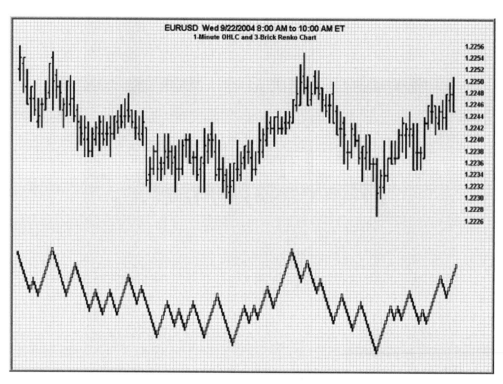

FIGURE 33.1   Renko Chart No. 1

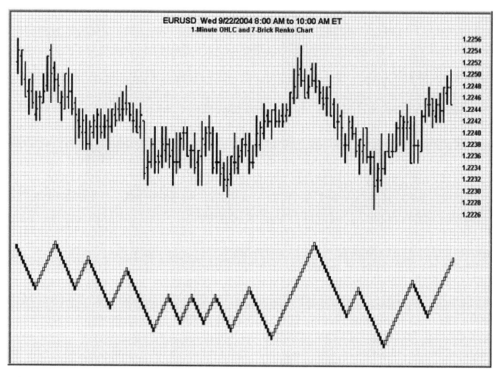

FIGURE 33.2   Renko Chart No. 2

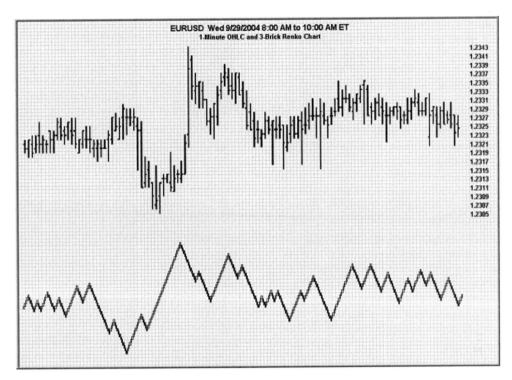

FIGURE 33.3 Renko Chart No. 3

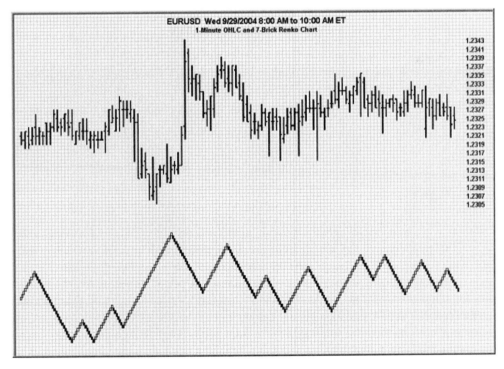

FIGURE 33.4 Renko Chart No. 4

219

Brick Size

Brick size is analogous to the point and figure box size and determines the minimum price change to display. Renko charts do not have an equivalent to point and figure reversal amount since the default is always one brick. To filter out noise, simply increase the brick size.

Algorithm

To draw renko bricks, today's close is compared with the high and low of the previous brick (white or black):

- If the closing price rises above the top of the previous brick by at least the box size, one or more white bricks are drawn in new columns. The height of the bricks is always equal to the box size.
- If the closing price falls below the bottom of the previous brick by at least the box size, one or more black bricks are drawn in new columns. Again, the height of the bricks is always equal to the box size.
- If prices move more than the box size, but not enough to create two bricks, only one brick is drawn. For example, in a two-unit ("2-brick") renko chart, if the prices move from 100 to 103, only one white brick is drawn from 100 to 102. The rest of the move, from 102 to 103, is not shown on the renko chart.

Programmatically, the same CalculateReversalColumns() function is called prior to plotting the chart (this function appears in Chapter 12 on point and figure charts).

Note that the x-axis does not represent time in a linear fashion, since there is one x-axis unit per brick.

KAGI CHART

Kagi charts are believed to have been created around the time that the Japanese stock market began trading in the 1870s. Kagi charts display a series of connecting vertical lines where the thickness (or color) and direction of the lines are dependent on the price action. The charts ignore the passage of time. If prices continue to move in the same direction, the vertical line is extended. However, if prices reverse by a minimum reversal amount, a new kagi line is then drawn in a new column. When prices penetrate a previous high or low, the thickness (or color) of the kagi line changes. Kagi charts were brought to the United States by Steven Nison in 1994 with the publication of his book *Beyond Candlesticks*.

Algorithm

The first closing price in a kagi chart is the starting price. To draw the first kagi line, the current close is compared to the starting price.

- If the current price is greater than or equal to the starting price, then a thick line is drawn from the starting price to the new closing price.
- If today's price is less than to the starting price, then a thin line is drawn from the starting price to the new closing price.

To draw subsequent lines, compare the closing price to the tip (i.e., bottom or top) of the previous kagi line:

- If the price continues in the same direction as the previous line, the line is extended in the same direction, no matter how small the move.
- If the price moves in the opposite direction by at least the reversal amount (this may take several days), then a short horizontal line is drawn to the next column and a new vertical line is drawn to the closing price.
- If the price moves in the opposite direction of the current column by less than the reversal amount no lines are drawn.
- If a thin kagi line exceeds the prior high point on the chart, the line becomes thick. Likewise, if a thick kagi line falls below the prior low point, the line becomes thin.

Kagi charts are designed to plot a single line until the price reverses by a predetermined amount, where another line is then begun. It is an attempt to smooth out the noise of daily trading activity so that the trend can be more clearly represented. The thickness of kagi lines is significant when prior highs and prior lows are exceeded.

Kagi charts use a modified form of the orthogonal line chart as a basis. When new highs above the previous column occur, the line color becomes green. When new lows below the previous column occur, the line color becomes red. Originally, the technique was to draw thick lines for new highs and thin lines for new lows, but the color alternation scheme accomplished the same end and has more visual appeal. (See Figures 33.5 through 33.8.)

Interpretation

Kagi charts illustrate the forces of supply and demand on a security:

- A series of thick (or green) lines shows that demand is exceeding supply (a rally).
- A series of thin (or red) lines shows that supply is exceeding demand (a decline).
- Alternating thick (or green) and thin (or red) lines show that the market is in a state of equilibrium (i.e., supply equals demand).

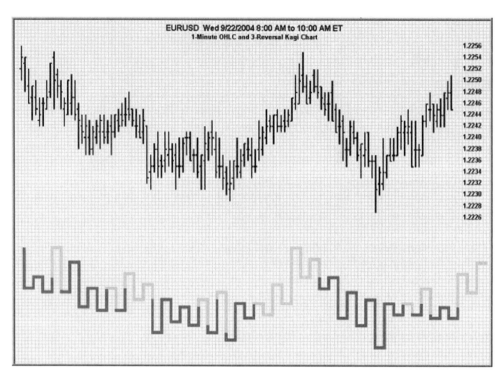

FIGURE 33.5 Kagi Chart No. 1

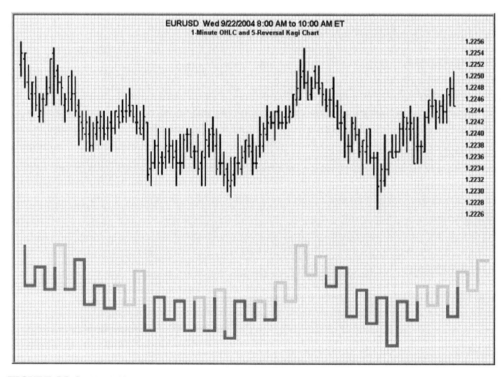

FIGURE 33.6 Kagi Chart No. 2

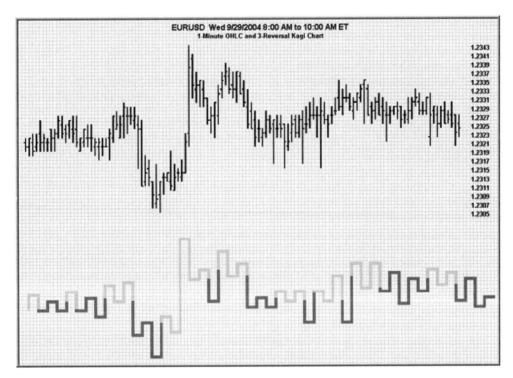

FIGURE 33.7 Kagi Chart No. 3

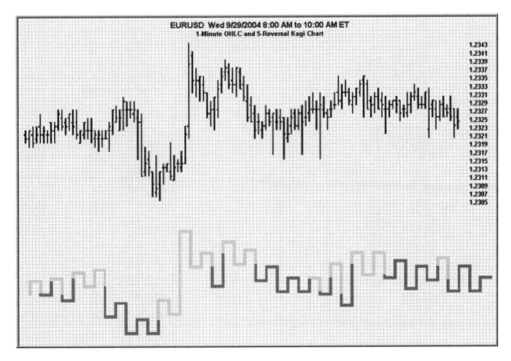

FIGURE 33.8 Kagi Chart No. 4

The most basic trading technique for kagi charts is to buy when the kagi line changes from thin to thick (or red to green) and to sell when the kagi line changes from thick to thin (or green to red). A sequence of higher highs and higher lows on a kagi chart shows that the underlying forces are bullish, whereas, lower highs and lower lows indicate underlying weakness.

THREE-LINE BREAK CHART

Three-line break charts display a series of vertical boxes (lines) that are based on changes in prices. As with kagi, point and figure, and renko charts, three-line break charts ignore the passage of time. The three-line break charting method is so named because of the number of lines typically used. Three-line break charts were first brought to the United States by Steven Nison in 1994 with the publication of his book *Beyond Candlesticks*. (See Figures 33.9 and 33.10.)

An advantage of three-line break charts is that there is no arbitrary fixed reversal amount. It is the price action that gives the indication of a reversal. The disadvantage of three-line break charts is that the signals are generated after the new trend is well under way. However, many traders are willing to accept the late signals in exchange for calling major trends.

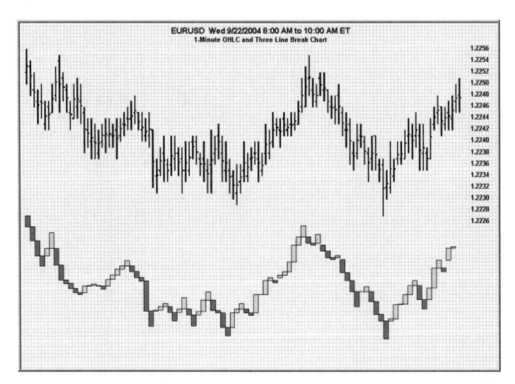

FIGURE 33.9 Three Line Break Chart No. 1

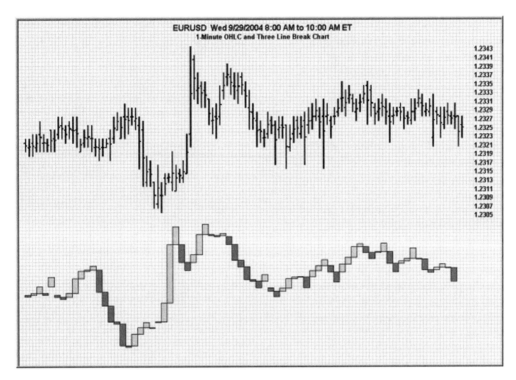

FIGURE 33.10 Three-Line Break Chart No. 2

Number of Lines

You can adjust the sensitivity of the reversal criteria by changing the number of lines in the break. For example, short-term traders might use two-line breaks to get more reversals, whereas a longer-term investor might use four-line or even 10-line breaks to reduce the number of reversals. Of these choices, the three-line break is the most popular in Japan. Steven Nison recommends using three-line break charts in conjunction with candlestick charts. He suggests using the three-line break chart to determine the prevailing trend and then using candlestick patterns to time your individual trades.

Algorithm

Line break charts are always based on closing prices. The general rules for calculating a line break chart are:

- If the price exceeds the previous line's high price, a new white line is drawn.
- If the price falls below the previous line's low price, a new black line is drawn.
- If the price neither rises above nor falls below the previous line, nothing is drawn.

In a three-line break chart, if rallies are strong enough to display three consecutive lines of the same color, then prices must reverse by the extreme price of the last three lines in order to create a new line:

- If a rally is powerful enough to form three consecutive white lines, then prices must fall below the lowest point of the last three white lines before a new black line is drawn.
- If a sell-off is powerful enough to form three consecutive black lines, then prices must rise above the highest point of the last three black lines before a new white line is drawn.

Interpretation

The following are some very basic trading rules for a three-line break chart:

- Buy when a white line emerges after three adjacent black lines (a white turnaround line).
- Sell when a black line appears after three adjacent white lines (a black turnaround line).
- Avoid trading in trendless markets where the lines alternate between black and white.

PART V

Goodman Swing Count System

CHAPTER 34

History

CHARLES B. GOODMAN

The principles of the Goodman Swing Count System (GSCS) were informally set forth in a series of annotated commodity charts from the late 1940s to the early 1970s. These trading studies, simply titled "My System," were the work of Charles B. Goodman and were never published.

I (Michael Archer) met Charles Goodman at the Denver, Colorado, offices of Peavey and Company (later, Gelderman) in the fall of 1971. It was the occasion of my maiden voyage in the great sea of commodity trading (later, futures). In 1971 silver prices were finally forging ahead to the $2.00/ounce level. A 10-cent limit move in soybeans elicited a full afternoon of postmortem analysis by traders and brokers alike.

The Peavey office, managed by the late and great Pete Rednor, employed eight brokers (later, account representatives). The broker for both Mr. Goodman and me was the colorful—and patient—Ken Malo. Brokers, resident professional traders—including Mr. Goodman and the Feldman brothers, Stu and Reef—and a regular contingent of retail customers drew inspiration from a Trans-Lux ticker that wormed its way across a long, narrow library table in the back of the office. Most impressive was a large clacker board quote system covering almost the entire front office wall. This electromechanical quotation behemoth made loud clacking sounds (thus its name) each time an individual price flipped over to reveal an updated quote. Green and red lights flashed, denoting daily new highs and lows. Pete, apart from being an excellent office manager, was also a fine showman who used the various stimuli to encourage trading activity.

THE RIGHT BRACKETS

Almost everyone made frequent reference to Charlie's *huge* bar charts posted on 2½-by-4-foot sheets of graph paper, mounted on heavy particle board and displayed on large easels. No one ever really knew what the numerous right brackets (])of varying lengths scattered throughout each chart meant. But there was always a great deal of speculation! The present work finally reveals the meaning of those mysterious trading hieroglyphics.

The quiet chatter of the tickertape, the loud clacking of the quote board, the constant ringing of the telephones. The news ticker that buzzed *once* for standing reports, *twice* for opinions, and *three* times for hot news. The squawk boxes and Pete Rednor's authoritative voice booming, "Merc! Merc!" What a spectacular scene it was! No wonder that this author, then a 21-year-old trading newbie, would soon make commodity futures and currency trading his life's work.

But nothing made a greater impression on me than the work of Charles B. Goodman. He instilled first some very simple ideas: "Avoid volatile markets when at all possible." "Trade only high-percentage short-term 'ducks.'" "Sit on your hands, Dad, sit on your hands." It didn't take long for me to adopt the ultraconservative "Belgian dentist" style of trading, that is, "Avoiding losing trades is more important than finding winning trades."

The Belgian dentist approach carried with me when I developed my artificial intelligence (AI) trading system in the 1980s—Jonathan's Wave. Even though it generated 48 percent annual returns with a zero expectation of a 50 percent drawdown (according to Managed Account Reports), it drove the brokers berserk because it could easily go a full month without making a single trade!

I am certain that Charlie's trading advice allowed me to survive the financial baptism by fire that destroys most commodity and currency trading newbies in a matter of months, if not weeks.

Mr. Goodman was to be my one and only trading mentor. Over the decade that followed he entrusted to me many, if not most, of his trading secrets. *To the best of my knowledge he shared this information on his work with no one else in such detail.*

LATER DEVELOPMENTS

Charlie and I spent hundreds of hours together analyzing the trade studies from My System. We also analyzed hundreds of other commodity, currency, and securities charts. Charlie was happy with My System being organized in his mind. But as a new-generation technical analyst, I was anxious to see it formalized on paper and eventually in source code on a computer. To be honest, this created a small amount of friction between the two of us—Charlie was dead set against formalized systems and believed strongly in the psychological and money management elements of trading.

Notwithstanding, by 1979 I was finally ready and able to formally state the principles of My System. Because of its equal concern for price measurements (parameters) and price levels interacting together (matrices), I originally renamed Charlie's My System "ParaMatrix." My first investment management company in the mid-1970s was Para-Matrix Investment Management, and I acted as both an investment advisor registered with the Securities and Exchange Commission (SEC) and a Commodity Trading Advisor registered with the Commodity Futures Trading Commission (CFTC).

Contrary to ongoing speculation, only two copies of my original 1979 *Principles of ParaMatrix* ever existed. I possess both of them. Charlie's original My System trade studies were mistakenly destroyed shortly after his death in 1984. What remains of them are fewer than 200 or so examples I had copied into *Principles of ParaMatrix*.

The present work (Part 5), "Goodman Swing Count System," is a reorganized reissue of *Principles of ParaMatrix* with updated charts and a simplified nomenclature that I am sure Charlie would have appreciated; "Keep it simple, Dad!" he would always advise. In a later work I hope to expand on Charlie's ideas by filling in some less formed ideas such as his market notation, or calculus as he referred to it, and a method for charting that I have dubbed Goodman charting. He also worked out a time-based, cyclical count system.

My own direction in futures and currencies turned in the 1980s to artificial intelligence (Jonathan's Wave) and in the 1990s and today to artificial life and cellular automata (the Trend Machine). In spite of, or perhaps because of, these complicated cutting-edge computer efforts, I continue to view the Goodman Swing Count System (GSCS) in a very positive light. To this day, the first thing I do when I see any chart is a quick Goodman analysis!

The GSCS is a natural system for pursuing the conservative Belgian dentist approach to trading, even without the aid of a computer. Part 5, in fact, could be used to make Goodman analysis without a computer at all!

Goodman Swing Count System trade opportunities are as frequent today as (perhaps more frequent than) they were 40 or 50 years ago. I believe that the system's foundations have stood the test of time well. Patterns today are no different than they were decades ago, nor are the twin human emotions—fear and greed—that create them. GSCS is an excellent method for finding support and resistance areas that no other method spots, and for locating *potential* turning points in any market. One of its best suits is that it can easily integrate into other trading techniques and methodologies.

I would never recommend using or advise anyone to use a 100 percent mechanical trading system, GSCS or any other!

Is it really a system? Depending upon your perspective, GSCS is between 70 percent and 90 percent mechanical. The program available from CommTools, Inc. (www.commtools.com) represents the kernel idea of mechanizing perhaps 80 percent of the system. I now believe attempting to completely code Charlie's work would be inadvisable.

Mr. Goodman passed away in 1984. It was always his desire to share with others, although as is usually the case with true genius—few wanted to listen. These days we are ever more bombarded with ever more cryptic and computer-dependent software programs and black boxes. Perhaps now is the time for the simple yet theoretically well-grounded ideas of GSCS to become popular.

The publication of this brief overview, I hope and pray, would meet with Charlie's wishes. His work in extracting an objective and almost geometrically precise (à la Benedict de Spinoza) trading system out of a simple trading rule (the 50 percent rule) is most remarkable. It has certainly earned him the right to be included in the elite group of early scientific traders along with George D. Taylor, Ralph N. Elliott, William D. Gann, and Burton Pugh.

Conforming to the spirit of the original My System, I have attempted to keep theoretical discussions and formulations to a necessary minimum. Trade studies at the end of Part 5 of this book must still be considered the crux of GSCS, even though I am pleased with the formalization of most relevant principles described in the following sections. The trader weary of theoretical discussions and intrigue will find all the concepts and principles delineated in the trade study examples. Nevertheless, those who invest time in the theory of GSCS will undoubtedly discover an area for further exploration where many new and fresh ideas are waiting to be mined.

In Mr. Goodman's worldly absence, the responsibility for this work and its contents is solely mine, for better or for worse.

CHAPTER 35

Ordinal Principles

ORDINAL VERSUS CARDINAL

Within the context of this book, ordinal refers to measurement without specific values; cardinal refers to measurement with specific values.

THE MEASURED MOVE

The cornerstone of the Goodman Swing Count System (GSCS) is the old "50 Percent Retracement and Measured Move" rule ("The Rule"). (See Figure 35.1.) This rule, familiar to most traders, is almost as old as the organized markets themselves. It has been traced to the times when insiders manipulated railroad stocks in the nineteenth century.

The first systematic description of The Rule was given in Burton Pugh's *The Great Wheat Secret*, originally published in 1933. In 1976, Charles L. Lindsay's *Trident* was published. This book did much—some say too much!—to quantify and mathematically describe The Rule. Nevertheless, it is must reading for anyone interested in this area of market methodology. Edward L. Dobson wrote *The Trading Rule That Can Make You Rich* in 1978. This is a good work with some nice examples. But none of these, in my humble opinion, even scratches the surface relative to Goodman's work.

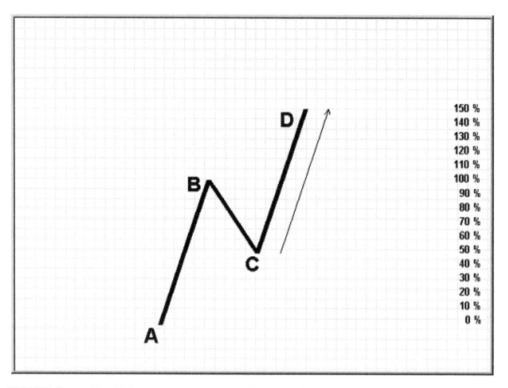

FIGURE 35.1 The 50 Percent Retracement and Measured Move Rule

CONGESTION PHASE

In 1975 a well-known Chicago grain floor trader, Eugene Nofri, published *Success in Commodities: The Congestion Phase System*. This small but power-packed volume detailed a short-term trading method using simple but effective congestion phases. (See Figure 35.2.) While not precisely a work on The Rule, it touched on some of Charlie's ideas from a different angle.

I mention Nofri's work also because Charlie was especially taken by its simplicity and because it can work well in conjunction with the GCSC. The idea of melding the GCSC with a congestion phase approach ought to produce a method of finding those high-percentage ducks that the Belgian dentist loves so much. Charlie also felt that Earl Hadady's work on contrary opinion was a natural fit, especially since the GCSC support and resistance points seldom lie where anyone else thinks they should.

Still, in the end, it was left for Charles B. Goodman, the great grain trader from Eads, Colorado, to extract all the logical consequences from The Rule and transform it into a robust, almost geometrically precise system.

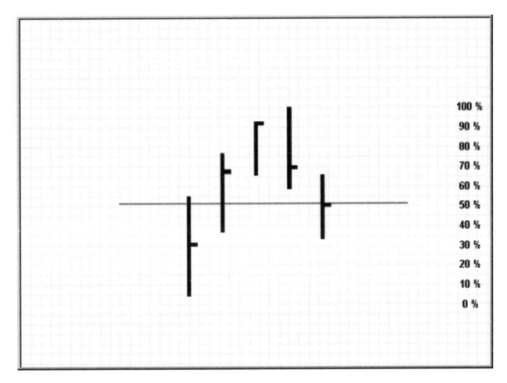

FIGURE 35.2 Simple Congestion Phase

EQUILIBRIUM OF BUYERS AND SELLERS

The logic of The Rule is quite simple. At a 50 percent retracement, both buyers and sellers of the previous trend (up or down) are ceteris paribus in balance. Half of each holds profits and half of each holds losses. (See Figure 35.3.)

The equilibrium is a tenuous one, indeed. The distribution of buyers and sellers over the initial price trend or swing is obviously not perfectly even: Some buyers hold more contracts than other buyers. They also have different propensities for taking profits or losses. Nor does it account for the buyers and sellers who have entered the market before the initial swing or during the reaction swing. Not all of the buyers and sellers from the original swing may be in the market any longer.

Remarkably, GCSC eventually takes all of this into account—especially the buyers and sellers at other price swing levels, called *matrices.*

Nevertheless, the 50 percent retracement point *is* often a powerful and very real point of equilibrium and certainly a known and defined hot spot of which one should be aware. Remember that both the futures markets and the currency markets are very close to a zero-sum game. It is only commissions, pips, and slippage that keep them from being zero-sum. At the 50 percent point it doesn't take much to shift the balance of power for that particular swing matrix.

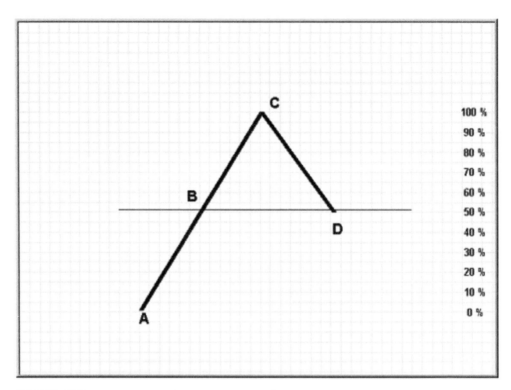

FIGURE 35.3 A Market Tug-of-War: Equilibrium of Buyers and Sellers

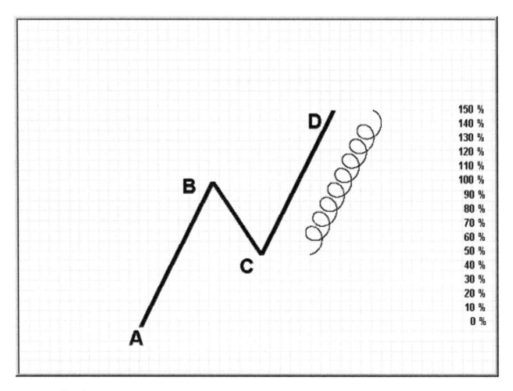

FIGURE 35.4 The Measured Move and Unwinding

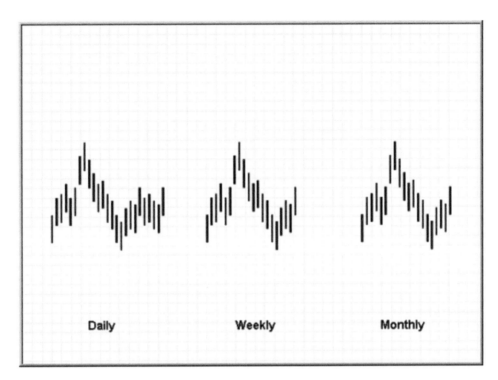

FIGURE 35.5 The Markets Are Recursive

The Rule also states that the final (third) swing of the move—again in the direction of the initial swing—will equal the value of the initial swing. The logic of this idea, called the measured move, is seen in Figure 35.4.

Examples of The Rule occur at *all* price levels or matrices, and many are being worked simultaneously in any given ongoing market. This is a critical point. In modern terminology it would be said that price movements are recursive. Simply stated, this means that without labeling you could not really tell the difference between a 10-minute chart and a daily or weekly chart—they all exhibit the same behavior and operate under the same principles of parameter and matrix. The bar graphs in Figure 35.5 were taken from actual market data. It is functionally impossible to tell the time units apart with respect to the chart action.

CHAPTER 36

Cardinal Principles

OVERVIEW

Now we can begin to informally define six of the seven concepts in The Rule that Mr. Goodman used to construct the Goodman Swing Count System (GCSC). What had been neglected by previous theorists, users, writers, and purveyors of the rule was this:

The 50 percent point is indeed an equilibrium point. As such, the equilibrium must give way, but either side (buyers or sellers) in either a downtrend or an uptrend may prevail at any given matrix or price level.

PRICE SURGE

Goodman realized both the possibilities for a reversal (as in the case of the completed measured move) and a price surge. A price surge would be equivalent to the sellers (in an uptrend) and the buyers (in a downtrend) winning the tug-of-war within a matrix. In price action this means prices would fall or rise to at least the beginning point of the initial swing.

In other words, the measured move is not a done deal—the 50 percent retracement in Figure 36.1 could also become a V or an inverted V. The 50 percent retracement is not necessarily a reversal point but should be considered as a point of interest where prices may be *more likely than randomly* to decide whether to continue or reverse.

It may not sound like much, but it is a major discovery.

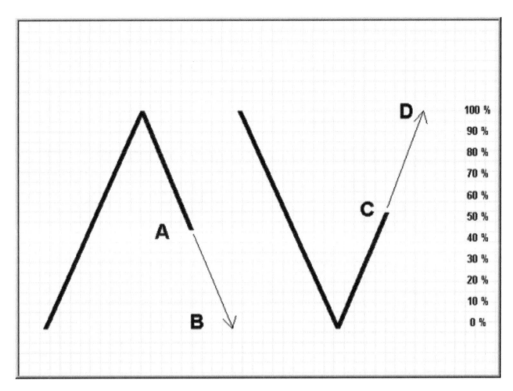

FIGURE 36.1   Price Surge—the First Concept

Clearly price surges are implicit in The Rule. But they are not visible on a chart unless you are looking for them and unless you are considering the 50 percent retracement as a point of interest and not necessarily a reversal. In fact, most practitioners perceive a price surge as a failure of The Rule!

MULTILEVEL MATRICES

What was even more important, Goodman discovered the implications of The Rule occurring simultaneously at all price levels. I remember exactly the day and place when Charlie showed me this one—it hit me as truly a grand revelation on the markets!

Here you are: The initial (primary) trend and secondary (reaction trend) as well as reversals (measured moves) and surges are relative to price matrix context. What is one thing in one price matrix may well be its opposite in a higher (or lower) matrix. (See Figure 36.2.)

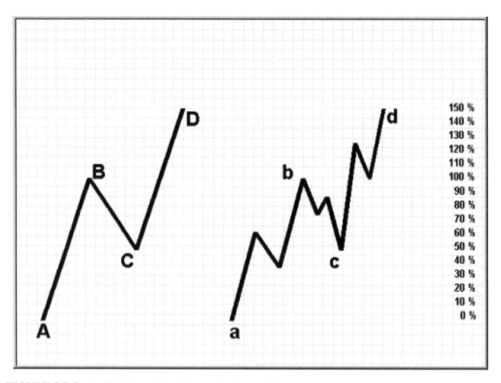

FIGURE 36.2 Multiple-Level Matrices—the Second Concept

It is true that Elliott wave theory contains the same concept. But with GCSC you can tell *before* (in many instances) which it is. In Elliott you can tell only *after*. GCSC is a predictive system, whereas Elliott wave theory, grand and elegant as it is, is primarily a descriptive system.

All price matrices are in theory part of a larger price matrix.

All price matrices are composed of smaller price matrices.

Of course there is the practical limitation of the smallest possible fluctuation.

Besides reversals and surges, GCSC matrix concepts include domination and generation.

Clearly, prices do not always seem to find any kind of equilibrium at the 50 percent retracement price area. Or so it may seem. This leads to the third grand discovery:

To the extent a price swing overshoots or undershoots its ideal 50 percent retracement, that price value will be made up on the next price swing within the matrix.

Now *this* is the trading rule that can make you rich!

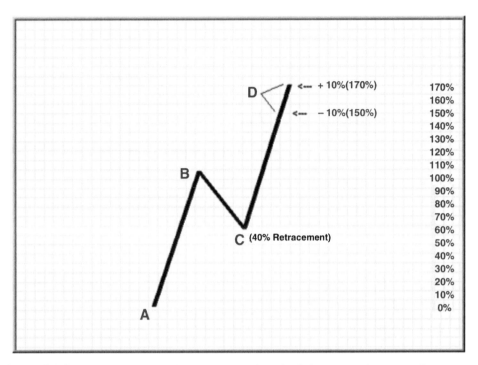

FIGURE 36.3 Compensation within a Matrix—the Third Concept: 40 Percent Retracement with Compensation

COMPENSATION

For example, if prices fall only 40 percent of the initial trend and reverse, the measured move will actually be either 90 percent or 110 percent of the measured move point and value of the primary (initial) swing in the matrix. The 10 percent difference—GCSC holds—must be made up eventually. This is the concept of compensation. See Figure 36.3.

CARRYOVER

Furthermore, if the difference is not fully made up in the final price swing of a matrix, the cumulative "miss" value will carry over through each subsequent price matrix until it does. This is the concept of carryover. (See Figure 36.4.) A carryover table is used to add and subtract cumulative carryover values until they cancel.

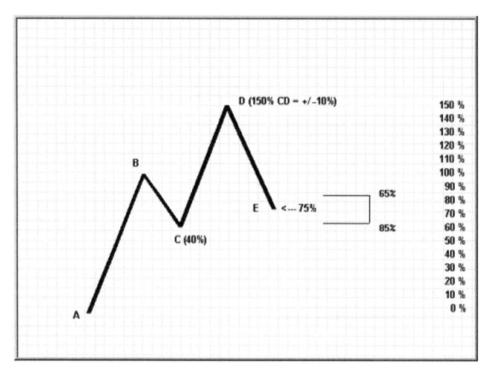

FIGURE 36.4 Carryover—the Fourth Concept

CANCELLATION

When no carryover remains, the price matrix is said to have cleared or cancelled. This is the GCSC concept of cancellation. Cancellation is critical to finding GCSC support and resistance points. These price areas or points indicate a higher degree of forecasting probability than would occur with a single matrix measurement. (See Figure 36.5.)

The exact method for these important concepts is more fully described in the following chapter. We can now get an early glimpse of what the strange brackets in Charlie's charts were all about. (See Figure 36.6 for an example.) The brackets indicate the measured area on a chart where prices have a higher degree of moving conclusively. The more bracketed areas surrounding a price, the higher the probability of forecasting.

The five points are: the beginning of the swing, the 50 percent measurement of the swing, the end of the swing, the measured move if the swing is a primary wave, and the end of the measured move if the swing is a secondary wave.

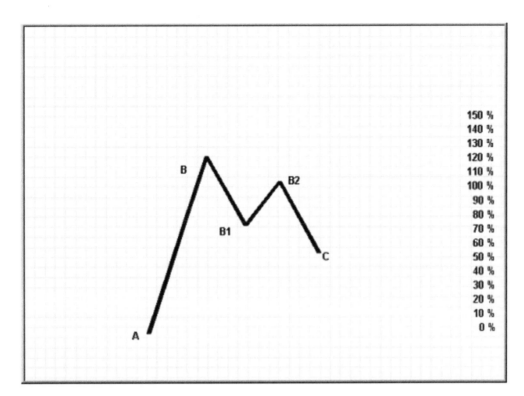

FIGURE 36.5 Cancellation—the Fifth Concept

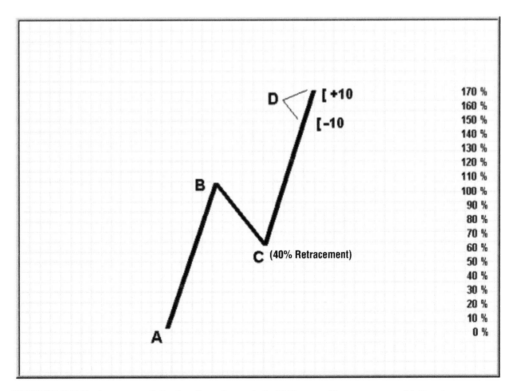

FIGURE 36.6 Meaning of the Brackets Revealed: 40 Percent Retracement with Brackets

INTERSECTIONS

Charlie had even more ideas:

The importance of a hot spot in relation to its likelihood of being an important point of support or resistance, reversal, or continuation, increases when two or more price matrices cancel at the same price or same price area. This is the key concept of intersection. There is no analogous concept in Elliott, the most common competitor to GSCS. Intersection makes GSCS much more objective and testable than other swing systems. (See Figure 36.7.)

This chapter has covered micro formations. Charlie also had compiled a dozen or so extremely valuable macro formations—combinations of micros. I encourage the reader to examine some charts and find simple areas of the intersection of two (or three) matrices. You will see at once that these points are golden to the trader. If I had after 30 years of studying the markets only one idea to impart, it would be to show you an example of a GSCS intersection in two or three matrices.

Remember, carryover is to the same or next larger price matrix. The above are examples of independent intersections. That is, each price level carryover calculation is kept separate from the others and tallied at the end of each matrix. Charlie had also de-

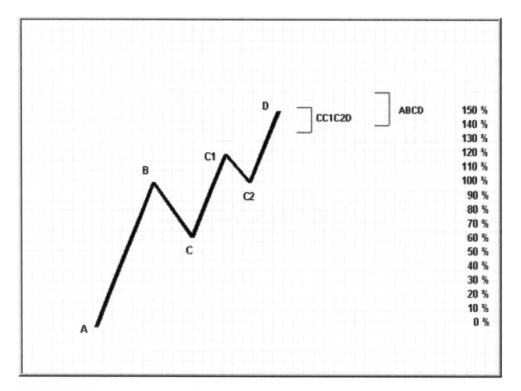

FIGURE 36.7 Intersections—the Sixth Concept

veloped (much less precisely) a concept of dependent intersections, but it is quite complex, beyond the scope of this chapter and worthy of further codification into software at a future date.

If you would like more information on ordinal and cardinal principles, comprising a complete tutorial on GSCS, or if you have questions, I would be happy to hear from you.

FIVE POINTS OF A GOODMAN WAVE

Here is another perspective to help you analyze a chart and understand GSCS. Given any component or matrix, there are five points worth watching. Remember, these points are constantly changing as the market develops.

The five points are: the 50 percent return, the top/bottom, the bottom/top, the measured move assuming the matrix or component is in the primary direction, and the measured move assuming the matrix or component is in the secondary direction. (See Figure 36.8.)

Sometimes it is easier to watch the points instead of totally focusing on the chart as it develops.

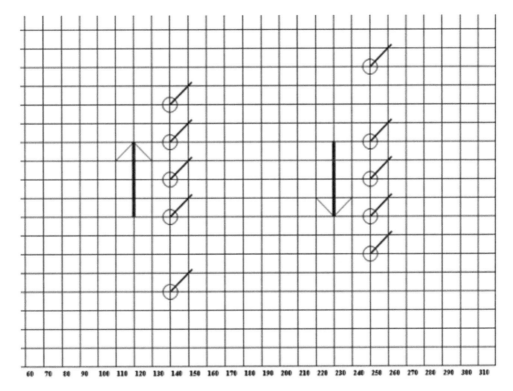

FIGURE 36.8 The Five Points of a Goodman Wave

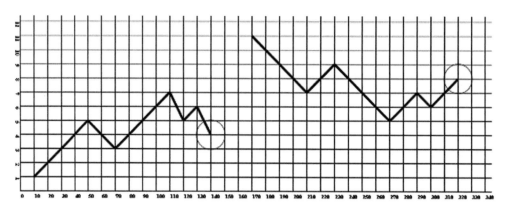

FIGURE 36.9   Double Intersection (at Circled Points)

DOUBLE AND TRIPLE INTERSECTIONS

The two key cardinal formations in GSCS are the double intersection and the triple intersection. These represent (respectively) the intersection of two and three matrix measurements.

The strong support and resistance at these areas may be used to enter the market in the direction of the dominant wave. (See Figure 36.9.)

CHAPTER 37

Goodman versus Elliott

OVERVIEW

When I tutor traders on Goodman, I break up the study into ordinal and cardinal.

We study Goodman wave theory (GWT) without respect to measurements first, and only then overlay a study of the Goodman measurement theory (GMT). These both involve Goodman ordinal rules and Goodman cardinal rules.

Here is a nice formation to look for in GWT. It has some high probabilities, especially with the use of filters and GMT (the latter beyond the scope of this short primer). Charlie called it the "Return."

Elliott identified the basic market wave as having five components (See Figure 37.1.)

This is incorrect. The basic market wave has three components. (See Figure 37.2.)

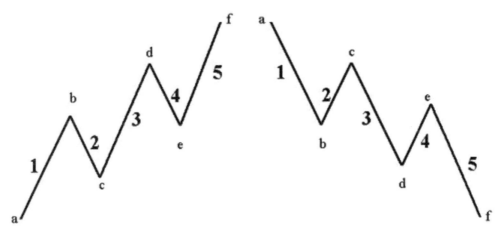

FIGURE 37.1 Elliott Market Components

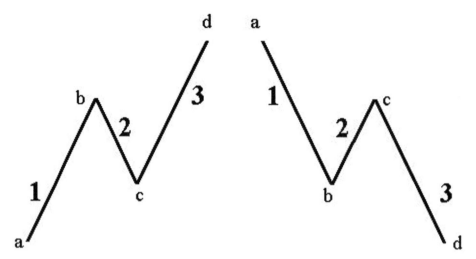

FIGURE 37.2   Goodman Market Components

PROPAGATION

According to Goodman, a wave propagates or builds in such a way that it *appears* to be five components, but the ordinal rule is actually this: If the first (primary) component of a wave is a simple, single component, the second (primary) component will be complex, consisting itself of three components, and vice versa. (See Figure 37.3.)

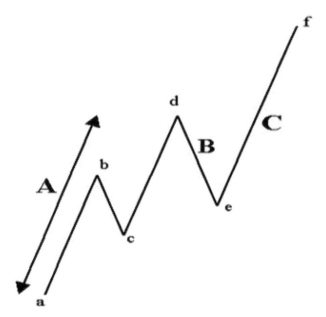

FIGURE 37.3   Propagation Rule

This propagation rule can be extremely useful in and of itself in anticipating the ordinal template of the market as it unfolds, but further details are beyond the scope of this short overview. There are 16 basic propagation schemes or templates.

THE RETURN

Charlie identified what he called a "return"—defined here as the price location (+/–) in a wave propagation where the secondary wave of the primary wave approaches the secondary wave of the complex component. (See Figure 37.4.)

This feature has some interesting ramifications for anticipating the basic market template. But for the purposes of this overview, I want to draw your attention to a single idea as a possible short-term trading tactic.

> The market will very often reverse from the "return" point for some price value. How much is variable, depending on other factors such as the market template and GMT, but as a short-term trade or spot play it can be quite useful.

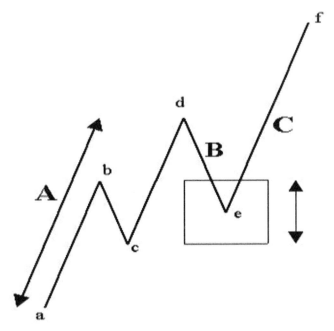

FIGURE 37.4 The Return

To use this in isolation as a short-term trading tool you will need a timing method—
I recommend a three-box reversal point and figure chart. Also helpful would be moni-
toring the Goodman templates at one higher and one lower matrix. The return can also
be useful in identifying the market template itself.

Typically (but not always) if the return falls short of the point of the BC wave, the
market will build a bit before reversing. If the return is past the point of the BC wave,
the market will often spike through the return point and then reverse.

When this is overlaid with the Goodman cardinal rules, it becomes a very powerful
tool in the broader scope of Goodman studies.

CHAPTER 38

Charting Study

OVERVIEW

The textbook Goodman wave from recent EUR/USD trading shown in Figure 38.1 gives us an opportunity to introduce a number of Goodman topics and ideas via a brief tour of the entire system.

NOTATION

The end points of a matrix ("M") are denoted by 1-2-3-4; going in to smaller matrices, i-ii-iii-iv; going out to a larger matrix, A-B-C-D. All matrix notation uses parentheses: M(1-2-3-4).

A wave is denoted by 1-2-3-4-5-6 (points of the wave); going in to smaller waves, i-ii-iii-iv-v-vi; going out to larger matrices, A-B-C-D-E-F-G. All waves are denoted as "G." The notation uses brackets G[1-2-3-4-5-6].

A matrix always has three components; of course, a component may also itself be a matrix. A Goodman wave has five components *at least for the purposes of notation.*

A matrix or wave segment or component is thus M(1-2) or G[3-4-5-6].

MATRIX

A matrix is a simple 1-2-3 swing (three components or segments). It may or may not have smaller matrices as some of its components. A matrix is either simple (no components) or complex (if it has components): M(1-2-3-4). (See Figure 38.2.)

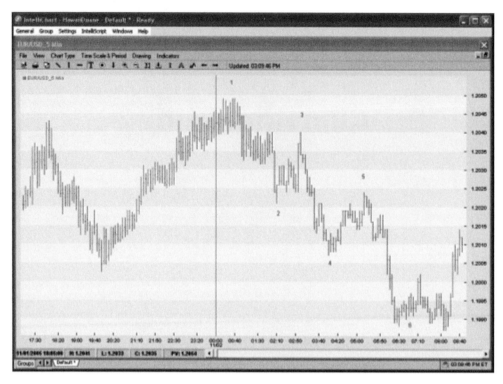

FIGURE 38.1 Chart Study
Source: Chart courtesy of www.FxTrek.com.

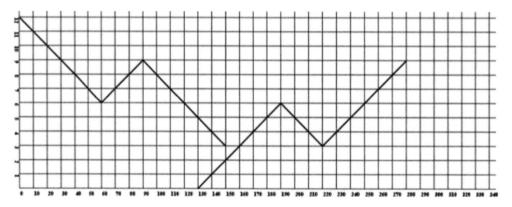

FIGURE 38.2 Example of a Matrix

A Goodman wave is the propagation or generation of a complex matrix in a specific manner and of a specific form: G[1-2-3-4-5-6].

Charlie's concept of how matrices propagate is different from Elliott's. Once you start looking for them, finding them, and analyzing them you will quickly realize how much more they conform to the real structure of the markets and—more importantly—how much more easily they may be traded. The propagation concept more accurately reflects the dynamic of markets than does a static wave concept.

Goodman waves are relatively easy to spot after they are built, or as part of a larger wave. But what we are most interested in—from the point of view of trading—is the propagation of a Goodman wave.

PROPAGATION

Any Goodman wave obviously begins with a segment S(1-2). The question becomes—and this is why the concept of propagation is important: Does the wave develop as a flat segment followed by a complex matrix—or vice versa?

According to GSCS theory, this segment or matrix now becomes the first component of a Goodman wave and is thereafter treated as a single segment or component for purposes of analysis.

We now look for a 50 percent secondary component retracement of the entire complex matrix or segment. On this chart study this is segment S(4-5). This component could easily be mistaken for a simple wave in a five-wave Elliott wave pattern, but it is not. In Goodman it is the key return or propagation segment.

Finally, we look for a component or matrix in the primary direction with a magnitude equal to the first component.

In Figure 38.3, note the return or propagation wave (the lighter wave).

These four wave formations (**templates**) are all you really need to know about the markets and all you really need to look for in your trading!

The four primary Goodman waves occur every day, over and over again, in all markets—forex, futures, and securities—and at all price levels. The wave is the foundation and basis of trading GSCS. The opportunities to trade it are only limited by your time to seek them out in the markets that most interest you.

Forget trading stations with five monitors; forget specialist short sales; forget complex volume and open interest calculations; forget Gann charts with 50 lines on them all leading to nowhere and Fibonacci charts with numbers carried out to 14 significant places. Look

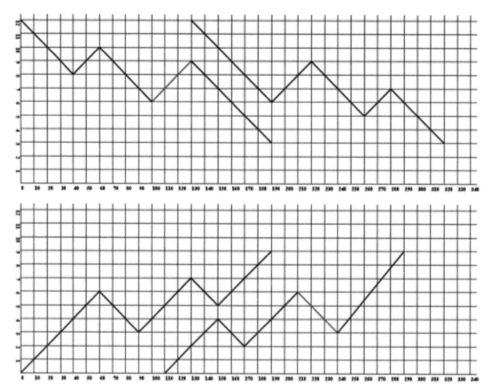

FIGURE 38.3 Examples of a Goodman Wave

for these four Goodman wave types. Learn everything you can about them; find them, study them, catalog them. *Learn how to template and anticipate them.*

Elliott mistakenly identified this as a five-component wave. This is not accurate or precise. What is occurring is that a three-component matrix is propagating in accordance with the 50 percent rule. It is *not* strictly a five-component wave but rather a matrix in generation or propagation. This propagation is critical and fundamental to GSCS.

SIMPLE/COMPLEX

Note: From a matrix point of view, two of the four Goodman waves appear to be a simple/complex matrix followed by a complex/simple matrix. It is important to think only in terms of the four Goodman wave types shown in Figure 38.3. By thinking in terms of propagation you will better anticipate the unfolding of the market through time.

For now just drill into memory the four Goodman wave types.

Keep in mind that—at least theoretically—Goodman waves propagate inward and outward, meaning that every wave is composed of smaller waves and every wave is a component of a larger wave. The same is true of matrices.

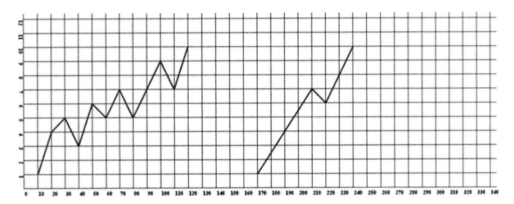

FIGURE 38.4 Fat/Thin

FAT/THIN

Note in the complex matrix of Figure 38.4 the first matrix is *fat* and the second is *thin*; this is another important alternating structure that assists in templating and trading.

By *fat* I mean there is a lot of back-and-fro motion (volatility) as prices move up or down (directional movement). By *thin* I mean there is little such motion.

The rhythm of the market is much determined by the fatness and thinness of price action. Rhythm can also give us important clues to templating. In GSCS templating is the nexus of theory and practice. Templating is the process of laying out the possible propagations of a wave and narrowing them down as events and prices unfold.

Fatness may simply represent price noise that may be filtered out of analysis. But it may occasionally represent significant internal matrices and demand deeper analysis.

GOODMAN AND COMPUTERS

The question arises: Is GSCS programmable? The answer is: probably. Software has been written to capture the basic elements of Goodman. A complete program would be a substantial undertaking and at least for me would go very much against the grain of what Charlie had in mind.

A small program to spot intersections, perhaps in TradeStation or StrategyBuilder format, would not be too difficult.

For further information about GSCS, contact Michael Duane Archer at Duane@ FxPraxis.com.

Appendixes

World Currencies

This is a list of global currencies and the three-character currency codes that we have found are generally used to represent them. Often, but not always, this code is the same as the ISO 4217 standard. (The ISO, or International Organization for Standardization, is a worldwide federation of national standards.)

In most cases, the currency code is composed of the country's two-character Internet country code plus an extra character to denote the currency unit. For example, the code for Canadian dollars is simply Canada's two-character Internet country code (CA) plus a one-character currency designator (D).

We have endeavored to list the codes that, in our experience, are actually in general industry use to represent the currencies. Currency names are given in the plural form. This list does not contain obsolete euro-zone currencies.

WORLD CURRENCIES

Symbol	Region	Currency Name
AED	United Arab Emirates	Dirhams
AFA	Afghanistan	Afghanis
ALL	Albania	Leke
AMD	Armenia	Drams
ANG	Netherlands Antilles	Guilders
AOA	Angola	Kwanza
ARS	Argentina	Pesos
AUD	Australia	Dollars
AWG	Aruba	Guilders

(continues)

Symbol	Region	Currency Name
AZM	Azerbaijan	Manats
BAM	Bosnia and Herzegovina	Convertible marka
BBD	Barbados	Dollars
BDT	Bangladesh	Taka
BGN	Bulgaria	Leva
BHD	Bahrain	Dinars
BIF	Burundi	Francs
BMD	Bermuda	Dollars
BND	Brunei Darussalam	Dollars
BOB	Bolivia	Bolivianos
BRL	Brazil	Brazil real
BSD	Bahamas	Dollars
BTN	Bhutan	Ngultrum
BWP	Botswana	Pulas
BYR	Belarus	Rubles
BZD	Belize	Dollars
CAD	Canada	Dollars
CDF	Congo/Kinshasa	Congolese francs
CHF	Switzerland	Francs
CLP	Chile	Pesos
CNY	China	Renminbi
COP	Colombia	Pesos
CRC	Costa Rica	Colones
CUP	Cuba	Pesos
CVE	Cape Verde	Escudos
CYP	Cyprus	Pounds
CZK	Czech Republic	Koruny
DJF	Djibouti	Francs
DKK	Denmark	Kroner
DOP	Dominican Republic	Pesos
DZD	Algeria	Algeria dinars
EEK	Estonia	Krooni
EGP	Egypt	Pounds
ERN	Eritrea	Nakfa
ETB	Ethiopia	Birr
EUR	Euro member countries	Euro
FJD	Fiji	Dollars
FKP	Falkland Islands	Pounds
GBP	United Kingdom	Pounds
GEL	Georgia	Lari
GGP	Guernsey	Pounds

GHC	Ghana	Cedis
GIP	Gibraltar	Pounds
GMD	Gambia	Dalasi
GNF	Guinea	Francs
GTQ	Guatemala	Quetzales
GYD	Guyana	Dollars
HKD	Hong Kong	Dollars
HNL	Honduras	Lempiras
HRK	Croatia	Kuna
HTG	Haiti	Gourdes
HUF	Hungary	Forint
IDR	Indonesia	Rupiahs
ILS	Israel	New shekels
IMP	Isle of Man	Pounds
INR	India	Rupees
IQD	Iraq	Dinars
IRR	Iran	Rials
ISK	Iceland	Kronur
JEP	Jersey	Pounds
JMD	Jamaica	Dollars
JOD	Jordan	Dinars
JPY	Japan	Yen
KES	Kenya	Shillings
KGS	Kyrgyzstan	Soms
KHR	Cambodia	Riels
KMF	Comoros	Francs
KPW	Korea (North)	Won
KRW	Korea (South)	Won
KWD	Kuwait	Dinars
KYD	Cayman Islands	Dollars
KZT	Kazakstan	Tenge
LAK	Laos	Kips
LBP	Lebanon	Pounds
LKR	Sri Lanka	Rupees
LRD	Liberia	Dollars
LSL	Lesotho	Maloti
LTL	Lithuania	Litai
LVL	Latvia	Lati
LYD	Libya	Dinars
MAD	Morocco	Dirhams
MDL	Moldova	Lei
MGA	Madagascar	Ariary

(continues)

Symbol	Region	Currency Name
MKD	Macedonia	Denars
MMK	Myanmar (Burma)	Kyats
MNT	Mongolia	Tugriks
MOP	Macau	Patacas
MRO	Mauritania	Ouguiyas
MTL	Malta	Liri
MUR	Mauritius	Rupees
MVR	Maldives	Rufiyaa
MWK	Malawi	Kwachas
MXN	Mexico	Pesos
MYR	Malaysia	Ringgits
MZM	Mozambique	Meticais
NAD	Namibia	Dollars
NGN	Nigeria	Nairas
NIO	Nicaragua	Gold cordobas
NOK	Norway	Krone
NPR	Nepal	Nepal rupees
NZD	New Zealand	Dollars
OMR	Oman	Rials
PAB	Panama	Balboa
PEN	Peru	Nuevos soles
PGK	Papua New Guinea	Kina
PHP	Philippines	Pesos
PKR	Pakistan	Rupees
PLN	Poland	Zlotych
PYG	Paraguay	Guarani
QAR	Qatar	Rials
ROL	Romania	Lei
RUR	Russia	Rubles
RWF	Rwanda	Rwanda francs
SAR	Saudi Arabia	Riyals
SBD	Solomon Islands	Dollars
SCR	Seychelles	Rupees
SDD	Sudan	Dinars
SEK	Sweden	Kronor
SGD	Singapore	Dollars
SHP	Saint Helena	Pounds
SIT	Slovenia	Tolars
SKK	Slovakia	Koruny
SLL	Sierra Leone	Leones
SOS	Somalia	Shillings

SPL	Seborga	Luigini
SRG	Suriname	Guilders
STD	São Tomé, Principe	Dobras
SVC	El Salvador	Colones
SYP	Syria	Pounds
SZL	Swaziland	Emalangeni
THB	Thailand	Baht
TJS	Tajikistan	Somoni
TMM	Turkmenistan	Manats
TND	Tunisia	Dinars
TOP	Tonga	Pa'anga
TRL	Turkey	Liras
TTD	Trinidad, Tobago	Dollars
TVD	Tuvalu	Tuvalu dollars
TWD	Taiwan	New dollars
TZS	Tanzania	Shillings
UAH	Ukraine	Hryvnia
UGX	Uganda	Shillings
USD	United States of America	Dollars
UYU	Uruguay	Pesos
UZS	Uzbekistan	Sums
VEB	Venezuela	Bolivares
VND	Vietnam	Dong
VUV	Vanuatu	Vatu
WST	Samoa	Tala
YER	Yemen	Rials
YUM	Yugoslavia	New dinars
ZAR	South Africa	Rand
ZMK	Zambia	Kwacha
ZWD	Zimbabwe	Zimbabwe dollars

Exchange Rates

The following table shows the international foreign exchange rates on April 21, 2006, compared with the U.S. dollar:

EXCHANGE RATES

Currency	Units/USD	USD/Units
Algerian dinar	0.01379	72.52500
Argentine peso	0.32701	3.05800
Australian dollar	0.74420	1.34373
Baharaini dinar	2.65266	0.37698
Bolivian boliviano	0.12508	7.99500
Botswana pula	0.18714	5.34360
Brazilian real	0.47279	2.11510
British pound	1.78280	0.56092
Canadian dollar	0.87827	1.13860
Chilean peso	0.00193	517.54999
Chinese yuan	0.12477	8.01450
Columbian peso	0.00043	2,337.00004
Cypriot pound	2.14777	0.46560
Czech koruna	0.04359	22.94200
Danish krone	0.16547	6.04350
Ecuador sucre	0.00004	25,000.00063
Euro	1.23450	0.81005

Ghanaian cedi	0.00011	9,106.99988
Guatemalan quetzal	0.13201	7.57500
Hong Kong dollar	0.12897	7.75400
Hungarian forint	0.00467	213.96001
Indian rupee	0.02216	45.13500
Indonesian rupiah	0.00011	8,882.99974
Israeli shekel	0.22015	4.54230
Japanese yen	0.00855	116.93001
Jordanian dinar	1.41143	0.70850
Kenyan shilling	0.01404	71.22000
Kuwaiti dinar	3.42407	0.29205
Malaysian ringgit	0.27319	3.66050
Mexican peso	0.09016	11.09120
Moroccan dirham	0.11191	8.93550
Namibian dollar	0.16587	6.02900
New Zealand dollar	0.63330	1.57903
Norwegian krone	0.15748	6.35000
Omani rial	2.59774	0.38495
Pakistan rupee	0.01668	59.97000
Peruvian nuevo sol	0.30233	3.30770
Qatari rial	0.27467	3.64070
Russian rouble	0.03639	27.48000
Saudi riyal	0.26663	3.75050
Singapore dollar	0.62661	1.59590
South African rand	0.16707	5.98550
South Korean won	0.00106	948.00005
Swedish krona	0.13248	7.54860
Swiss franc	0.78475	1.27430
Taiwan dollar	0.03098	32.27500
Tanzanian shilling	0.00083	1,211.99996
Thai baht	0.02645	37.81000
Tunisian dinar	0.74738	1.33800
Turkish lira	0.75683	1.32130
United Arab Emirati dirham	0.27228	3.67270
U.S. dollar	1.00000	1.00000
Venezuelan bolivar	0.00047	2,144.00005
Vietnamese dong	0.00006	15,924.99916
Zimbabwean dollar	0.00001	99,202.00100

It is interesting to note that as of the list's date only seven world currencies have a parity rate with the U.S. dollar greater than 1.0000: Kuwaiti dinar (3.42407), Bahraini dinar (2.65266), Omani rial (2.59774), Cypriot pound (2.14777), British pound (1.78280), Jordanian dinar (1.41143), and euro (1.23450). Coincidentally, at the bottom of the list both alphabetically and parity-wise, is the Zimbabwean dollar, which requires over 99,000 to equal one U.S. dollar.

Additional information on current exchange rates can be found at http://money central.msn.com/investor/market/rates.asp.

Euro Currency

O n January 1, 1999, 11 of the countries in the European Economic and Monetary Union (EMU) decided to give up their own currencies and adopt the new euro (EUR) currency: Austria, Belgium, Finland, France, Germany, Ireland, Italy, Luxembourg, the Netherlands, Portugal, and Spain. Greece followed suit on January 1, 2001. The Vatican City also participated in the changeover. This changeover is now complete.

It is worth noting that any place that previously used one or more of the currencies listed below has now also adopted the euro. This applies to the Principality of Andorra, the Principality of Monaco, and the Republic of San Marino. This of course applies automatically to any territories, departments, possessions, or collectivities of euro-zone countries, such as the Azores, the Balearic Islands, the Canary Islands, Europa Island, French Guiana, Guadeloupe, Juan de Nova, the Madeira Islands, Martinique, Mayotte, Réunion, Saint-Martin, Saint Pierre, and Miquelon, to name just a few.

Euro banknotes and coins began circulating in the euro-zone countries on January 1, 2002. At that time, all transactions in those countries were valued in euros, and the old notes and coins of those countries were gradually withdrawn from circulation.

OFFICIAL FIXED EURO RATES FOR PARTICIPATING COUNTRIES

Symbol	Region	Legacy (Old) Currency	Conversion to Euro	Conversion from Euro
ATS	Austria	Schilling	ATS/13.7603 = EUR	EUR × 13.7603 = ATS
BEF	Belgium	Franc	BEF/40.3399 = EUR	EUR × 40.3399 = BEF
DEM	Germany	Mark	DEM/1.95583 = EUR	EUR × 1.95583 = DEM

(continues)

Symbol	Region	Legacy (Old) Currency	Conversion to Euro	Conversion from Euro
ESP	Spain	Peseta	ESP/166.386 = EUR	EUR × 166.386 = ESP
FIM	Finland	Markka	FIM/5.94573 = EUR	EUR × 5.94573 = FIM
FRF	France	Franc	FRF/6.55957 = EUR	EUR × 6.55957 = FRF
GRD	Greece	Drachma	GRD/340.750 = EUR	EUR × 340.750 = GRD
IEP	Ireland	Punt	IEP/0.787564 = EUR	EUR × 0.787564 = IEP
ITL	Italy	Lira	ITL/1936.27 = EUR	EUR × 1936.27 = ITL
LUF	Luxembourg	Franc	LUF/40.3399 = EUR	EUR × 40.3399 = LUF
NLG	Netherlands	Guilder	NLG/2.20371 = EUR	EUR × 2.20371 = NLG
PTE	Portugal	Escudo	PTE/200.482 = EUR	EUR × 200.482 = PTE
VAL	Vatican City	Lira	VAL/1936.27 = EUR	EUR × 1936.27 = VAL

For convenience, and because their values are now irrevocably set against the euro as listed in the preceding table, the XE.com Universal Currency Converter will continue to support these units even after their withdrawal from circulation. In addition, most outgoing euro currencies will still be physically convertible at special locations for a period of several years. For details, refer to the official eEuro site.

Also note that the euro is not just the same thing as the former European Currency Unit (ECU), which used to be listed as XEU. The ECU was a theoretical basket of currencies rather than a currency in and of itself, and no ECU banknotes or coins ever existed. At any rate, the ECU has been replaced by the euro, which is a bona fide currency.

Global Banking Hours

P rice fluctuations in the spot currency markets are essentially news-driven. Or more accurately, it is the human reaction to news-driven events that makes trading possible and profitable. How traders interpret these news events determines which direction the market will travel. As in all financial markets, foreign exchange also has its share of contrarians who keep runaway breakouts in check while supplying additional volatility to the overall situation.

Despite all the fundamental and technical influences on the foreign exchange market, one major constant in determining periods of high volatility is the hours of operation for the central banks of each major currency country.

Figure D.1 emphasizes the importance of the effect of time of day on forex market activity and volatility based on hours of operation around the globe. Because banking hours vary from country to country, we have arbitrarily set hours of operation from 9:00 A.M. to 5:00 P.M. for consistency. The top row is expressed as central european time (Greenwich mean time + 1 hour), which aligns with the Central Bank of Europe in Frankfurt, the most prestigious central bank in the European Monetary Union.

The table allows traders to view overlapping time periods when central banks for different currencies are operating and thus guarantee a certain degree of mutual activity.

For example, when banks open in New York City at 9:00 A.M. EST, the Frankfurt bank has already been operating for six hours. So there is a two-hour overlap of trading in the EURUSD currency pair on both sides of the Atlantic Ocean (9:00 A.M. to 11:00 A.M. EST). This can be readily recognized in the time of day activity chart for the EURUSD pair (Figure 2.4 in Chapter 2).

If we are interested in initiating a trade in the EURHKD cross-rate pair, we note that

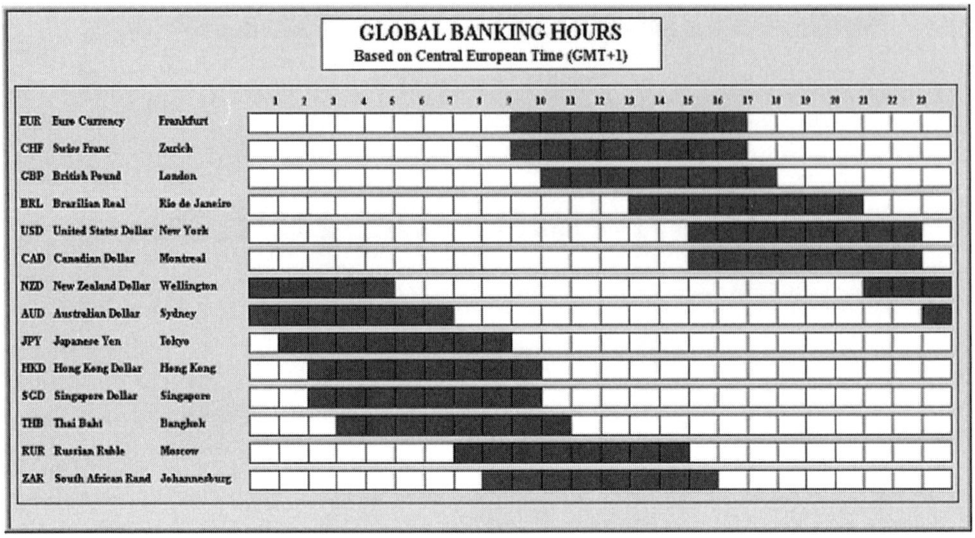

FIGURE D.1 Global Banking Hours

there is a one-hour overlap in banking operations between central Europe and Hong Kong that occurs between 9:00 A.M. and 10:00 A.M. in Frankfurt (or 3:00 A.M. to 4:00 A.M. in New York).

Dedicated currency traders may have to adjust their sleeping schedules to take advantage of increased activity and volatility when trading non-USD cross-rate currency pairs.

Monthly OHLC and Activity Charts

In this appendix, we present monthly OHLC and activity charts for the 10 most frequently traded USD currency pairs. Beneath each chart are the corresponding statistics for the time period January 2000 through December 2005.

In the statistics block, we use the following definitions:

$$\text{Midrange} = \frac{\text{High} + \text{Low}}{2}$$

$$\text{Absolute Range} = \text{High} - \text{Low}$$

$$\text{Relative Range} = 100 \times \frac{\text{Absolute Range}}{\text{Midrange}}$$

The currency pairs in this appendix are arranged in the following order:

EURUSD	AUDUSD
GBPUSD	NZDUSD
USDCHF	USDSEK
USDJPY	USDNOK
USDCAD	USDDKK

In the charts (Figures E.1 through E.10), activity is represented as the vertical bars at the bottom. The upper (lighter) portion is the number of upticks, while the lower (darker) portion is the number of downticks. Their sum equals the total activity for the corresponding month.

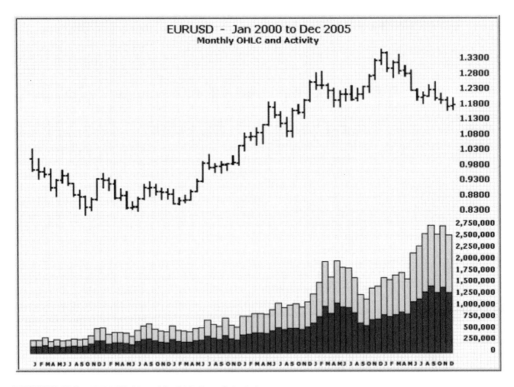

FIGURE E.1 EURUSD Monthly OHLC and Activity

Open	1.0088
High	1.3667
Low	0.8229
Close	1.1849
Mean	1.0656
Midrange	1.0948
Absolute Range	0.5438
Relative Range	49.6712
Standard Deviation	0.1573

It is interesting to note that activity increased by 1,060 percent from January 2000 to December 2005.

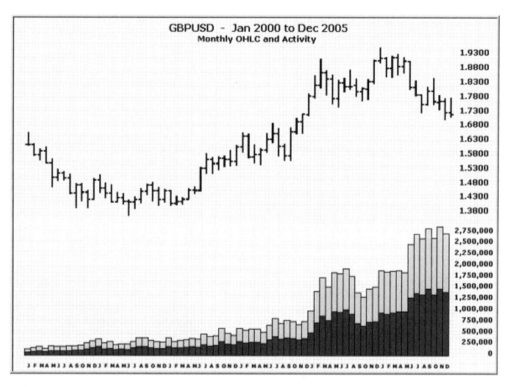

FIGURE E.2 GBPUSD Monthly OHLC and Activity

Open	1.6147
High	1.9550
Low	1.3685
Close	1.7232
Mean	1.6266
Midrange	1.6618
Absolute Range	0.5865
Relative Range	35.2941
Standard Deviation	0.1646

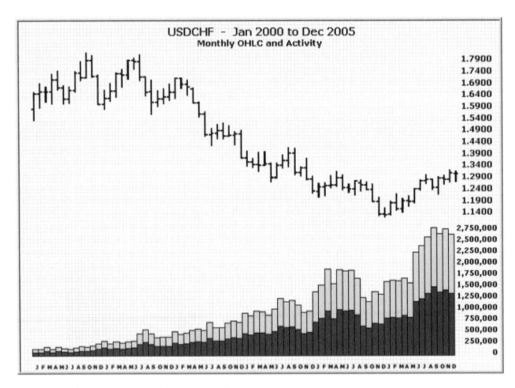

FIGURE E.3   USDCHF Monthly OHLC and Activity

Open	1.5908
High	1.8309
Low	1.1288
Close	1.3136
Mean	1.4594
Midrange	1.4799
Absolute Range	0.7021
Relative Range	47.4440
Standard Deviation	0.2043

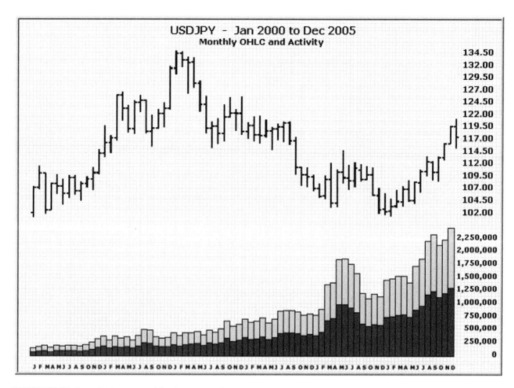

FIGURE E.4 USDJPY Monthly OHLC and Activity

Open	102.2600
High	135.1600
Low	101.3600
Close	117.7500
Mean	114.9319
Midrange	118.2600
Absolute Range	33.8000
Relative Range	28.5811
Standard Deviation	8.0282

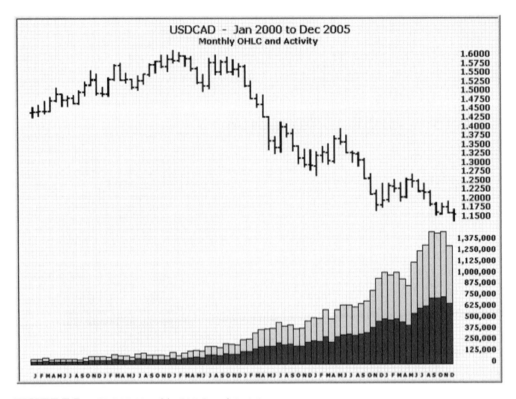

FIGURE E.5 USDCAD Monthly OHLC and Activity

Open	1.4450
High	1.6188
Low	1.1425
Close	1.1619
Mean	1.4166
Midrange	1.3807
Absolute Range	0.4763
Relative Range	34.4982
Standard Deviation	0.1404

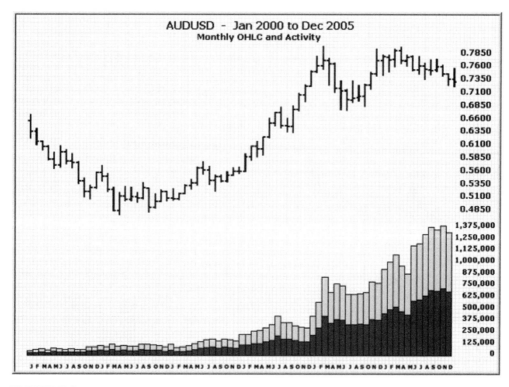

FIGURE E.6　AUDUSD Monthly OHLC and Activity

Open	0.6570
High	0.8008
Low	0.4778
Close	0.7329
Mean	0.6325
Midrange	0.6393
Absolute Range	0.3230
Relative Range	50.5240
Standard Deviation	0.0996

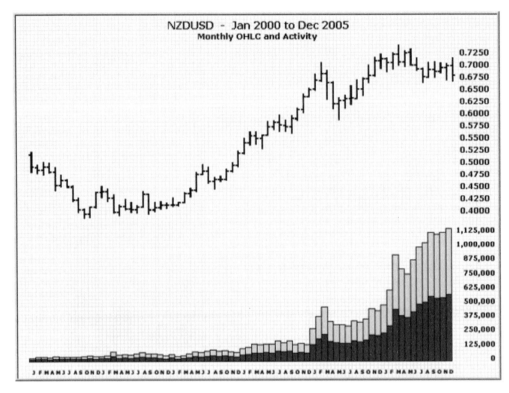

FIGURE E.7 NZDUSD Monthly OHLC and Activity

Open	0.5213
High	0.7465
Low	0.3900
Close	0.6837
Mean	0.5492
Midrange	0.5683
Absolute Range	0.3565
Relative Range	62.7365
Standard Deviation	0.1137

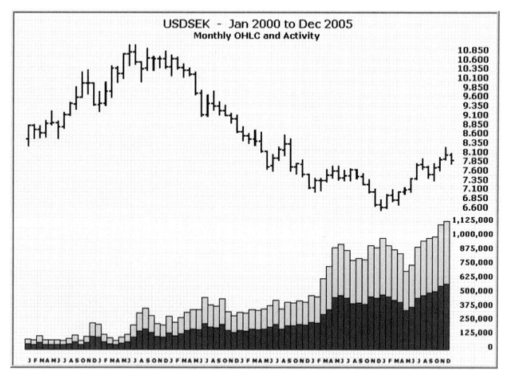

FIGURE E.8   USDSEK Monthly OHLC and Activity

Open	8.4894
High	11.0510
Low	6.5701
Close	7.9378
Mean	8.6906
Midrange	8.8106
Absolute Range	4.4809
Relative Range	50.8583
Standard Deviation	1.2345

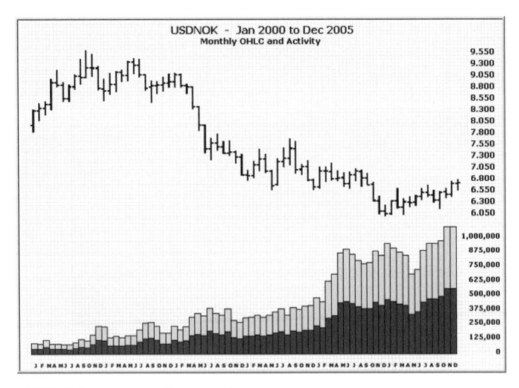

FIGURE E.9 USDNOK Monthly OHLC and Activity

Open	8.0147
High	9.6520
Low	6.0320
Close	6.7442
Mean	7.6666
Midrange	7.8420
Absolute Range	3.6200
Relative Range	46.1617
Standard Deviation	1.0694

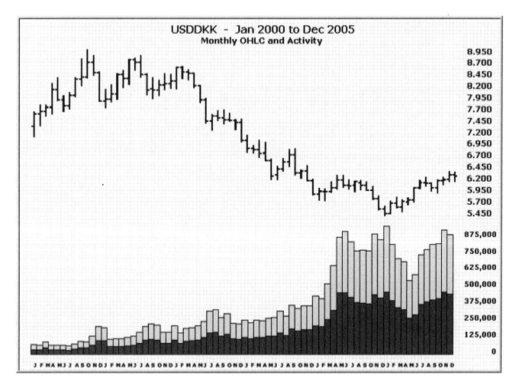

FIGURE E.10   USDDKK Monthly OHLC and Activity

Open	7.3780
High	9.0425
Low	5.4443
Close	6.2978
Mean	7.1353
Midrange	7.2434
Absolute Range	3.5982
Relative Range	49.6756
Standard Deviation	1.0510

Daily OHLC and Activity Charts

The current appendix is analogous to the preceding appendix except the time frame spans 1/1/2006 to 4/14/2006 and the time interval has been changed from monthly to daily in order to scrutinize recent market characteristics in greater detail.

The numeric values in the statistical blocks beneath each chart are defined as in the preceding appendix.

The currency pairs in this appendix (Figures F.1 through F.10) are arranged in the following order:

EURUSD	AUDUSD
GBPUSD	NZDUSD
USDCHF	USDSEK
USDJPY	USDNOK
USDCAD	USDDKK

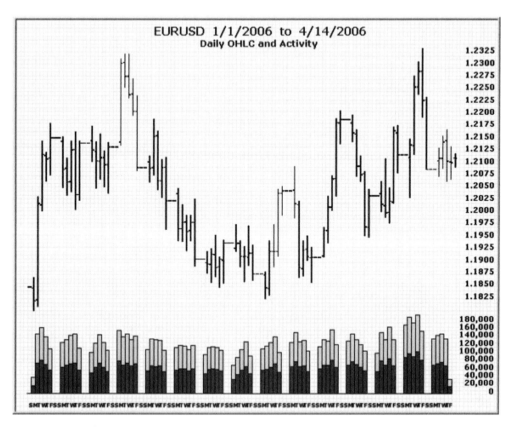

FIGURE F.1 EURUSD Daily OHLC and Activity

Open	1.1849
High	1.2335
Low	1.1801
Close	1.2111
Mean	1.2048
Midrange	1.2068
Absolute Range	0.0534
Relative Range	4.4249
Standard Deviation	0.0111

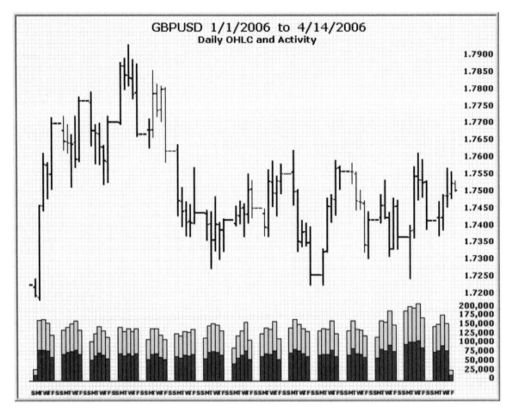

FIGURE F.2   GBPUSD Daily OHLC and Activity

Open	1.7232
High	1.7937
Low	1.7187
Close	1.7509
Mean	1.7523
Midrange	1.7562
Absolute Range	0.0750
Relative Range	4.2706
Standard Deviation	0.0147

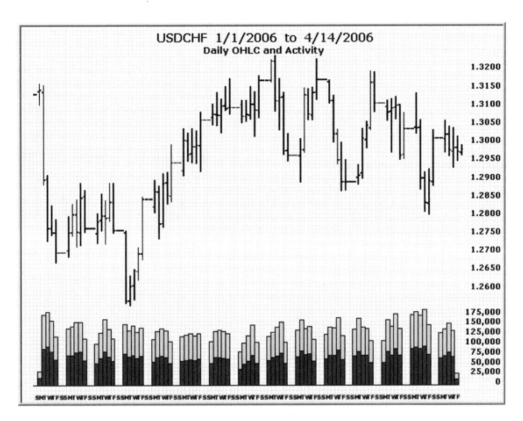

FIGURE F.3 USDCHF Daily OHLC and Activity

Open	1.3136
High	1.3242
Low	1.2556
Close	1.2984
Mean	1.2964
Midrange	1.2899
Absolute Range	0.0686
Relative Range	5.3182
Standard Deviation	0.0150

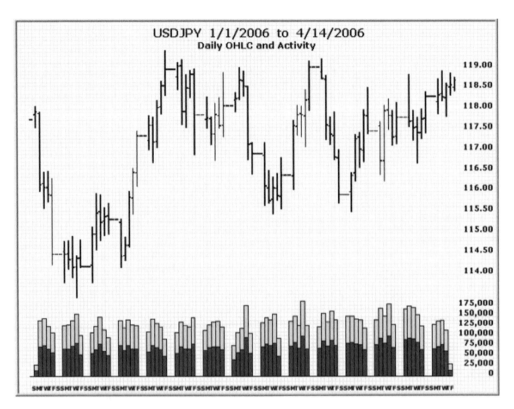

FIGURE F.4   USDJPY Daily OHLC and Activity

Open	117.7500
High	119.4200
Low	113.4100
Close	118.6900
Mean	117.0547
Midrange	116.4150
Absolute Range	6.0100
Relative Range	5.1626
Standard Deviation	1.4004

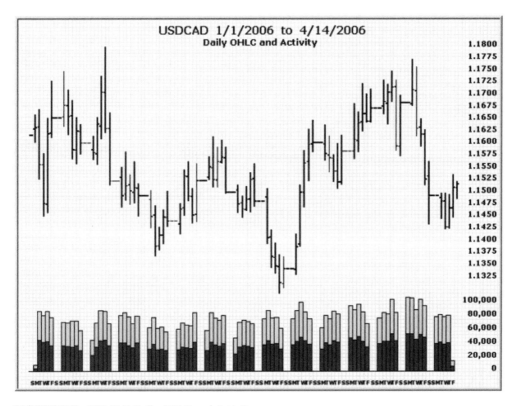

FIGURE F.5 USDCAD Daily OHLC and Activity

Open	1.1619
High	1.1800
Low	1.1294
Close	1.1519
Mean	1.1545
Midrange	1.1547
Absolute Range	0.0506
Relative Range	4.3821
Standard Deviation	0.0095

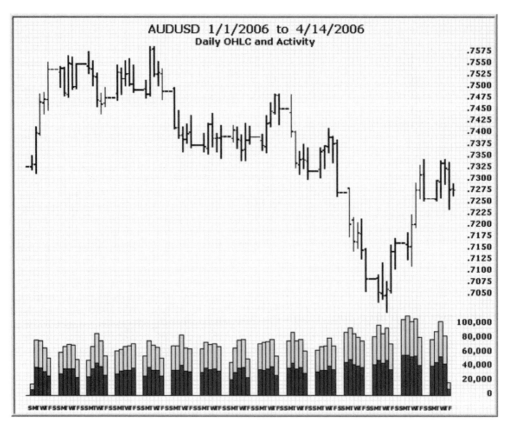

FIGURE F.6   AUDUSD Daily OHLC and Activity

Open	0.7329
High	0.7590
Low	0.7015
Close	0.7279
Mean	0.7376
Midrange	0.7303
Absolute Range	0.0575
Relative Range	7.8740
Standard Deviation	0.0133

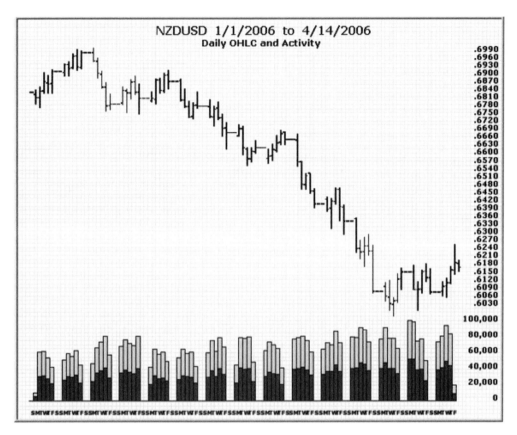

FIGURE F.7 NZDUSD Daily OHLC and Activity

Open	0.6837
High	0.7004
Low	0.5991
Close	0.6175
Mean	0.6581
Midrange	0.6498
Absolute Range	0.1013
Relative Range	15.5906
Standard Deviation	0.0302

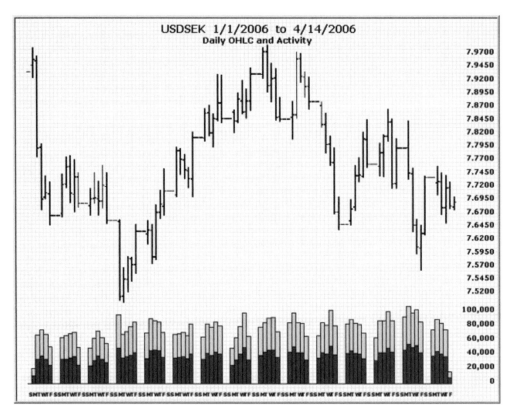

FIGURE F.8 USDSEK Daily OHLC and Activity

Open	7.9378
High	7.9882
Low	7.5042
Close	7.6927
Mean	7.7619
Midrange	7.7462
Absolute Range	0.4840
Relative Range	6.2482
Standard Deviation	0.1022

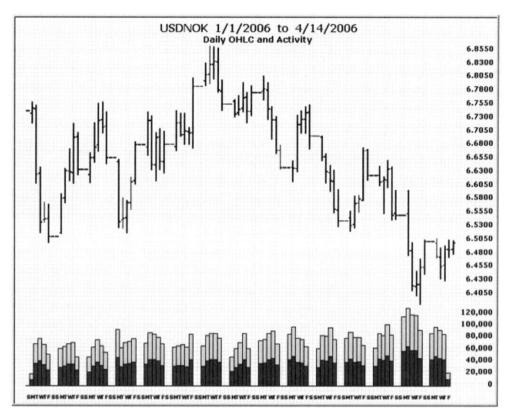

FIGURE F.9 USDNOK Daily OHLC and Activity

Open	6.7442
High	6.8636
Low	6.3880
Close	6.5014
Mean	6.6440
Midrange	6.6258
Absolute Range	0.4756
Relative Range	7.1780
Standard Deviation	0.0990

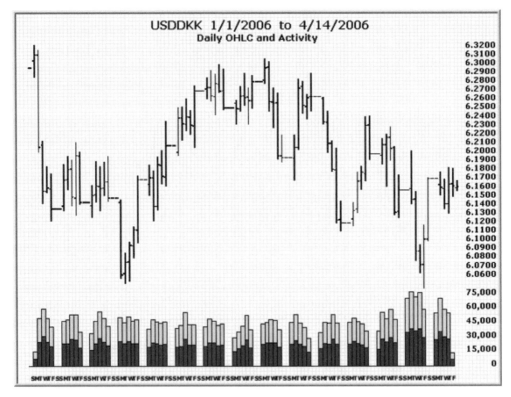

FIGURE F.10   USDDKK Daily OHLC and Activity

Open	6.2978
High	6.3233
Low	6.0470
Close	6.1622
Mean	6.1946
Midrange	6.1852
Absolute Range	0.2763
Relative Range	4.4672
Standard Deviation	0.0576

Time of Day Charts (Activity)

The time frame in the following charts spans 1/1/2005 through 4/14/2006. Composite charts are calculated by averaging the sum of the upticks and downticks over that period using one-minute time intervals. Their purpose is to assist traders in determining when to schedule online trading sessions based on traders' predilections to the nebulous risk/reward factor and the volatility of the targeted currency pair (in this case, EURUSD).

The vertical numeric scale on the right of each chart (Figures G.1 through G.6) is activity expressed in total number of ticks (upticks plus downticks) during each time interval. The bottom band (the darkest) represents the activity for the current minute. The central band plus the lower band represents three-minute activity. The sum of all three vertical bars represents the five-minute activity.

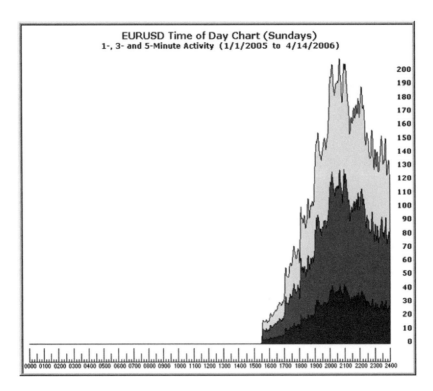

FIGURE G.1 Sunday Composite Activity Chart

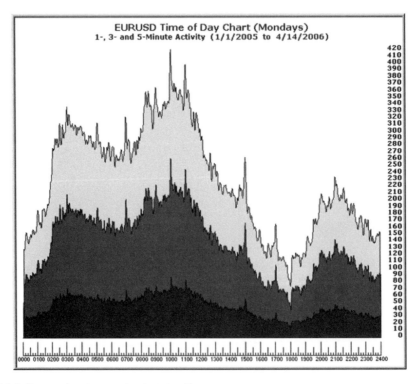

FIGURE G.2 Monday Composite Activity Chart

294

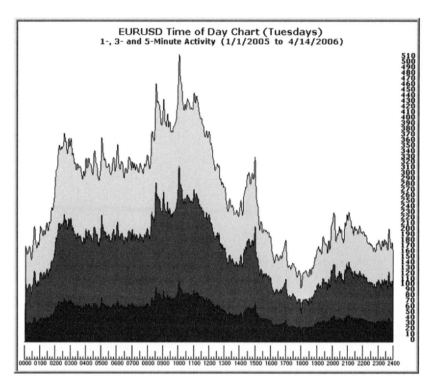

FIGURE G.3 Tuesday Composite Activity Chart

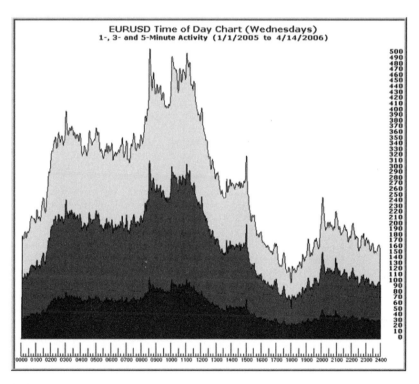

FIGURE G.4 Wednesday Composite Activity Chart

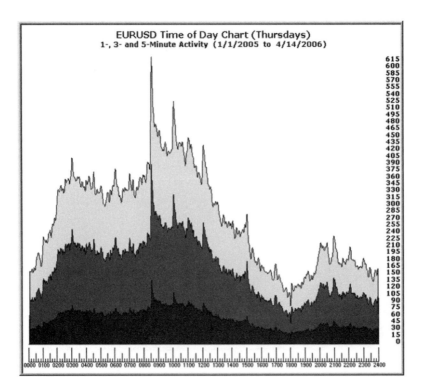

FIGURE G.5 Thursday Composite Activity Chart

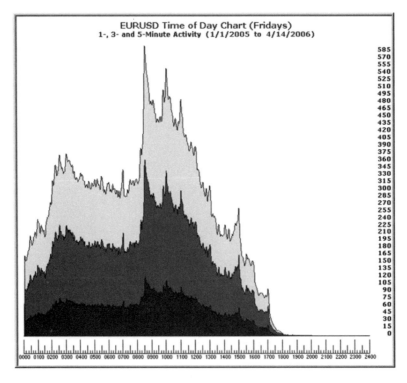

FIGURE G.6 Friday Composite Activity Chart

Time of Day
Charts (Range)

The time frame in the following charts spans 1/1/2005 through 4/14/2006.

The vertical numeric scale on the right of each chart (Figures H.1 through H.6) is absolute range expressed in integer pips of the quote currency. The bottom band (the darkest) represents the range for the current two-minute interval. The sum of the central band plus the lower band represents the seven-minute range. The sum of all three vertical bands represents the 15-minute absolute range.

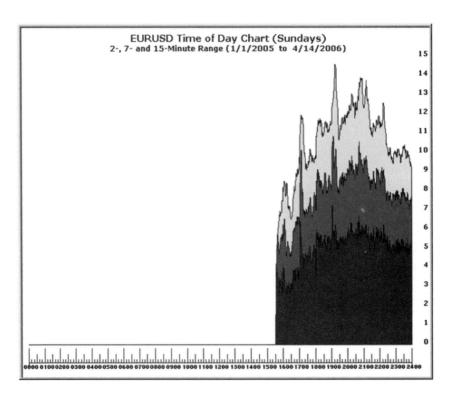

FIGURE H.1 Sunday Composite Range Chart

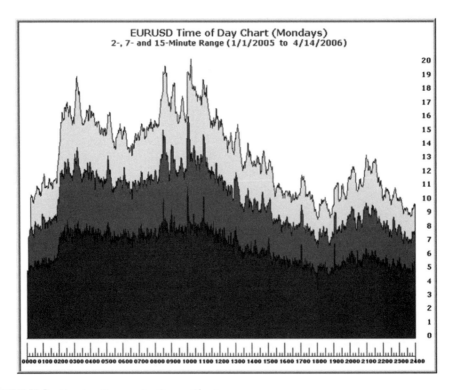

FIGURE H.2 Monday Composite Range Chart

298

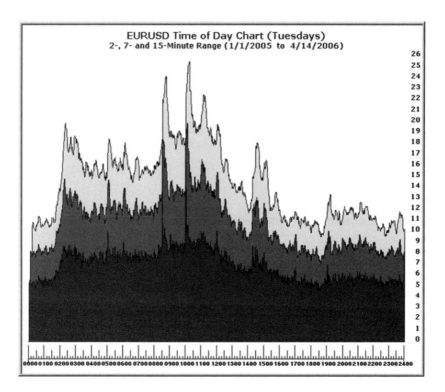

FIGURE H.3 Tuesday Composite Range Chart

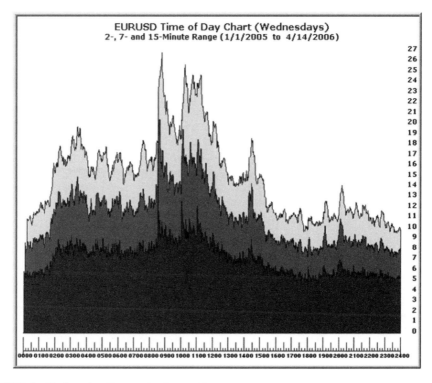

FIGURE H.4 Wednesday Composite Range Chart

299

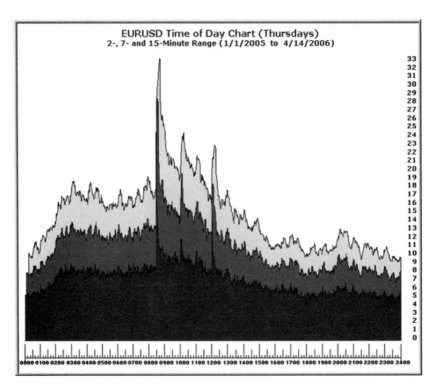

FIGURE H.5 Thursday Composite Range Chart

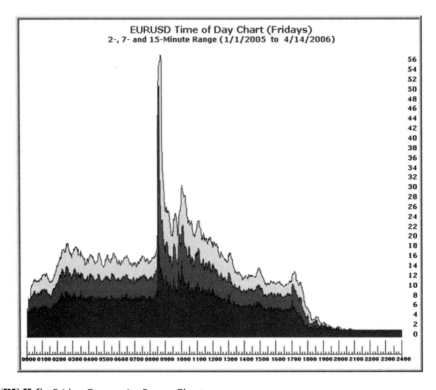

FIGURE H.6 Friday Composite Range Chart

Time of Day Charts (Momentum)

The time frame in the following charts spans 1/1/2005 through 4/14/2006.

The vertical numeric scale on the right of each chart (Figures I.1 through I.6) is absolute momentum expressed in integer pips of the quote currency. The bottom band (the darkest) represents the momentum for the current one-minute interval. The sum of the central band plus the lower band represents five-minute momentum. The sum of all three vertical bands represents the 15-minute absolute momentum.

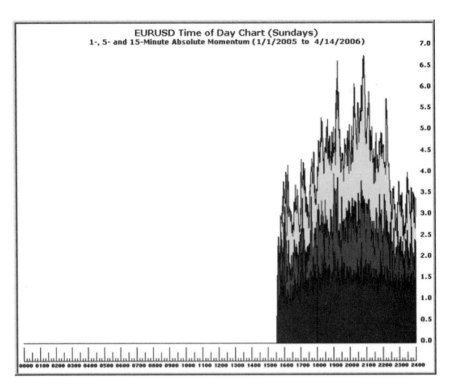

FIGURE I.1   Sunday Composite Momentum Chart

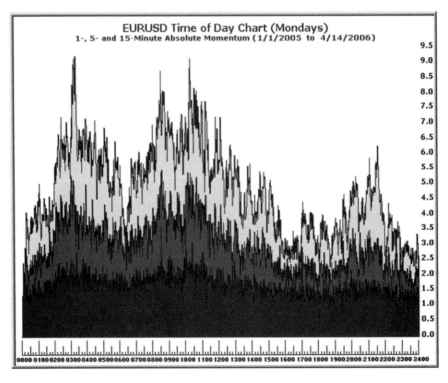

FIGURE I.2   Monday Composite Momentum Chart

302

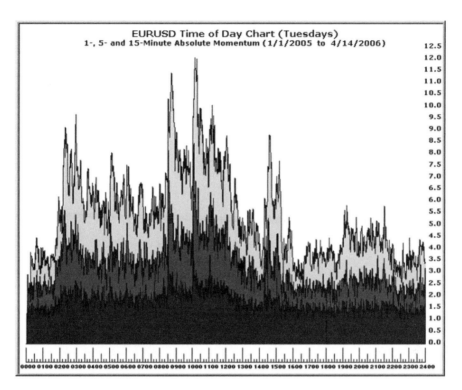

FIGURE I.3 Tuesday Composite Momentum Chart

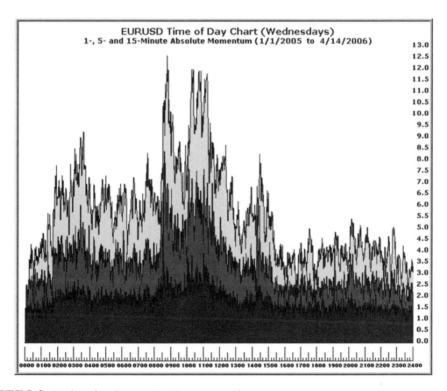

FIGURE I.4 Wednesday Composite Momentum Chart

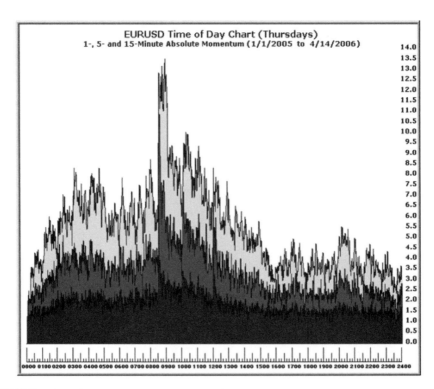

FIGURE I.5 Thursday Composite Momentum Chart

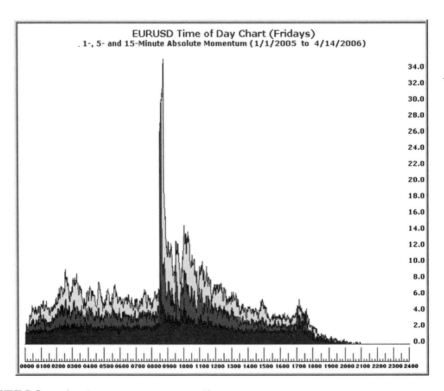

FIGURE I.6 Friday Composite Momentum Chart

Day of Week
Charts (Activity)

his and the following two appendixes are the composite of six day of week charts (Sunday through Friday) for the 10 most frequently traded USD currency pairs, using the same statistical method (activity, range, or momentum). Saturdays are not included since the liquidity of trading diminishes drastically at 5:30 P.M. Friday eastern time.

The time frame again spans 1/1/2005 through 4/14/2006. Time of day charts employed one-minute raw data intervals, whereas day of week charts use hourly data as the basis.

The currency pairs in these three appendixes are arranged in the following order:

EURUSD	AUDUSD
GBPUSD	NZDUSD
USDCHF	USDSEK
USDJPY	USDNOK
USDCAD	USDDKK

In Figures J.1 through J.10, the vertical numeric scale on the right is activity expressed in total number of ticks (upticks plus downticks) during each time interval. Each lower (dark) vertical bar represents the activity for the current hour. The sum of the two vertical bars (light and dark) represents the activity for each two-hour period (the current hour plus the previous hour).

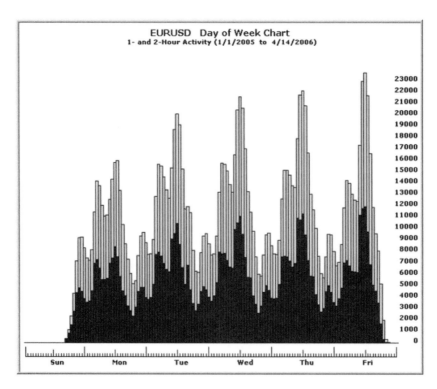

FIGURE J.1 EURUSD Composite Activity Chart

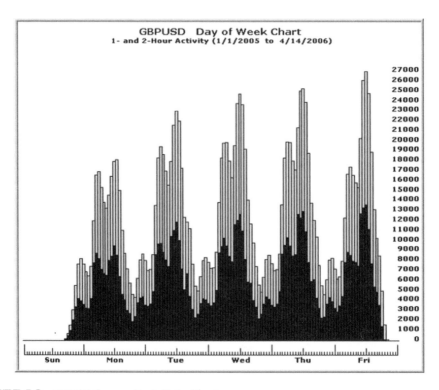

FIGURE J.2 GBPUSD Composite Activity Chart

306

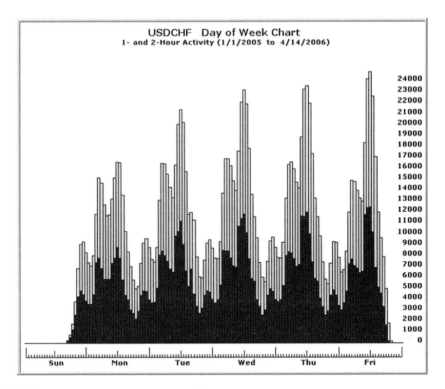

FIGURE J.3 USDCHF Composite Activity Chart

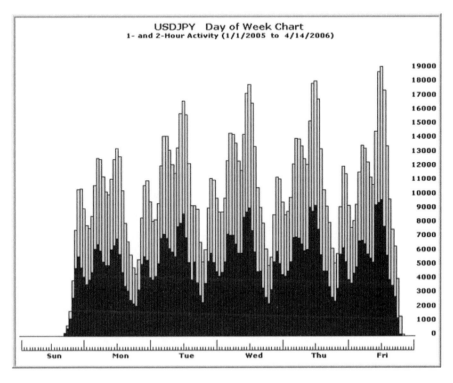

FIGURE J.4 USDJPY Composite Activity Chart

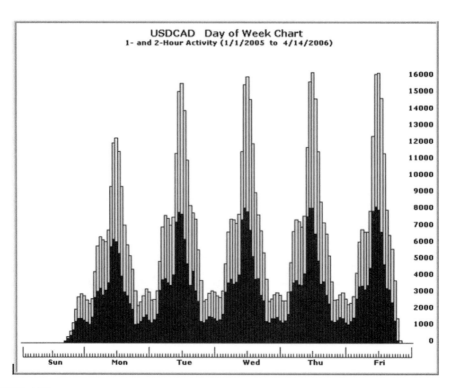

FIGURE J.5 USDCAD Composite Activity Chart

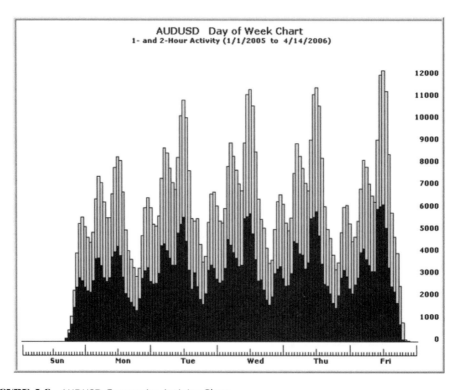

FIGURE J.6 AUDUSD Composite Activity Chart

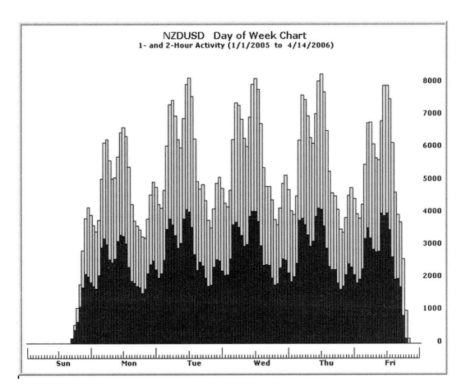

FIGURE J.7 NZDUSD Composite Activity Chart

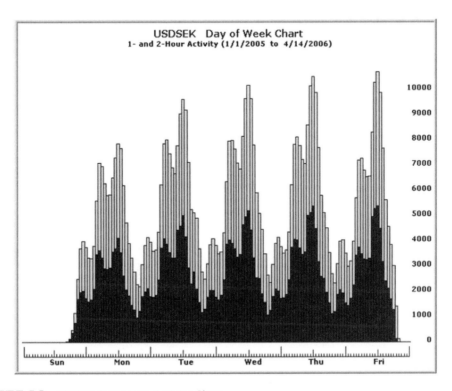

FIGURE J.8 USDSEK Composite Activity Chart

309

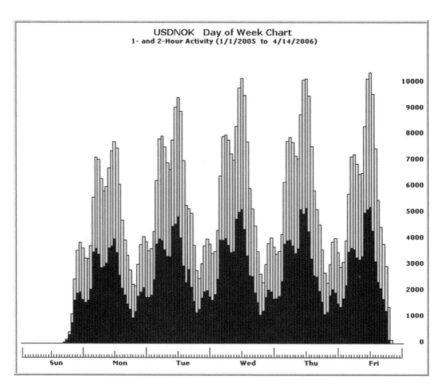

FIGURE J.9 USDNOK Composite Activity Chart

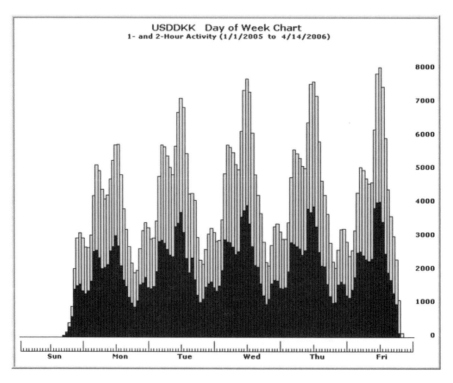

FIGURE J.10 USDDKK Composite Activity Chart

Day of Week Charts (Range)

See the comments at the beginning of Appendix J for a general description of weekly composite charts.

In Figures K.1 through K.10, the vertical numeric scale on the right of the composite range chart is the absolute range expressed in total number of pips during each time interval. Each lower (dark) vertical bar represents the range for the current hour. The sum of the two vertical bars (light and dark) represents the range for each two-hour period (the current hour plus the previous hour).

Pips are expressed in units of the quote (rightmost) currency in the pair and calculated by multiplying the exchange rate by the corresponding pip conversion factor.

PIP CONVERSION FACTORS

Pair	Factor
EURUSD	10,000
GBPUSD	10,000
USDCHF	10,000
USDJPY	100
USDCAD	10,000
AUDUSD	10,000
NZDUSD	10,000
USDSEK	1,000
USDNOK	1,000
USDDKK	1,000

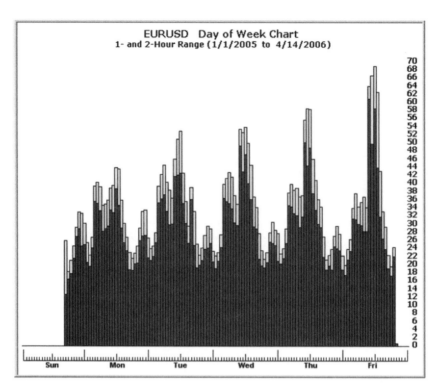

FIGURE K.1 EURUSD Composite Range Chart

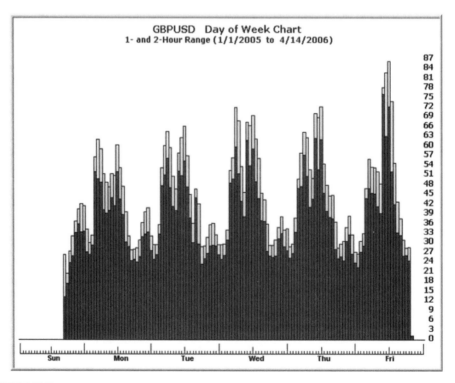

FIGURE K.2 GBPUSD Composite Range Chart

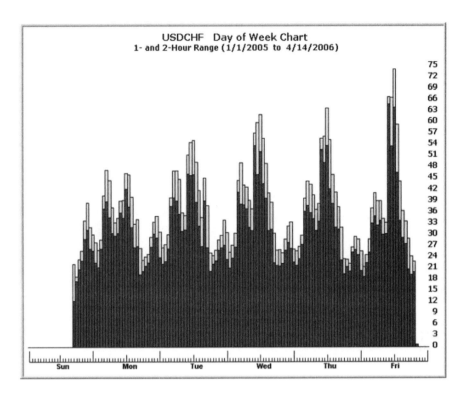

FIGURE K.3 USDCHF Composite Range Chart

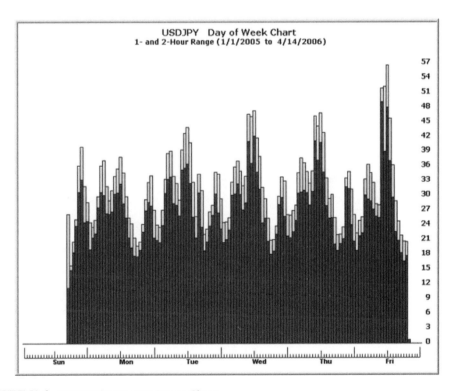

FIGURE K.4 USDJPY Composite Range Chart

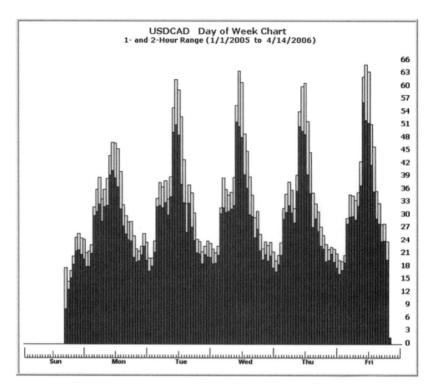

FIGURE K.5 USDCAD Composite Range Chart

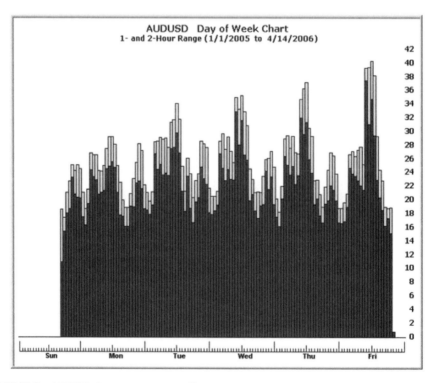

FIGURE K.6 AUDUSD Composite Range Chart

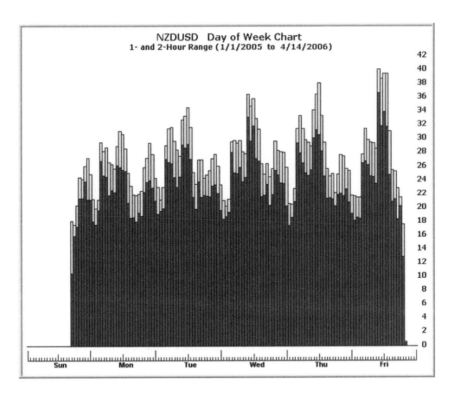

FIGURE K.7   NZDUSD Composite Range Chart

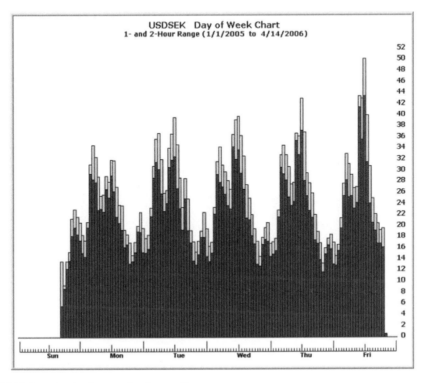

FIGURE K.8   USDSEK Composite Range Chart

315

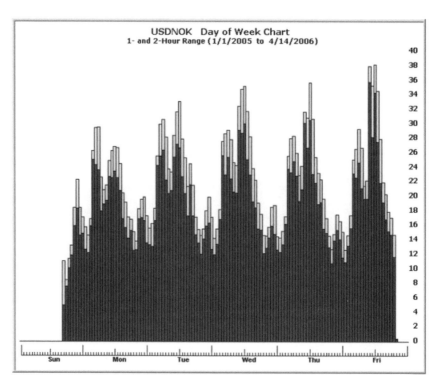

FIGURE K.9 USDNOK Composite Range Chart

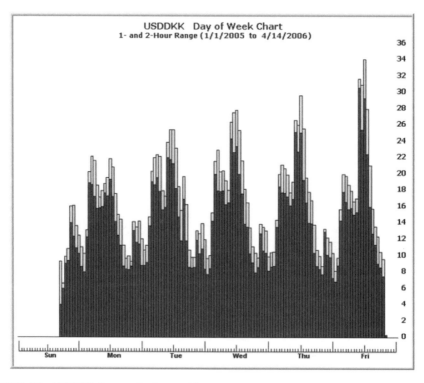

FIGURE K.10 USDDKK Composite Range Chart

Day of Week Charts (Momentum)

See the comments at the beginning of Appendix J for a general description of weekly composite charts.

In Figures L.1 through L.10, the vertical numeric scale on the right of the composite momentum chart is the absolute momentum expressed in total number of pips during each time interval. Each lower dark band represents the absolute momentum for the current hour. The sum of the two vertical lower and upper bands represents the momentum for each two-hour period (the current hour plus the previous hour).

Pips are expressed in units of the quote (rightmost) currency in the pair and calculated by multiplying the exchange rate by the corresponding pip conversion factor.

Pair	Factor
EURUSD	10,000
GBPUSD	10,000
USDCHF	10,000
USDJPY	100
USDCAD	10,000
AUDUSD	10,000
NZDUSD	10,000
USDSEK	1,000
USDNOK	1,000
USDDKK	1,000

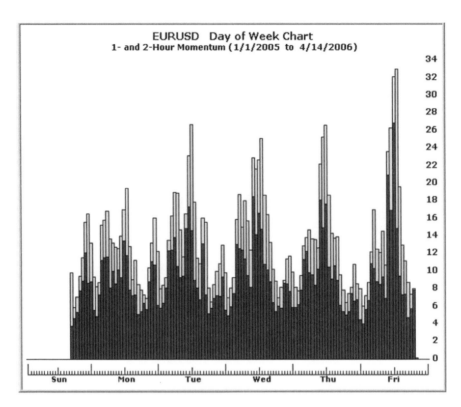

FIGURE L.1 EURUSD Composite Momentum Chart

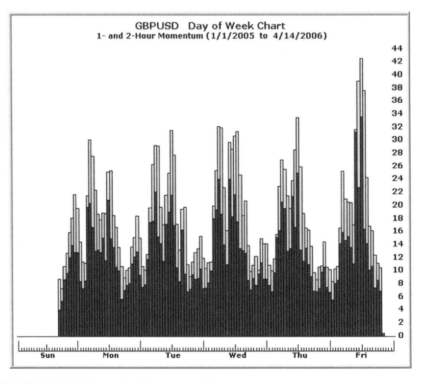

FIGURE L.2 GBPUSD Composite Momentum Chart

318

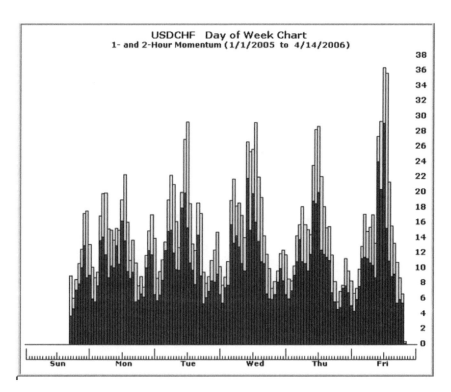

FIGURE L.3 USDCHF Composite Momentum Chart

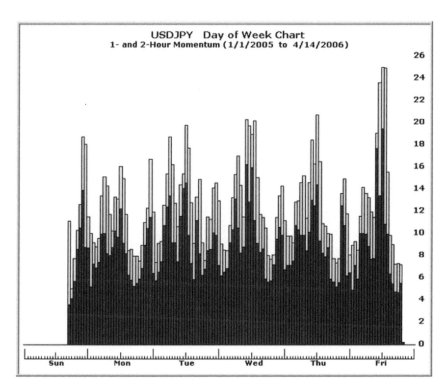

FIGURE L.4 USDJPY Composite Momentum Chart

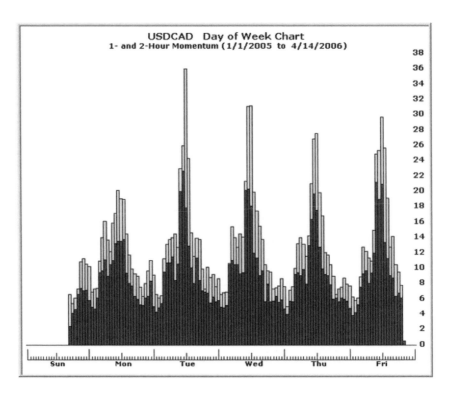

FIGURE L.5 USDCAD Composite Momentum Chart

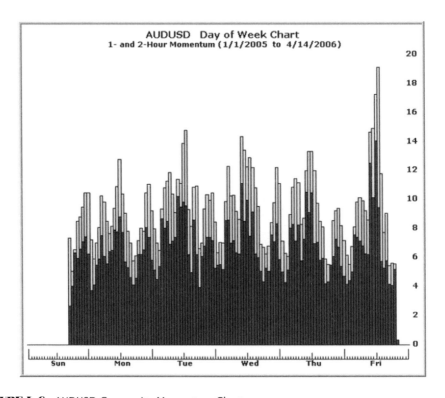

FIGURE L.6 AUDUSD Composite Momentum Chart

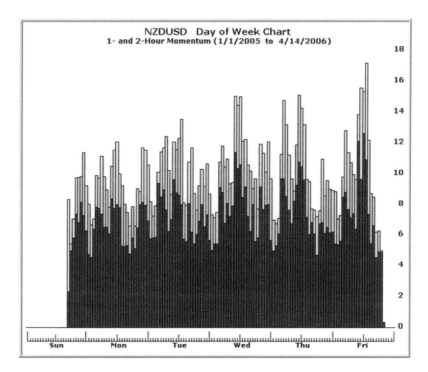

FIGURE L.7 NZDUSD Composite Momentum Chart

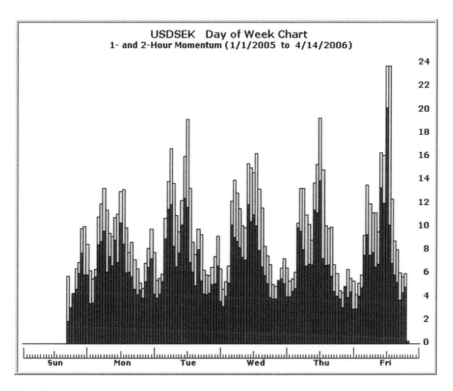

FIGURE L.8 USDSEK Composite Momentum Chart

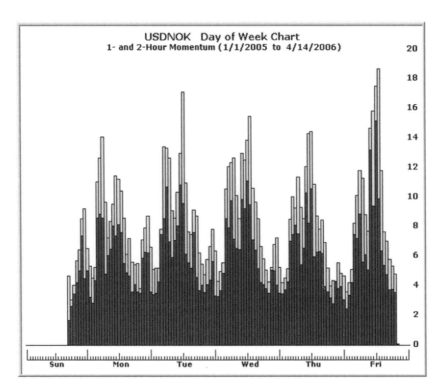

FIGURE L.9 USDNOK Composite Momentum Chart

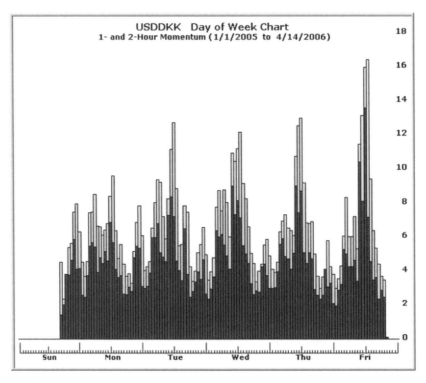

FIGURE L.10 USDDKK Composite Momentum Chart

Comparative Statistics

Throughout the body of this book and the preceding appendixes, we have presented a voluminous number of charts and diagrams in keeping with our goal of assisting traders with a visual approach to technical analysis. For the most part, each chart elucidated one or two specific characteristics about a single currency pair.

This appendix, though not graphic in nature, was included to inform traders how the individual currency pairs compare with each other. The definitions for the statistical results listed in Table M.1 are:

$$\text{Midrange} = \frac{\text{High} + \text{Low}}{2}$$

$$\text{Absolute Range} = \text{High} - \text{Low}$$

$$\text{Relative Range} = 100 \times \frac{\text{Absolute Range}}{\text{Midrange}}$$

$$\text{Coefficient of Variation} = 100 \times \frac{\text{Standard Deviation}}{\text{Mean}}$$

First, activity is expressed in millions of ticks.

Second, the time period for the underlying data is 1/1/2006 through 4/14/2006. We could have started with data from the 1970s, but preferred to restrict this study to the most recent quotes available, thereby ensuring the statistical results are representative of current market behavior.

Third, columns 2 through 8 are descriptive statistics for *individual* currency pairs. This is fine when analyzing one currency pair by itself.

TABLE M.1 Comparison of Currency Pairs

Pair	High	Low	Midrange	Absolute Range	Mean	Standard Deviation	Activity	Relative Range	Coefficient of Variation
NZDUSD	0.7469	0.3897	0.5683	0.3572	0.5530	0.1118	25.2	62.8541	20.2254
AUDUSD	0.8010	0.4775	0.6393	0.3235	0.6366	0.0979	36.4	50.6062	15.3802
USDDKK	9.0450	5.4430	7.2440	3.6020	7.0983	1.0327	31.8	49.7239	14.5488
EURUSD	1.3670	0.8227	1.0949	0.5443	1.0686	0.1545	84.8	49.7146	14.4594
USDSEK	11.051	6.5686	8.8098	4.4824	8.6461	1.2039	39.5	50.8797	13.9241
USDNOK	9.6540	6.0295	7.8418	3.6245	7.6271	1.0507	38.6	46.2206	13.7759
USDCHF	1.8313	1.1285	1.4799	0.7028	1.4551	0.1990	84.1	47.4897	13.6730
USDCAD	1.6190	1.1294	1.3742	0.4896	1.4086	0.1447	37.2	35.6280	10.2728
GBPUSD	1.9552	1.3682	1.6617	0.5870	1.6289	0.1616	78.7	35.3253	9.9206
USDJPY	135.19	101.39	118.29	33.80	114.92	7.7004	73.4	28.5738	6.7006

Fourth, the currency pairs have been sorted in descending order of the final column, the coefficient of variation.

The final two columns (relative range and coefficient of variation) are true *group* statistical tools. Both methods have been massaged into *index numbers* by dividing a statistical value by a central value (the midrange and the mean respectively). These two group statistics allow the currency pairs to be compared without bias toward the prevailing parity ratio. Activity can be considered both an individual and a group statistic since it is not influenced by parity ratios.

For example, note that the Japanese yen has the highest standard deviation in the table but ranks last in the sorted table. This is because it has the highest number of currency units per U.S. dollar (that is, 114 yen equals one U.S. dollar). This is called the parity ratio and differs in purpose from the exchange rate.

Thus, speculators wishing to trade high volatility should select currency pairs from the top of the table, while traders interested in less risky pairs should select from the bottom of the table. However, this does not mean to imply that unexpected breakouts will not occur in currency pairs near the bottom of the table.

Unraveling
Bar Quotes

Most currency data vendors provide historical quote data in many different time intervals. Most typical are streaming ticks (closes only), 1-minute OHLC, 10-minute OHLC, 30-minute OHLC, hourly OHLC, and daily OHLC. However, most traders rarely have the need or the patience to deal directly with tick data (except during live trading sessions) because of its pure bulk and storage overhead. Critical analysts and statisticians do this job for the average trader.

When dealing with swing reversal algorithms such as point and figure (P&F), renko, kagi, and so on, tick data may seem superfluous since the analyst is trying to filter out minor fluctuations anyway. Thus, equispaced interval data is almost always employed.

All OHLC interval data has an intrinsic flaw by the mere fact that it is unknown which extreme occurred first, the high or the low. In our algorithms that convert raw data to both swing data and P&F data, we found it necessary to interject a preliminary process before actually filtering out fluctuations of a specified magnitude (that is, lack of magnitude).

This process unravels the four OHLC quotes into four consecutive "closes," as it were, thus creating a stream of univariate data ideal for the swing reversal algorithm (also four times the size of the input data). Obviously, the opening and closing quotes pose no problems with regard to temporal order. The following rules determine which extreme occurred first.

Case 1: The open is closer to the high than the close is. (See Figure N.1.)
Case 2: The open is closer to the low than the close is. (See Figure N.2.)
Case 3: The open equals the close and the open is closer to the high than to the low. (See Figure N.3.)
Case 4: The open equals the close and the open is closer to the low than to the high. (See Figure N.4.)

FIGURE N.1 Order = O → H → L → C

FIGURE N.2 Order = O → L → H → C

FIGURE N.3 Order = O → H → L → C

FIGURE N.4 Order = O → L → H → C

Case 5: This is the rare instance where the open equals the close and they are equidistant from the extremes. (See Figure N.5.)

Rather than opt for a random determination of the H-L order, we decided to check the previous bar for any pertinent information and found two solutions. (See Figure N.6.)

The two new rules for these conditions are:

Case 5-A: If the previous close is less than the current open (the left diagram), then the direction is upward. Therefore:

$$\text{Order} = O \rightarrow H \rightarrow L \rightarrow C$$

Case 5-B: If the previous close is greater than the current open (the right diagram), then the direction is downward. Thus:

$$\text{Order} = O \rightarrow L \rightarrow H \rightarrow C$$

FIGURE N.5   Open = Close

FIGURE N.6   Two Cases

FIGURE N.7   Order = O → ? → ? → C

Unfortunately, there remains one final case:

Case 5-C: If the previous close equals the current open, then it is time to generate an equal-distribution random number. (See Figure N.7.)

We searched our 7,000,000+ EURUSD 2005 database and found several instances of this condition. Fortunately, in every case, the high equaled the low. Thus, this occurs during periods of low activity and lateral congestion. We therefore feel justified in our very limited use of random numbers in a science where deterministic numbers are treasured.

Just as a matter of curiosity, currency traders may be interested to know just how many ticks can occur within a single minute since this quantity less four quotes is being discarded by the "intervalizing" process. We searched our historical and more recent files and isolated the following:

Date:	Wednesday, August 4, 2004
Time:	8:07 A.M. ET
Open:	1.2004
High:	1.2006
Low:	1.1970
Close:	1.1975
Upticks:	142
Downticks:	157

This amounts to 299 ticks in one minute with a range of 36 pips. Currency trading continues to grow at a phenomenal rate so we expect this record to be broken in the very near future, quite possibly in one of the other major USD pairs or even a cross rate.

The Visual Basic 6.0 source code to perform the preceding is:

```
Option Explicit

Global Const MAX_QUOTES = 8000
Global Const MAX_CLOSES = MAX_QUOTES * 4
Global Const UP = 1
Global Const DOWN = -1
```

```
Global Const vbLightGray = &HC0C0C0
Global Const vbGray = &H808080
Global Const vbLightYellow = &HC0FFFF

Type QUOTE_TYPE
Date As String
Time As String
O As Double
H As Double
L As Double
C As Double
U As Double
D As Double
End Type

Global NumQuotes As Long
Global NumCloses As Long
Global NumColumns As Long
Global Pair$, StartDate$, EndDate$
Global BoxSize As Double, RevAmt As Double
Global Q(MAX_QUOTES) As QUOTE_TYPE
Global C(MAX_QUOTES) As Double
Global Column(MAX_CLOSES) As Integer

Public Function ConvertBarDataToSingleData(C() As Double) As Long
Dim i&, j&

On Error GoTo Err_ConvertBarDataToSingleData

j = 0
For i = 1 To NumQuotes
        j = j + 1
        C(j) = Q(i).O
        j = j + 1
        If Q(i).H - Q(i).O < Q(i).H - Q(i).C Then
            C(j) = Q(i).H
            j = j + 1
            C(j) = Q(i).L
        ElseIf Q(i).H - Q(i).O > Q(i).H - Q(i).C Then
            C(j) = Q(i).L
            j = j + 1
            C(j) = Q(i).H
        Else ' case open=close
```

```
        If Q(i).O = Q(i).H Then
            C(j) = Q(i).H
            j = j + 1
            C(j) = Q(i).L
        ElseIf Q(i).O = Q(i).L Then
            C(j) = Q(i).L
            j = j + 1
            C(j) = Q(i).L
        ElseIf Q(i).H - Q(i).O < Q(i).O - Q(i).L Then
            C(j) = Q(i).H
            j = j + 1
            C(j) = Q(i).L
        ElseIf Q(i).H - Q(i).O > Q(i).O - Q(i).L Then
            C(j) = Q(i).L
            j = j + 1
            C(j) = Q(i).H
        Else ' case O=C and H-O = O-L !!!
            If Q(i - 1).C < Q(i).O Then
            C(j) = Q(i).H
            j = j + 1
            C(j) = Q(i).L
            ElseIf Q(i - 1).C > Q(i).O Then
            C(j) = Q(i).L
            j = j + 1
            C(j) = Q(i).H
            Else ' case Q(i - 1).C = Q(i).O then ARBITRARY!!!
            C(j) = Q(i).H
            j = j + 1
            C(j) = Q(i).L
        End If
    End If
End If
j = j + 1
C(j) = Q(i).C
Next i
ConvertBarDataToSingleData = j
Exit Function
Err_ConvertBarDataToSingleData:
MsgBox Err.Description
ConvertBarDataToSingleData = 0
End Function
```

Visual Basic
Source Code
(Point and Figure)

For those illustrious traders who home-brew their own trading programs, we provide the source code for the point and figure (P&F) reversal algorithm and the chart-plotting routines in Microsoft Visual Basic 6.0:

```
Option Explicit

Global Const MAX_QUOTES = 8000
Global Const MAX_CLOSES = MAX_QUOTES * 4
Global Const UP = 1
Global Const DOWN = -1
Global Const vbLightGray = &HC0C0C0
Global Const vbGray = &H808080
Global Const vbLightYellow = &HC0FFFF

Type QUOTE_TYPE
Date As String
Time As String
O As Double
H As Double
L As Double
C As Double
U As Double
D As Double
End Type
```

```
Global NumQuotes As Long
Global NumCloses As Long
Global NumColumns As Long
Global Pair$, StartDate$, EndDate$
Global BoxSize As Double, RevAmt As Double
Global Q(MAX_QUOTES) As QUOTE_TYPE
Global C(MAX_QUOTES) As Double
Global Column(MAX_CLOSES) As Integer

Public Function CalculateColumns(C#(), NumCloses&, BoxSize#, RevAmt#) As Integer
Dim i&, col&, start#, last#, direction%

On Error GoTo Err_CalculateColumns

' initialize the global column array

For i = 1 To NumCloses
Column(i) = 0
Next i
last = C(1)

' calculate first value of column array

For i = 2 To NumCloses
If C(i) - last >= RevAmt * BoxSize Then
Do
If last + BoxSize > C(i) Then
Exit Do
End If
last = last + BoxSize
Column(1) = Column(1) + 1
Loop
direction = UP
start = i + 1
Exit For
ElseIf last - C(i) >= RevAmt * BoxSize Then
Do
If last - BoxSize < C(i) Then
Exit Do
End If
last = last - BoxSize
Column(1) = Column(1) - 1
Loop
```

```
direction = DOWN
start = i + 1
Exit For
Else
' Do nothing if Q(i).C = Q(1).C
End If
Next i

' loop through remainder of closes filling the column array

col = 1
For i = start To NumCloses
If direction = UP Then
If C(i) - last >= BoxSize Then
Do
If last + BoxSize > C(i) Then
Exit Do
End If
last = last + BoxSize
Column(col) = Column(col) + 1
Loop
ElseIf last - C(i) >= RevAmt * BoxSize Then
col = col + 1
Do
If last - BoxSize < C(i) Then
Exit Do
End If
last = last - BoxSize
Column(col) = Column(col) - 1
Loop
direction = DOWN
End If
ElseIf direction = DOWN Then
If last - C(i) >= BoxSize Then
Do
If last - BoxSize < C(i) Then
Exit Do
End If
last = last - BoxSize
Column(col) = Column(col) - 1
Loop
ElseIf C(i) - last >= RevAmt * BoxSize Then
col = col + 1
```

```
Do
If last + BoxSize > C(i) Then
Exit Do
End If
last = last + BoxSize
Column(col) = Column(col) + 1
Loop
direction = UP
End If
End If
Next i
CalculateColumns = col
Exit Function
Err_CalculateColumns:
MsgBox Err.Description
End Function


Public Sub PlotPafChart(obj As Object)
Dim Xinc# ' width of each graph paper square in twips
Dim Yinc# ' height of each graph paper square in twips
Dim Xmrg# ' left margin of plotting zone
Dim Ymrg# ' top margin of plotting zone
Dim PipFactor# ' converts prices to integers, ie, 10000 for EURUSD
Dim Fmt$ ' format string for PipFactor
Dim dnum# ' floating point loop index
Dim st$ ' local discard string
Dim i&, j& ' integer loop indexes
Dim max# ' maximum high
Dim start# ' first close in raw data
Dim last# ' last plotted X or Y
Dim x1#, x2# ' x-axis coordinates
Dim y1#, y2# ' y-axis coordinates
Dim HdrMrg# ' header margin

On Error GoTo Err_PlotPafChart

' Initialize variables ==============================

Xinc = 150
Yinc = Xinc
Xmrg = 5.5 * Xinc
Ymrg = 10 * Yinc
PipFactor = 100 '10000
```

```
' Plot background graph paper ========================

obj.Cls
For dnum = 0 To obj.Height Step Xinc
obj.Line (0, dnum)-(obj.Width, dnum), vbGray
Next dnum
For dnum = 0 To obj.Width Step Yinc
obj.Line (dnum, 0)-(dnum, obj.Height), vbGray
Next dnum

' Print two-line header ============================

HdrMrg = 0.21
obj.Line (HdrMrg * obj.Width, 80)-((1# - HdrMrg) * obj.Width, 650), vbLightYellow, BF
For i = 0 To 12
obj.Line (0.21 * obj.Width + i, 100 - i)-(0.79 * obj.Width - i, 650 + i), vbBlack, B
Next i

obj.FontName = "Times New Roman"
obj.ForeColor = vbBlack
obj.FontSize = 10
obj.FontBold = True
st = "USDJPY December 2004"
obj.CurrentX = (obj.Width - obj.TextWidth(st)) / 2
obj.CurrentY = 150
obj.Print st

obj.FontSize = 9
st = "P&F Chart Box Size = " + CStr(BoxSize) + " Rev Amt = "
st = st + CStr(RevAmt) + " Boxes"
obj.CurrentX = (obj.Width - obj.TextWidth(st)) / 2
obj.Print st

' Find maximum close ==================================

max = 0
For i = 1 To NumCloses
If C(i) > max Then max = C(i)
Next i
' Adjust max to be a multiple of boxsize units from C(1)
' This ensures Xs and Os land in center of squares

last = C(1)
Do
```

```
last = last + BoxSize
Loop While last < max
max = last
Debug.Print max

' Print vertical scale ================

x1 = 1
y1 = Yinc * (Ymrg / Yinc - 3)
x2 = Xmrg
y2 = obj.Height - 2 * Yinc
obj.Line (x1, y1)-(x2, y2), vbWhite, BF
obj.FontSize = 8
obj.FontBold = True
i = -1
Do
i = i + 1
dnum = max - i * BoxSize
st = Format(dnum - 0.0001, "##0.00")
obj.CurrentX = (Xmrg - obj.TextWidth(st)) / 2
obj.CurrentY = Ymrg + (i - 3) * Yinc + 10
If obj.CurrentY > obj.Height - 3 * Yinc Then Exit Do
obj.Print st
Loop While obj.CurrentY <= 0.98 * obj.Height

' Plot Xs and Os columns =================

last = -4 + (max - C(1)) / BoxSize
For i = 1 To NumColumns
x1 = Xmrg + (i * Xinc)
If Column(i) > 0 Then
For j = 1 To Column(i)
y1 = Ymrg + (last - j + 0.45) * Yinc
PrintX obj, x1, y1, 0.3 * Xinc
Next j
Else
For j = -1 To Column(i) Step -1
y1 = Ymrg + (last - j + 0.45) * Yinc
PrintO obj, x1, y1, 0.3 * Xinc
Next j
End If
last = last - Column(i)
Next i
```

```vb
Exit Sub
Err_PlotPafChart:
MsgBox Err.Description
Resume
End Sub

Public Sub PrintX(obj As Object, cx#, cy#, side#)
Dim i%
cy = cy + 5
For i = 0 To 15
obj.Line (cx - 0.7 * side + i, cy - side)-(cx + 0.7 * side + i, cy + side), vbBlack
obj.Line (cx + 0.7 * side - i, cy - side)-(cx - 0.7 * side - i, cy + side), vbBlack
Next i
End Sub

Public Sub PrintO(obj As Object, cx#, cy#, radius#)
Dim i%
cy = cy + 5
For i = 0 To 15
obj.Circle (cx + i, cy), radius, vbBlack, , , 1.85
Next i
End Sub
```

Visual Basic
Source Code (Swing)

T he following Visual Basic code calculates both the price array and the time index array for open, high, low, close (OHLC) quotes. The main function CalculateSwing Data() requires a single passed parameter, the reversal amount expressed as an integer.

FILE: modSwing.bas

The module uses the global variables:

```
Q() As QUOTE_TYPE
S() As SWING_TYPE
NumQuotes As Long
NumSwings As Long
```

The calling format is:

```
NumQuotes = GetData()
NumSwings = CalculateSwingData(3)
```

```
Option Explicit

Public Function CalculateSwingData(RevAmt%) As Long
Dim i&, j&, Direction&

    On Error GoTo Err_CalculateSwingData
```

```
    ' Initiatialize first swing pair
    S(1).Price = Q(1).C
    S(1).ArIdx = 1
    ' Initialize first direction
    For i = 2 To NumQuotes
    If Q(i).H >= Q(1).H Then
        Direction = UP
        S(2).Price = Q(i).H
        S(2).ArIdx = i
        Exit For
    ElseIf Q(i).L < Q(1).L Then
        Direction = DOWN
        S(2).Price = Q(i).L
        S(2).ArIdx = i
        Exit For
    End If
Next i
j = i
' Calculate remaining swing pairs iteratively
For i = j + 1 To NumQuotes
    If Direction = UP Then
        If Q(i).H > S(j).Price Then
            S(j).Price = Q(i).H
            S(j).ArIdx = i
        ElseIf S(j).Price - Q(i).L >= RevAmt Then
            Direction = DOWN
            j = j + 1
            S(j).Price = Q(i).L
            S(j).ArIdx = i
        End If
    ElseIf Direction = DOWN Then
        If Q(i).L < S(j).Price Then
            S(j).Price = Q(i).L
            S(j).ArIdx = i
        ElseIf Q(i).H - S(j).Price >= RevAmt Then
            Direction = UP
            j = j + 1
            S(j).Price = Q(i).H
            S(j).ArIdx = i
        End If
    End If
```

```
If j = MAX_SWINGS Then
    Exit For
    End If
Next i
If S(j).ArIdx < NumQuotes Then
    j = j + 1
    S(j).Price = Q(NumQuotes).C
    S(j).ArIdx = NumQuotes
End If
    CalculateSwingData = j
    Exit Function
Err_CalculateSwingData:
    MsgBox Err.Description
End Function
```

Resources

PERIODICALS

Active Trader —www.activetradermag.com

Currency Trader—www.currencytradermag.com

eForex—www.eforex.net

Euromoney —www.euromoney.com

Futures—ww.futuresmag.com

FX&MM—www.russellpublishing.com/FX&MM/index.html

FX Week—www.fxweek.com

Technical Analysis of Stocks & Commodities—www.traders.com

Traders Journal —www.traders-journal.com

BOOKS

Aby, Carroll D., Jr. *Point and Figure Charting*. Greenville, SC: Traders Press, 1996.

Archer, Michael, and James Bickford. *Getting Started in Currency Trading*. Hoboken, NJ: John Wiley & Sons, 2005.

Arms, Richard W., Jr. *Volume Cycles in the Stock Market*. Revised Edition, Salt Lake City, UT: Equis International, Inc., 1994.

Bickford, James. *Chart Plotting Techniques For Technical Analysts*. Boulder, CO: Syzygy, 2002.

Bigalow, Stephen. *Profitable Candlestick Trading*. New York: John Wiley & Sons, 2002.

Bulkowski, Thomas. *Encyclopedia of Chart Patterns*. Hoboken, NJ: John Wiley & Sons, 2005.

De Villiers, Victor and Owen Taylor. *Point and Figure Method of Anticipating Stock Market Price Movements*. New York, NY: Traders Library, 1934.

Dobson, Edward L. *The Trading Rule That Can Make You Rich.* Greenville, SC: Traders Press, 1978.

Dorsey, Thomas. *Point & Figure Charting*. New York: John Wiley & Sons, 1995.

DraKoln, Noble. *Forex for Small Speculators.* Long Beach, CA: Enlightened Financial Press, 2004.

Henderson, Callum. *Currency Strategy.* New York: John Wiley & Sons, 2002.

Horner, Raghee. *Forex Trading for Maximum Profit.* Hoboken, NJ: John Wiley & Sons, 2005.

Klopfenstein, Gary. *Trading Currency Cross Rates.* New York: John Wiley & Sons, 1993.

Lien, Kathy. *Day Trading the Currency Market.* Hoboken, NJ: John Wiley & Sons, 2004.

Louw, G. N. *Begin Forex.* FXTrader, 2003.

Luca, Cornelius. *Technical Analysis Applications in the Global Currency Markets.* Upper Saddle River, NJ: Prentice Hall, 2000.

Luca, Cornelius. *Trading in the Global Currency Markets.* Upper Saddle River, NJ: Prentice Hall, 2000.

Murphy, John. *Intermarket Financial Analysis.* New York: John Wiley & Sons, 2000.

Murphy, John. *Technical Analysis of the Financial Markets.* Upper Saddle River, NJ: Prentice Hall, 1999.

Reuters Limited. *An Introduction to Foreign Exchange & Money Markets.* London: Reuters Financial Training, 1999.

Rosenstreich, Peter. *Forex Revolution.* Upper Saddle River, NJ: Prentice Hall, 2004.

Schlossberg, Boris. *Technical Analysis of the Currency Market.* Hoboken, NJ: John Wiley & Sons, 2006.

Shamah, Shani. *A Foreign Exchange Primer.* Hoboken, NJ: John Wiley & Sons, 2003.

Thousands of books have been written on the subject of technical analysis. Here are a few with possible topical interest to this volume:

Lindsay, Charles. *Trident: A Trading Strategy.* Thousand Oaks, CA: Trident, 1976.

McGee, John. *Technical Analysis of Stock Trends.* New York, NY: American Management Association, 2001.

Nison, Steven. *Beyond Candlesticks: More Japanese Charting Techniques Revealed.* New York: John Wiley & Sons, 1994.

Nison, Steven. *Japanese Candlestick Charting Techniques.* Upper Saddle River, NJ: Prentice Hall, 1991; rev. ed. 2001.

Nofri, Eugene, and Jeanette Nofri-Steinberg. *Success in Commodities: The Congestion Phase System.* Elizabeth, NJ: Pageant-Poseidon Press, 1975.

Pugh, Burton. *The Great Wheat Secret.* Miami, FL: Lambert-Gann, 1933.

Ross, Joe. *Trading by the Minute.* Cedar Park, TX: Ross Trading, 1991.

Zieg, Kermit C., Jr. *Point and Figure: Commodity and Stock Trading Techniques.* Greenville, SC: Traders Press, 1997.

The world's largest supplier for mail-order trading books is Traders Press at www.traders press.com.

INTERNET

The amount of information now on the Internet about currency trading is enormous—a Google search finds over 2.2 million entries for "forex"; inclusion of a web site herein does not represent an endorsement of any kind. We suggest beginning with one of the major portals such as www.goforex.net.

Online Brokers and Dealers

www.abwatley.com/forex

www.ac-markets.com

www.admisi.com

www.advancedfinancialworldwideinc.com

www.akmos.com

www.alipes.net

www.alphaonetrading.com

www.ancofutures.com

www.apexforex.com

www.arcadiavest.com

www.axistrader.com

www.cbfx.com

www.charterfx.com

www.choicefx.com

www.cmc-forex.com

www.coesfx.com

www.csfb.com

www.currencyconnect.net

www.currencytradingusa.com

www.currencyuk.co.uk

www.currenex.com

www.cytradefutures.com

www.dfgforex.com

www.directfx.com

www.dukascopy.com

www.eminilocal.com

www.enetspeculation.com/pub/en/defaut.asp

www.etradeprofessional.co.uk

www.fibo-forex.it

www.finanza.saav.biz

www.FlashForex.com

www.forex.com

www.forex.ukrsotsbank.com

www.forex-arabia.com

www.forexcapital.com

www.forex-day-trading.com

www.forexforyou.com

www.forex-mg.com

www.forex-millenium.com

www.forexsolutions.com

www.forexsystembroker.com

www.forextradingdirect.com

www.forextradingusa.com

www.fxadvantage.com

www.fxall.com

www.fxcm.com

www.fxdd.com

www.fxonline.co.jp

www.fxpremier.com

www.fxsol.com

www.fxtrader.net

www.fxtrading.com

www.gaincapital.com

www.gcitrading.com

www.gfsbroker.com

www.gftforex.com

www.ggmk.com

www.gnitouch.com

www.goldbergforex.com

www.guardianfx.com

www.hawaii4x.com

www.hotspotfx.com

www.ifxmarkets.com

www.interactivebrokers.com

www.interbankfx.com

www.invest2forex.com

www.kshitij.com

www.mvpglobalforex.com

www.oio.com

www.pfgbest.com

www.powerforex.com

www.proedgefx.com

www.propfx.com

www.rcgtrader.com

www.realtimeforex.com

www.realtrade.lv

www.refcofx.com

www.rjobrien.com

www.saxobank.com

www.sncinvestment.com

www.socofinance.com

www.spencerfx.com

www.strategybroker.com

www.strikefx.com

www.superfutures.com

www.swissnetbroker.com

www.synthesisbank.com

www.titanfingroup.com

www.tradeamerican.com

www.tradestation.com

www.x-trade.biz

www.zaner.com

Data

www.comstock-interactivedata.com/index.shtml

www.cqg.com/products/datafactory.cfm

www.csidata.com

www.datastream.com

www.disktrading.is99.com/disktrading

www.dukascopy.com

www.ebs.com/products/market-data.asp

www.forexcapital.com/database.htm

www.infotecnet.com

www.netdania.com

www.olsendata.com

www.ozforex.tradesecuring.com/misc/ozchart.asp

www.pctrader.com

www.tenfore.com

Charts

www.esignal.com

www.forexcharts.com

www.forexdirectory.net

www.forex-markets.com

www.fxstreet.com

www.fxtrek.com

www.global-view.com/beta

www.kabuto.com/charts.shtml.

www.linnsoft.com/welcome/charts.htm

www.moneytec.com

www.naviamarkets.com/dzine/TechAnal.htm.

Portals, Link Page, and Forums

www.currencypro.com

www.forexcentral.net

www.forexdirectory.net

www.forexpoint.com

www.forex-registry.com

www.forexsites.com

www.forexvision.com

www.fxstreet.com

www.global-view.com/beta

www.goforex.com

www.investorsresource.info

www.moneytec.com

www.piptrader.com

Software Development

www.fxpraxis.com

www.snapdragon.co.uk

Performance Evaluation

www.barclaygrp.com

www.marhedge.com

www.parkerglobal.com

Professional and Regulatory

www.aima.org

www.cftc.gov

www.fiafii.org

www.mfainfo.org

www.nfa.futures.org

Co-Author Archer's Forex Web Site

www.fxpraxis.com, affiliated with www.gaincapital.com

Index

Underlying
  currency, 170
  instruments, 4
  security, 201
Undershot price swings, 240
Upticks, 6, 12–13, 271, 293
Upward trends/trending, 45, 63–64, 83,
  199
U.S. dollar (USD), 23, 104–108, 264–266.
  See also specific currency pairs
USDCAD, 29, 32, 201, 271, 276, 282, 287,
  305, 308, 311, 314, 317, 320
USDCHF, 29–30, 32, 201, 271, 274, 282,
  285, 305, 307, 311, 313, 317, 319
USDDKK, 29, 32, 271, 281, 282, 292, 305,
  310, 311, 316, 317, 322
USDJPY, 29, 32, 201, 271, 275, 282, 286,
  305, 307, 311, 313, 317, 319
USDNOK, 29, 32, 271, 280, 282, 291, 305,
  310, 311, 316, 317, 322
USDSEK, 29, 32, 271, 279, 282, 290, 305,
  309, 311, 315, 317, 321

Valley, implications of, 126, 128
Velocity, 128, 199
Visual Basic source code
  point and figure, 331–337
  swing, 338–340

Volatility, significance of, 33, 42, 170,
  197–198, 269–270
Volume, 21, 253
Volume Cycles in the Stock Market
  (Arms), 10

Walls, defined, 96
Wave(s), *see specific types of waves*
  anatomy, 191
  defined, 126
Web sites, as information resources, 124,
  180, 266, 343–347
Western reversal charts
  geometric chart, 211–213
  pivot chart, 215–216
  trend outline chart, 213–215
Width ratio, 192
Wilder, J. Welles, 14, 49

X-axis, 19, 44, 50, 62, 84, 135, 137, 139,
  191, 196, 213, 220
XE.com Universal Currency Converter,
  268

Y-axis, 50, 135, 137, 139, 191, 196

Zero-mean oscillator, 168
Zieg, Kermit C., Jr., 200

About the Authors

Michael D. Archer has been an active commodity futures and forex trader for more than 30 years. Mike has also worked in various registered advisory capacities, notably as a Commodity Trading Advisor (CTA) and as an investment advisor. He is currently CEO of CommTools, Inc., a corporation focusing on nonlinear solutions to trend forecasting, with a special emphasis on cellular automata models.

James L. Bickford is a senior software engineer, technical analyst, and very active forex day trader with an academic background in applied mathematics and statistics. He has numerous books to his credit, most recently *Chart Plotting Algorithms for Technical Analysts*.

The co-authors also collaborated on *Getting Started in Currency Trading* (John Wiley & Sons, 2005).

5593 136